4.0

Bar Flower

Bar Flower

my Decadently Destructive
Days and nights as a
tokyo nightclub Hostess

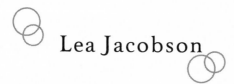

Lea Jacobson

St. Martin's Press ✻ New York

www.stmartins.com

Library of Congress Cataloging-in-Publication Data

Jacobson, Lea.
  Bar flower : my decadently destructive days and nights as a Tokyo nightclub hostess / Lea Jacobson,—1st ed.
      p.   cm.
  ISBN-13: 978-0-312-36897-5
  ISBN-10: 0-312-36897-6
  1. Jacobson, Lea.   2. Women alcoholics—Japan—Tokyo—Biography.   3. Alcoholics—Japan—Tokyo—Biography.   4. Cocktail servers—Japan—Tokyo—Biography.   5. Bars (Drinking establishments)—Japan—Tokyo.   I. Title.

HV5137.J33   2008
362.292092—dc22   2007048125
[B]

First Edition: April 2008

10   9   8   7   6   5   4   3   2   1

For Alecia Atlas, my first real writing teacher,
and for Fran Killilea, my first Japanese sensei.
Although a memoir like this could not have been
what either of you had in mind when you first
opened these doors for me at Northport High
School, I give it to you anyway.

Bar Flower

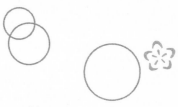

prologue
interview with a vampire

Just after nine o'clock one morning, I was unpleasantly awoken by a digital ringing sound. When I finally rolled over and flicked open my cell phone, I did not recognize the number that flashed before me. This made sense, since no one who knew me would ever call at so ungodly an hour.

"*Moshi-moshi,*" I grumbled.

"Hello. Is this Lea?" a male voice said nervously.

"Yeah, it's me." I switched to English.

"This is Michel," the voice responded in a thick French accent.

"Oh, hello," I said automatically. "How are you?"

Who the hell is Michel? I racked my brain. *A customer? It can't be. I haven't entertained any English-speaking customers in quite a while.*

"I'm well," he replied. "I was wondering if you'd be available for the interview today."

Suddenly it hit me: Michel was a friend of a friend. More specifically, he was the Japan correspondent for a French Internet magazine who, a week earlier when we met at a bar, had requested an interview with me for an article he was writing about hostess bars in Tokyo.

Having been asleep for only three hours, I desperately searched my half-sleeping brain for excuse to cancel. "Okay," I said when I couldn't think of anything. "But can you come over to my place?"

After he agreed to this condition I gave him the directions to my new apartment in Nihonbashi, then grudgingly forced myself out of bed.

"Do you want anything to drink?" I asked him when he arrived. "A beer maybe?" I shot a tired smile in his direction as I took an Asahi Super Dry out of the refrigerator for myself. I could barely talk to anyone without a drink in me anymore.

"No, thank you," he politely refused. It was before noon after all.

"So what does working as a bar hostess entail, exactly?" Michel asked me after taking out his notebook and making himself comfortable on my couch.

"Basically filling my clients' glasses with fine whiskeys," I replied casually, "lighting their cigarettes, and entertaining them with dancing, karaoke, and flirtatious conversation. And smiling. Lots and lots and lots of smiling."

"And that's really it?" He raised his eyebrows.

"That's it." I looked him straight in the eyes. "We flirt, seduce, and sometimes even have mock-relationships with the clients. Still, we always pull away at the last possible moment when they try to kiss us or something."

"So it's like a game?" he asked.

"Exactly," I agreed. "A game that many men spend obscene amounts of money on in order to play."

"I don't understand it." He looked up from his notebook.

"Most Westerners don't," I said flatly. "It is a ritualized spectacle of male dominance in which a woman cares for a man's every need with a smile. Symbolism and ritual are much more powerful forces in the East than they are in the West, I find."

"What does a nightclub hostess have in common with the geisha?" he inquired.

"Everything and nothing," I replied as I lit up a cigarette. "We both work in a facet of Japanese entertainment culture that is called 'the Floating World,' where we are at the top rungs of the *mizu shobai,* or *water trade,* which refers to the business of ephemeral pleasures."

"By that you mean sex?"

"Yes and no." I rolled my eyes. "Both occupations are considered to be part of the sex industry, yet neither of us deals in sex. Instead, we sell fantasies. It is in the nature of these fantasies that the hostess differs from the geisha. While the geisha is a cultural relic, the hostess is modern and exotic. The geisha is rigorously trained in traditional Japanese music, dance, and etiquette. So the fantasy is one of authenticity. By contrast, the foreign hostess offers a fantasy of escape from the rigid rules of Japanese society."

"You seem very tired today," he commented after I let out a giant yawn that likely smelled of alcohol.

"Good assumption," I said mockingly. "I don't get home from work until early morning. Actually," I reflected, "hostesses are as nocturnal as vampires. Sometimes, especially in the winter when the sun goes down early, I can get accustomed to going a week or so without ever seeing the light of day."

"How old are you?" he asked.

"I'm twenty-five," I replied. "That's pretty old for a hostess, you know. Once you hit my age in the profession you're practically considered damaged goods, so I have to lie about it all the time. That fucking pisses me off about Japanese society."

"You've got a sharp tongue for a bar girl," he observed.

"I guess," I said through my sleepy laughter. "But I act like a completely different person when I'm on the job. You might not even recognize me. If you want me to play nice, you've gotta pay for it. And I'm not selling cheap."

"Would you recommend this type of job to other foreign women?" He read the next question printed in his notebook.

"Absolutely not." My expression turned severe.

"But from your tone of voice until now"—Michel's face revealed some confusion—"you seem to enjoy the job very much."

"I do enjoy it," I clarified, "definitely. And I also enjoy smoking marijuana, but I'm not about to give some girl her first joint. Do you know what I mean? It's more of an addiction than a job really."

"So did you first come to Tokyo with the intention of becoming a nightclub hostess?" he then asked.

"Interesting you ask that." I grinned at him with my eyes half-open. "Actually it's a very long story . . ."

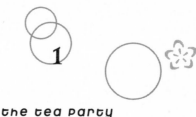

the tea party

carting my luggage across Tokyo's Narita Airport without anyone else's help, I was quite pleased with myself. I bought a ticket for
the limousine bus to YCAT (Yokohama City Air Terminal), where I
would meet a woman named Yumika Ito, the personal secretary to
the president of the Happy Learning English School, with whom I
would soon sign a one-year teaching contract. A recent college graduate, I accepted the teaching job in order to secure my visa to Japan.

I had always hoped, since I began studying the Japanese language in high school, that I could spend some time living by myself in
Japan, immersing myself in her language and culture. And I was finally there. I did it. I thought this much to myself as I sat upright on
the airport bus. My face glued to the window, I sounded out the
Japanese characters on buildings and street signs, or at least the ones
I could decipher, before the sun gave way to evening twilight.

My new coworker was able to find me easily when I disembarked at YCAT. As a five-foot-eight, blond, young, and foreign
woman, I was becoming aware of just how conspicuous I would be

in my new environment. "You are Lea Jacobson, I presume?" the woman politely asked. I assured her that was my name. She introduced herself with a handshake, although she bowed as a reflex at the same time, and then moved to help me bring my luggage toward her car.

Ito-san (or Ms. Ito in English) was a quaint young woman with a seemingly delicate frame, a high-pitched voice, and a pretty face that only gave a hint of the constant strain underneath. After loading my luggage into her miniature minivan with Hello Kitty cushions on the front seats, we were off.

"This is Kanagawa Prefecture," she informed me in her careful yet accented English. "It is just south of Tokyo, bordering the sea. Your homestay family's house is in Yokohama city and our office is in Yokosuka city. Tokyo and Yokohama are nearby cities. It will be about a forty-five-minute commute for you by car in the morning. Is that fine for you?"

"It's fine," was all I could reply, feeling overwhelmed.

"Tonight I will take you to your homestay family's house," she continued, her speech possibly rehearsed. "They are all very happy you are coming. Your car is already parked in their driveway. Tomorrow is Saturday, and I will come over at ten A.M. to give you your first driving lesson. I will show you the directions to the office in Yokosuka so you can drive there by yourself on Monday morning for your first day of training. The teachers at Happy Learning English usually spend the mornings in the office planning their lessons, then after lunch you will drive to various classrooms around Kanagawa Prefecture. Once you learn to drive on the left side of the road it might be interesting for you to explore different parts of Kanagawa by car."

"I'm looking forward to it," I assured both Ito-san and myself. "I'm very excited to begin working for your company." At that she gave me a nervous smile to which I would soon be accustomed.

With such business taken care of, for the remainder of the trip Ito-san and I chatted in English and Japanese about my college Japanese courses, Miyazaki films, sushi, her daughters, and Hello Kitty. She told me that when she was in college she once stayed with an American family in Wisconsin whose house was so large it had its own golf course. "Everything in America was so big," she sighed. "You have so much space over there for recreation."

As we drew nearer to my homestay family's dwelling I didn't feel as nervous as I thought I might. This was likely due to the ongoing assault on my senses caused by a combination of jet lag and culture shock; with all the adrenaline in my system, I could only feel eager and energized. "As I told you on the phone," Ito-san relayed to me, "the husband and wife have one four-year-old little girl. Her name is Ayu and she is sort of a genius at English. She learned to speak English on a native level by watching children's videos and Disney movies in the English language."

"That's incredible," I said.

"I know," Ito-san agreed. "Throughout my life in Japan I have never heard of such a child. Her parents brought her to a class at Happy Learning School and she just started speaking perfect English to one of our instructors. Her parents didn't even know she could speak the language well, since neither of them can converse in English at all."

"She's a regular miracle," I exclaimed in delight.

Ayu's parents had encouraged their daughter to watch television in English almost since the girl's birth, seeing as the kindergarten entrance exams for Japanese students will often test English comprehension. It was under these circumstances that the family came to invest in imported Disney movies, and learned of their child's genius for the foreign language before Ayu ever entered school.

"The mother has agreed to let you stay on the condition that you communicate with Ayu in English during some of your spare time, since the girl is too advanced for any of our classes and her family cannot afford sending her to an international school," Ito continued. "In return, Mrs. Nakano has pledged to give you room and board, as well as to converse with you in Japanese so as to help you learn the language."

"Sounds great," I said eagerly.

"The parents are a little anxious that Ayu not lose this astounding ability of hers."

"That makes sense," I agreed.

"So please try to spend as much time with her as you can."

"No problem," I said as I relaxed in my seat. "I love kids."

Upon our arrival, a middle-aged woman opened the door of a house that seemed small yet cozy. There was a small child hiding behind the woman's legs, but her mother soon shoved her out into the light where Ayu became less shy. She looked straight up at me and without hesitating asked, "Will you be my sister?"

"Sure!" I happily responded. And with that she grabbed my arm, telling me to "Come this way!" up the stairs. Without properly introducing myself to the mother, I followed the child's orders and we were on our way.

"What's with the blue doily on her head?" I heard Ito-san ask Mrs. Nakano in Japanese as we ascended the stairs.

"Today she thinks she is Princess Jasmine from *Aladdin*," her mother replied with a smile. "Yesterday she was Belle."

"Don't step on the mome raths! Don't step on the mome raths!" Ayu advised me to my confusion while we scurried up the stairs. It was only later that I realized she was quoting from the movie *Alice in Wonderland*.

Already arranged in what would be my room on the second floor was an impromptu tea party. After closing the door carefully to prevent the intrusion of parents, Ayu sat down next to the teacups and settled into character. I figured I should do the same but she swiftly interrupted me: "No room, no room," she squeaked with a smile.

"Um," I said, suddenly remembering how tired I was from my flight, "I'm pretty sure there's plenty of space for me to sit down. I'm not as big and fat as you might think." Her tiny voice exploded with laughter while I wondered to myself what I'd said or done that could possibly be that funny. At any rate, I made space for myself and sat down.

"Have some wine!" she said staring at me, eagerly anticipating what I might reply to such an absurd offer. "Wha—?" I began to ask and was interrupted when she blurted out, "There isn't any!" While Ayu was unable to restrain her laughter, I smiled politely to humor her. *I am surely the best toy her parents have ever given her,* I thought to myself.

"Okay, well, I'll have tea then," I replied. She poured my tea first, politely asking if I desired milk or sugar in proper English before attending to her own cup. She was truly delightful. I sat confused for a while, drinking invisible tea. I understood that this child was a genius, but could she be mad as well? Suddenly something inside of me clicked and I understood the situation. "Miss Ayu," I asked, rather sure of myself. "Would this by any chance be a *mad* tea party?"

"Of course!" she said with a smile.

"And did you watch the movie *Alice in Wonderland* today?" I asked her.

"Mommy lets me watch it every day," she said rather seriously, it being my turn to laugh.

I hesitated, and then said, "But today you are dressed up like Princess Jasmine, not Alice."

"But I'm not Alice," she chirped knowingly. "You are!"

I had no idea how true the child's words would turn out to be, nor could I ever have anticipated how many mad gatherings still awaited me in this new country.

2

wind-up women and
child soldiers

Obedience to authority, instilled in people from the time they are small children, makes Japanese society work very smoothly, with far less of the social turmoil and violent crime that have plagued other countries. . . . But there is a minus side, which, like so many other modern Japanese problems, has to do with once-good ideas carried too far.

—ALEX KERR, *Dogs and Demons:
the Fall of Modern Japan*

the boys stood in one line, the girls in the other.

Upon noticing the parade of tiny people crossing the playground to enter my classroom on my first day of teaching, I felt as if I had entered into another dimension entirely. For a foreigner, the sight of a uniform-clad kindergarten class marching across a playground and chanting, "*Hai . . . hai . . . hai . . . hai . . . ,*" is quite a spectacle to behold.

As they marched into the auditorium, I was given my microphone and a large chalkboard. While I decorated the board by writing a large letter *A* with colored chalk, the children performed some convoluted, though perfectly in-sync, combination of claps and calisthenics and then promptly sat down in rows on the floor. I turned around just as one of the three classroom teachers that accompanied the large group of students scolded a little boy for not sitting with his legs crossed like everyone else.

Japanese kindergartens, or *youchien*, are separate from elementary schools and have three grade levels to accommodate children aged three to six. This was the first-year class.

After lunch all of the teachers at Happy Learning typically finished up our lesson plans and traveled in our company cars to various kindergartens and elementary schools throughout the Kanagawa Prefecture. Most of my teaching was in kindergarten classrooms and auditoriums.

I far preferred my teaching hours to the time I spent behind a desk in the office. This was due to the fact that the camaraderie among the foreign English teachers at work was anything but harmonious. Aside from Ito-san, there were three other female office workers, our president, and six native English teachers including myself. Of the four American women on the teaching staff, I was the only American who wasn't from "the base."

Among the women who lived on the U.S. naval base at Yokosuka, two were right-wing religious zealots who had met their husbands on the Internet and one was a recent high school graduate from Kentucky. I had far more in common with the two Canadian women on staff than I did with the Navy wives, but that comparison doesn't say much.

Japan, being so densely populated, generally forces people closer to one another than they care to be. The Japanese typically cope with these environmental inconveniences by having manners, but we nonnatives cannot be bothered by such sensitivities. Thus our workplace's narrow parking lots, close leisure quarters, and tight office spaces gave rise to a considerable amount of petty arguments and tension.

And this was *before* the Navy wives began draping various prowar paraphernalia around the office preceding the commencement of the Iraq War in March of 2003.

Ito-san's assigned tasks were to help the teachers adjust to Japanese customs and to mitigate any internal conflicts among the foreign employees. Although this was no small feat, the woman was often far too busy making tea to tend to any such thing.

We could never interrupt Ito-san when she had tea duty. It was far too important. When the electric buzzer sounded its high-pitched ring notifying the office of visitors, Ito-san would leap up from her desk—usually with stacks of photocopies still in her hands—and head off to greet the visitor. She would answer the door, seat the guest(s), bow deeply, then head to the kitchen to prepare traditional green tea for the prospective students, accountants, company consultants, interviewees, cable guys, or whoever else rang.

Ito-san always had the same nervous smile on her face, an expression that wasn't entirely fake yet could hardly be called happy. If the teachers at Happy Learning could agree on anything, it was that Ito-san behaved like a wind-up secretary whose abrupt and circular scuttling would one day run her straight into the ground.

So leaving the office after lunch was a great reprieve. The children I taught were far more clever than most of the teachers I worked with, and I learned from them a great deal more about Japanese society. Thus my afternoons tended to be far more enjoyable than the mornings I spent in the stuffy office.

Truth be told, teaching English to small children in Japan is a lot like being employed as a birthday party clown. My appearance alone set me far outside the norm at these kindergartens, begging the normal expectation to be entertained. It didn't take long to accustom myself to such a role, which I didn't mind so long as the students still obeyed me. Since my small white Suzuki model was literally packed to the ceiling with educational toys, balloons, and stuffed animals, some coworkers nicknamed my ride "the traveling circus."

As the weeks passed, I learned to differentiate the various levels of kindergarten by the children's uniforms, which demarcated grade levels as well as gender. Among the first-year students, the boys wore blue smocks with matching hats, and the girls sported a yellow variation of essentially the same outfit. A hat was tightly fastened to each student's head with an elastic band, and all rims pointed forward.

On the upper levels, the uniforms worn by the second- and third-level kindergarteners progressively began to resemble the types of uniforms typically worn by elementary, middle, and high school students; that is to say they consisted of military jackets and shorts for the boys and plaid skirts and ties for the girls.

For the Japanese, it is important to distinguish differences in rank and sex at the earliest possible age. From my understanding, this has to do with the distinctly Confucian notion that the way to impose ultimate order and peace is through a rigid hierarchical system. That said, the Japanese reverence of *wa*, or "group harmony," cannot be overstated.

As for me, I never thought that the Hokey Pokey could go so well in an auditorium full of fifty or so four-year-olds. Japanese kindergartens stand as a powerful testament to how impressionable and trainable the very young human actually is.

In my afterschool classes, however, designed only for students whose parents were hefting the bills for English tutoring, the roundtable setting was much more relaxed than the norm, and the children acted differently. As I came to realize, the simple fact that I was a foreigner functioned as their ticket out of having to behave like child soldiers.

In these classes, the students called me "spaghetti-head sensei" (referring to my blond curls, while sensei is "teacher") and drew portraits of me with yellow crayons that they presented to me afterward.

One of the more charming little ones was called Asahi-kun. While the name Asahi translates to "morning sun," the suffix "kun" is often added to the end of boys' names. (The little girls take "chan" at the end of their names instead, as if the boys and girls needed to be differentiated any further.) As he marched into my classroom with his fellow students, he would broadly declare *"Sensei no tonari,"* which means "I get to sit next to the teacher!" Standing three feet tall in his military uniform, Asahi was distinguishable by his rosy cheeks, puckered lips, and otherwise compactly squished-together facial features. Suffice to say he endeared himself to me quickly.

I was likewise amused one day when a small boy named Nobuya-kun bravely came up to me before class to show me the cast on his wrist.

"Nobuya is broken," he solemnly told me in English. Japanese tends to allow one to speak of oneself in the third person, a nuance that is widely used among children under five years old, so the boy apparently assumed that the same was true for English.

"You broke your wrist." I was far too struck by the utter cuteness of his phrasing to correct his speech for the time being. "Oh no! What happened?" I asked slowly.

"Nobuya . . ." he uttered as he began to act out a curious set of charades that inevitably ended with his falling upon his wrist. *"Boom! Boom!"* the child explained with a far too serious glance.

"Be careful next time." I stroked his cast in a nurturing manner as

I tried not to laugh. "You speak English so well," I complimented his efforts. "How smart you are!"

"Nobuya smart!" he echoed, cracking a smile as he walked away to join the rest of the class.

It sometimes felt impossible for me not to favor particular students in each class when certain children would often act so dementedly adorable.

For a culture that frowns on individualism, my students certainly did love to shout their own names in my class. This was especially true for a first-year student called Maya-chan.

"Maya is pink!" she proclaimed once, after I asked them who wanted to use the pink-colored construction paper. "Maya! Maya! Maya!" She could not contain her excitement.

"You mean, 'I want pink,'" I corrected her.

"I am pink! Maya! Maya! Maya!" At that I gave her the paper, since there wasn't enough class time to correct every mistake and the rest of the class was waiting for their colored paper as well.

Sadly, however, Maya's audacity was not typical of my female students, most of whom spoke so faintly that it begged me to tilt my ear just beside their mouths. Even then I couldn't make out what some of them were saying. Such behavior (or lack thereof) was encouraged by society to the extent that there was even a girl in my class called Shizuka-chan, a name that—at least phonetically—means "silence." A popular name for young girls recently, *shizuka* is likewise the word one uses when telling someone else to "shush" or even to "shut up."

The classroom teachers at Japanese kindergartens more or less encourage such discrimination. Once when I was using balloons to teach the large class in the auditorium about colors, a small boy began to cry because he apparently feared that a balloon might pop. Upon noticing this, his regular classroom teacher pulled him aside and lectured: *"Nakanai de ne. Otoko no ko dakara. Otoko jya nai ka?"* which translated to something along the lines of "Don't cry, okay, because you are a boy. Aren't you a boy?"

Conversely, the instructors often allowed the female students to sit out of activities that required too much strenuous exercise. Within the context, the mere condition of being female was reason enough to lower certain expectations.

The Japanese teachers themselves were an interesting phenomenon as well. Of the classroom teachers I encountered at the kindergartens I visited, all were female and basically every instructor appeared to be under thirty. In fact, I often pondered what happened to all of the *youchien no senseis* when they outgrew the role. The two Canadian teachers at my job, Karen and Pam, shared in my curiosity. Pam once joked that perhaps there was a well out in the back of the school that the women are thrown into after they reach a certain age.

"I wouldn't put it past them," I recall saying.

I remember sitting in traffic on the long commute home from work one evening, pondering how flawlessly conditioned these children were becoming as a result of such training.

My thoughts then turned to my unmistakable favorite, Maya-chan. Only four years old, she had yet to learn that she was most likely to receive the affections of adults by acting quiet and cute. It saddened me to know that Maya would inevitably learn to stifle her speech in the future, be it by her second or third year at *youchien.* For on all levels of the Japanese educational system, conformity is nothing short of survival.

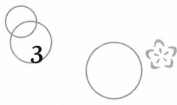

super·cute syndrome

There will never be more than a thin glass barrier between
your present and the wreckage of your past.

—WEI HUI, *Shanghai Baby*

IT WAS SATURDAY, so I took the train from Yokohama over to Tokyo in order to meet up with an old friend.

"Hey, gaijin!" I shouted toward Rachel as I arrived outside the Starbucks building that towered over the massive Shibuya train station. *Gaijin* is a derogatory term utilized by right-leaning Japanese to belittle foreigners residing on the Asian archipelago. And, like any spirited minority, we couldn't get enough of using the term ourselves to insult one another.

Rachel was an old friend from college; the two of us had graduated together the previous May and had ended up working for our respective English schools in the Tokyo metropolitan area entirely by chance.

This was the latest in the series of coincidences that had brought us together over the years. During my second year of college, Rachel and I found that we both lived in the same apartment complex in the student ghetto by McGill, and that we had many of our Cultural Studies courses in common.

But most memorably, we likewise encountered each other in a school-sponsored support group for students who were recovering from eating disorders. That said, it was a great relief for both of us to know that we had each other's support when we departed across the globe.

There is generally a point in the recovery process from any eating disorder where, after getting through years of therapy and reading Naomi Wolf's *The Beauty Myth* twice, one is acutely aware that everything she's been fed by society that equates attractiveness and success to thinness is basically patriarchal bullshit with an underlying motive to keep women from reaching our full potential.

At the same time, however, self-destruction is a powerful coping mechanism that is not about to let any such knowledge—no matter how painfully true—get the best of it. Thus in times of stress or grief, Rachel and I knew that we had to be on constant guard against various impulses to fast, binge, purge, overexercise, abuse laxatives, or even cut ourselves—as a way to disengage from the current situation.

Before we respectively departed for Japan, many people warned us that Japan "is not a good place for women." I generally appreciated their concern, but usually replied that I was willing to put aside my judgmental nature in order to most effectively explore this new and exciting territory.

That day we were sitting by the window on the second floor of Starbucks, or *Sutaabakusu* as it was pronounced. Overlooking Shibuya crossing, I was nothing short of stunned. The plain act of watching people make their way across an intersection had never been so enthralling. When each light changed a mass of citizens, hundreds it seemed, flooded the intersection to cross the street. Since I was relatively new to the country, even the simplest of activities still felt like an adventure.

That afternoon, from the window of the Starbucks over Shibuya crossing, I spotted my first authentic flock of Japanese *gyaru*.

"Are those chicks for real?" I asked my friend as I stared down at two seemingly bowlegged young women attempting to cross the street in platform heels. Walking arm-in-arm, the contrast between the white sparkling makeup and the artificially tanned faces it was caked upon made them impossible to miss.

"Yeah," Rachel said. Having arrived two months before me, her urban knowledge was far superior to mine. "Girls like that are practically a tourist attraction here in Shibuya."

"What's with Snoopy?" I asked rhetorically, nodding at a heavily painted woman with a stuffed Snoopy doll ostensibly poking its head out of her massive Louis Vuitton bag.

"It's the *suupa-cyuuto* syndrome," Rachel joked. "It's on the rise out here and it's highly contagious."

"Those high school girls over there are also carrying stuffed animals," I added, "but why are they wearing their uniforms on the weekend?"

"Where?" Rachel asked

"Oh," she said after I pointed over at the station, "those girls are not in high school." She smirked.

As I was to learn very quickly, the *gyaru* of Shibuya can be subdivided into two rare species of girl known as *kogyaru* (childlike gal) and *ganguro-gyaru* (black-faced gal). The *kogyaru* dressed up in used schoolgirl uniforms, which the women uniformly sexualized by hiking up the skirts and forgetting important buttons. The *ganguro-gyaru,* on the other hand, burned their skin in tanning salons until it was near black, wore streaky eyeliner, and bleached their hair to appear as white as possible.

Although the Japanese women who dressed to embody both stereotypes were usually in their mid-twenties, all harbored unhealthy obsessions with all things *kawaii* (so cute). The vast majority of them were middle school or high school dropouts who—for one reason or another—couldn't take the heat of the country's notoriously strict school system.

"Most high school students wouldn't be allowed to dye their hair like that, or even curl it," she went on to remind me.

"Oh, yeah," I said, "that's harsh. You know," I reflected, "if I were about to become a women in this society, I seriously doubt that I'd want to grow up, either."

"Me neither," my friend replied emphatically. "By the way, Lea, have you heard about this phenomenon called *'kireru'* among students here?" she inquired.

"No, what is it?" I asked with interest.

"It's when these otherwise normal school kids just snap under all of the pressure and suddenly become violent. There are stories of perfectly behaved kids who will all of a sudden 'lose it' and go chopping up another student with a butcher knife or the like."

"How do you know all this?" I questioned.

"We had to attend a workshop about it in the international high school where I work."

"That's so creepy . . . yet so interesting," I said, speaking my mind.

"What does *kireru* mean exactly," she asked, "in Japanese?" I was the Japanese major among us after all.

"It's the intransitive form of the verb 'to cut.'"

"Oh," Rachel said, slightly surprised.

"Yeah, I guess it's only fitting that it translates to 'snap apart' or to 'be severed.'"

"How are you doing with that by the way"—Rachel used this opportunity to check on my sanity—"with *cutting*, I mean."

"One year and five months." I stated how long it had been since I'd abstained from injuring myself in that way.

"Congrats," she encouraged me.

"Thanks," I said dismissively, searching for a way to change the subject.

"No really," she continued, "you should be proud of how far you've come."

"Whatever." I looked out the window.

At that, we both noticed another large group of *gyaru* wobbling their way across the intersection.

"They all have the same Louis Vuitton handbag," Rachel said with a twinge of disgust in her voice. "Even in their degeneration they conform."

"You know," I said, "if I had so few options in life I might just freak out like those girls."

"How so?" she asked.

"Well, if you're taught that the only thing you can do that has any worth is to be cute," I said with my experience in Japanese kindergartens in mind, "going garishly overboard with fashion and supercharged cuteness could be some kind of outlet or symptom of their frustration."

"Yeah," Rachel replied then paused, though her mind seemed to be drifting elsewhere. "I still go to the gym a lot," she said then, seemingly out of nowhere.

"It's like," she continued after I hadn't spoken for a few moments, "I know in my head that I don't need to lose any weight"— she lowered her voice, despite the likelihood that no one in our immediate vicinity could understand English—"but it's tough not to exercise too much when I feel so guilty when I don't work out."

"I know how you feel," I agreed.

"And all my female students are always talking about their diets," she continued.

"It's crazy," I replied, "that these Japanese women all have bone structures of twigs but they still think they're so fat!"

"Exactly!" my friend concurred. "You know," she went on, "in America you could say that the diet industry makes so much money because our country does have an obesity problem. Yet when I look at these Japanese women, so many of whom are going on fad diets and restricting foods even though their traditional cuisine is very healthy and they obviously don't need to be any thinner, I just don't get it."

"Me neither," I said, pondering.

"If anything," she continued, "it just shows how fishy this grand expansion of the weight loss industry really is."

"You're so right," I agreed.

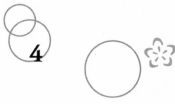

4

ayu in wonderland

Anon, to sudden silence won,
In fancy they pursue
The dream-child moving through a land
Of wonders wild and new,
In a friendly chat with bird or beast—
And half believe it true.

—LEWIS CARROLL,
Alice's Adventures in Wonderland

"nakano ayako desu," my homestay mother said as she bowed in
the traditional manner the night we were first introduced. That was
the first and last time I ever heard her use "Ayako," her given name, a
name time nearly forgot since the woman never used it. To Ayu she
was called *okaasan* (mom) and her husband referred to her as
okaasan as well, which was quite customary. Outsiders called her by
Nakano-san, her married name. And I, fittingly, vacillated between
calling her by "Okaasan" and "Nakano-san." To me, the title mother
didn't have as much to do with my affections for her as it did with her
general rank around the house.

Okaasan took her work as a housewife extremely seriously. Her cooking was brilliant, and it pleased her very much that I enjoyed Japanese food and ate well. I didn't meet Okaasan's husband until three days after I moved into the family's home, on one of the few evenings he returned from the *kaisha* during normal waking hours. Although Ayu-chan and Okaasan both referred to the man as otō-san (father) I always used Nakano-san, be it out of respect or because "father" seemed just too familiar for the man who was so often absent.

As the months passed, I was astonished by how busy Okaasan kept herself at all times. The Japanese traditionally use separate dishes for each of the many courses served to every family member, be it breakfast, lunch, or dinner, and this left a tedious amount of tableware to wash and dry afterward, seeing as the family did not own a dishwasher. Okaasan had a special way of washing clothes that did not require detergent, and almost no Japanese use a dryer for their laundry. She scrubbed her husband's shirt collars with a toothbrush, dusted and vacuumed the house from top to bottom every day, and she got an average of four or five hours of sleep each night.

As well, I had to notice that in this land of technological wonders such as cell phone karaoke and frighteningly precise subways, the housewife I lived with did not know how to use the Internet or drive a car. Still, I dealt with all these inequities passively. Like a polite guest or an efficient sponge, I spent my first six months in Japan learning tradition, submissively taking in customs, and trying to understand dialect. Naturally, such a living situation did wonders for my Japanese skills.

"they're kind of strict," I warned Rachel, my less than conservative friend, who had been invited by Okaasan to dinner and to spend the night at the Nakanos one weekend. Having picked her up in my car at Yokohama Station, I explained to Rachel that my agreeing to live with a Japanese family for an extended period of time was a bit akin to joining a cult. There were many many rules. In spite of this, I rationalized, there were many benefits to reap if one could just obey *the Commandments* . . .

Thou shalt hold rice bowl upright with left hand and chopsticks with the right. Should thou attempt to eat rice from a bowl resting on the table, other members will concur that thou resembleth an animal.

Thou shalt not leave chopsticks inside rice or soup bowls unattended lest thou will cause thine companions to gasp and shudder.

Thou shalt not pass food from one set of chopsticks to another, as such a sight is equally horrifying.

Thou shall not blow thy nose in the presence of other members.

Thou shalt not let the dog into the house unless he is performing tricks for guests.

Thou shall not take the first bath at night even when it is offered to thyself.

Thou shalt understand that members only mean what they say about 20 percent of the time. As for the remainder, thou must becometh a detective and dutifully decode subtle indications.

Thou shalt not leave the premises for more than one night without bringing back a confectionary gift of sorts.

Thou shalt not make use of heating or hot water without being reminded of Japan's astronomically high utility bills. Thus, the space heater in thy bedroom is only for decoration.

Because and only because thou possesseth a vagina, thou must
· sit up straight with legs closed at all times

- help mother to prepare dinner
- serve dinner to the penis-possessing members first
- assist in cleanup and dishwashing
- babysit and entertain five-year-old child
- not bare thy shoulders even in August, and pretend not to notice when the penis-possessing members stride about in their underwear
- never ever leave any evidence, visible or otherwise, that thou owneth underwear thyself
- and whenever possible, thou shalt not acknowledge thine own presence.

"You fucking kidding me?" Rachel protested before I'd finished my recital.

"Well." I thought it over. "I guess you don't have to follow all the rules that I do since you're only staying for the night. They'll expect you to screw up a little 'cause you're foreign."

"Yeah, I'm used to that." Rachel smirked.

"It will be fine," I assured her, "really."

Though Rachel didn't care much for kids, I explained to her that Ayu was a sweet-tempered and highly intelligent girl. How, in a country where adults who hold university degrees in English often find conversation with native speakers near impossible, Ayu began to speak English on a native level after watching some Disney movies. This was the only explanation, as her parents could barely speak a word in English.

Upon our arrival, Ayu was wearing her princess dress again, a Halloween costume her mother made for her some months ago. The girl had taken to changing into the dress immediately upon returning home from kindergarten every day that week. Ayu's way of introducing herself to Rachel, as it happened, was to lightly tap my friend over the head with her toy wand and pronounce, "Ha ha! Now you are a frog!" then run away squealing with laughter.

"You're right"—Rachel turned to me—"her English is really good."

Soon Rachel and I were called into the kitchen to help prepare dinner.

"So the leftover radish," I had to clarify, "the part that is sliced and placed under the sashimi for decoration, that is called 'the wife'?"

"Yes," replied Okaasan, who taught me something new every time I helped her out in the kitchen, "*tsuma,* that is the expression, because it decorates the main dish."

"Oh, that's interesting," I responded.

"What are you guys talking about?" Rachel inquired, unable to decode our Japanese.

"Tell you later," I said, brushing her off. Some things were better left untranslated.

Luckily Rachel enjoyed sashimi and the dinner went very well, though I was exhausted from the constant interpreting.

"I usually can't stand kids," Rachel told me as we got ready for bed, "but Ayu is really delightful. I wouldn't be able to live in a situation like this because I like my privacy, but I am still a little jealous of you: I mean, good food, lots of space, and your very own child prodigy to play with. I want one for myself!"

"Ayu loves speaking English because she thinks she is in a movie," I told Rachel in the privacy of my room. "Ayu's parents are so strict with her," I said thoughtfully, "that she lives inside these American cartoons instead."

"Really." Rachel seemed interested.

"And when she says to us 'let's pretend' this or that," I continued, "she doesn't really know what 'pretending' means; she thinks that she *actually becomes* each character in the fantasy."

"Ayu's life would be a brilliant case study for postmodernism." Rachel was feeling intellectual. "I mean, she learned all of her language—in English anyway—from an electronic device, instead of from any human tongue."

"Postmodernism makes my head hurt."

"Come on, just think about it," my friend persuaded. "All of her English language patterns come from the media, like she is some by-product of the Disney corporation."

"She is a little girl," I corrected emphatically.

"I know, I know." Rachel was apologetic.

"And I'm just worried," I continued, "about when she grows up, when all the fantasies crash, you know?"

"It happens," Rachel said coolly.

"It sucks." I knew too well.

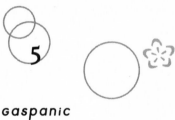

5

gaspanic

> *I felt myself being replaced . . . like reaching the vaporiza-tion point or the melting point or the boiling point or what-ever, there are certain temperatures at which any substance will change its state.*
>
> —MARI AKASAKA, *Vibrator*

RUSH-HOUR TRAFFIC HAS a peculiarly maddening quality about it. There is nothing quite like having to drive at two miles an hour in a vehicle that's fully capable of going sixty to bring out the more in-sane aspects of human nature. Trapped on a stagnant highway, we vehemently curse the existence of all our fellow commuters regard-less of the fact that we are all in precisely the same predicament.

Life on the left side of the highway barrier proved to be no dif-ferent.

And Yokohama's residential roads were no reprieve. A narrow al-ley that Americans might consider to be wide enough to barely clear a small car was a typically bustling two-way street in Japan. Due to space restrictions, it was also typical for bicycles, motorcycles, scooters, and herds of schoolchildren to share the same road. In short, everything was on a collision course with everything else.

I was sitting in Yokohama traffic when I first decided that the real world sucked, and that I should have stayed in college as long as possible. I often cursed myself for opting to graduate from university a year ahead of schedule, lamenting that I could not skip classes at will anymore—since I was the teacher after all—and that feeling emotionally unstable was no longer a reasonable excuse to stay at home for a week.

Then one day on the job, as if I needed more stress in my life, the brakes on my tiny car ceased to function properly. Each time I tried to stop, I would come upon a new and unique adventure. Sometimes the brakes squeaked, while at other times they grumbled, jerked, and caused the entire car to vibrate as if in a vehicular earthquake.

I naturally reported this dilemma to Ito-san immediately, which resulted in her sending my car off to the shop to be inspected and repaired.

"I can't believe they won't just get you a new car," Karen said, with a look of utter disgust for the establishment.

"Fukuda is a stingy asshole," Pam said as they gave each other knowing glances.

At the time I had yet to become a full-fledged member of their complaining club. That took two more weeks, when my brakes began to squeal again, almost immediately after being fixed.

"The president wants to drive your car around the block later this morning," Ito informed me after I voiced my second complaint. "So make sure the car is clean," she insisted. I agreed with her because I had no other options.

Ito-san approached my desk for a second time later that same day, with a somewhat nervous look in her eyes.

"The boss said that your car works fine," she said quietly, her eyes on the floor.

"What?" I was sure I had heard her wrong.

"Mr. Fukuda just drove your car around the block once, and he instructed me to report to you that there is nothing wrong." Ito was visibly ashamed to be the bearer of such news. At the same time, however, she wasn't taking any stand to defend me.

"Are you crazy?" I asked her sincerely, my tone drawing the attention of everyone in the office. It was her turn to stand in shocked silence. *"The brakes don't fucking work on my car!"* I exclaimed.

"It's *shō ga nai,* Lea," she replied, switching over to her native Japanese. "He is our boss." *Shō ga nai* is an overused Japanese expression that connotes a situation that "can't be helped." While all the foreign workers looked angry and concerned when they came to realize the situation, Ito still showed no emotion, saving her chronic anxiety.

"No, it's not," I affirmed. "It's *shō ga nai* for Mr. Fukuda that I will quit right now if he doesn't get me a new car!" I had tried to adapt to the culture all I could, but at the same time, I wasn't about to risk my life for the good of the company. Foreigners *are* unalterably different from many Japanese in this respect.

At that, I made my way to the bathroom where I sobbed angrily for five minutes before returning to work. Another nuisance about having an adult job was that I couldn't cry in public anymore.

The outburst did result in my eventually receiving a new company car, but at a price. The Japanese staff around the office began to view and treat me differently. Conversations among them either stopped entirely or became covert whispers as soon as I entered certain rooms. They viewed me as volatile, unsafe, and a detrimental obstacle to the group harmony.

Around the same time, after many months of living with my

homestay family, my Japanese had gotten quite good. Too good, in fact, to maintain the peace any longer. When I finally blew my lid at home, regurgitating all of my homestay mother's "lessons," so to speak, my rage centered in upon women's underwear of all things.

In order to put this conflict into its proper context, it merits a moment's digression to explain the history of women's underwear in Japan. Actually, traditional dress for Japanese females does not include underwear underneath kimonos or wraparound skirts. From the early 1900s however, Japanese women gradually westernized their wardrobe. An important catalyst was the fatal fire in a high-rise Tokyo department store in 1932, through the course of which a significant number of casualties were women clad in traditional Japanese dress who fell from safety ropes because they only used a single hand to grip the ropes while the other was used to keep their skirts from flying about and exposing themselves.

Born from this tragedy was a call for the westernization of women's wardrobes—particularly with respect to undergarments, which in theory could allow women more freedom of movement. So it was that underwear was thereby deemed a symbol of gender equality and containment of the female private parts was deemed liberating. Yet from a feminist perspective, the freedom was short-lived, as Japan gradually became a mecca for panty thieves by the end of the twentieth century. Western feminists will justifiably criticize the Japanese for selling schoolgirls' used underpants in vending machines, still this is done with little understanding that underwear, in itself, is a gift from the West.

As it happened one night, my homestay mother came into my room to tell me that I had to hide my underwear on the bottom of my laundry basket. She was concerned, you see, that someone outside might be able to view my unmentionables through my open windows. She tried to explain that women's underwear and stockings are very shameful things in Japan. Meanwhile, I thought to myself about how I had to fold her husband's underwear yet still I couldn't leave my own underwear atop my laundry basket in my own room.

I snapped. This particular point enraged me if only because I had spent so much time in therapy and support groups learning that I need not be ashamed of my body, and I was not about to allow all of my progress to be undone. There was a point, I assured myself, where "accepting other cultures" had to end and the universality of gender oppression begin.

In probably my most daring act, I spoke to my host mother in English for the first time I can remember.

"That's so stupid," I huffed as I turned around and left the scene.

"Eh?" She was truly shocked.

"Nandemonai," I mumbled, meaning "nothing."

When she left my room in a huff I almost thought I'd won, but she appeared at my door ten minutes later holding my electronic Japanese-English dictionary. It read the Japanese translation of the word *stupid, bakabakashii.* We fought about underwear in Japanese. I refused to eat breakfast at her table the next morning.

In the days to follow I made arrangements with my employer to stay temporarily at a teacher's residence at my school, where Karen and Pam also resided. There, I happily drank orange juice from the carton, sat at the table improperly, stayed out late partying in Tokyo, and spitefully strung up my underwear around my room. I became a full-fledged member of Karen and Pam's bitterness society, and the three of us began to socialize much more often.

There is a chain of bars in the area called Gaspanic, which were known for their foreign staff and clientele. Inside of Gaspanic, it was a house rule that all customers should have drinks in their hands at all times, or else they would be asked to leave.

I came one Thursday night with Pam, Karen, and some other

coworkers. Trouble started earlier in the night when I lost my wallet. We later found my wallet under the seat of a companion's car, but at the time my dilemma was such that I found it missing when I needed cash for a new drink. I searched frantically, being repeatedly bothered by an obnoxious bartender who warned me to order another drink or leave. It was the club's policy after all. No exceptions.

I inevitably forgot my manners and lashed out at him, "Fuck you, I lost my wallet okay!" At that I was chased out of the place kicking and screaming. I was furious, refusing to leave until I spoke to a manager. Then Pam and Karen came down the stairs to speak to me. Pam said that I should calm down and just leave if I didn't want to be taken away by the police. When I finally reached fresh air, I screamed "I hate Japan!" with drunken tears in my eyes.

I left the club alone.

Drunken fury notwithstanding, I was more disheartened with Pam that night than with Japan or even with those who threw me out of the club. By turning against me although she was a supposed semi-friend, she effectively slammed shut a small oxygen vent, leaving me to suffocate alone with my rage. I woke up the next morning with new gashes on my left forearm. The year and a half of temperance during which I had successfully abstained from hurting myself was as broken as my skin.

Luckily it was winter, and long sleeves were the norm.

In the aftermath, I missed Ayu fiercely. So the following week, I took a deep breath, gathered my patience, and went back to my homestay. On Monday night, I returned with my suitcase in one hand and a confectionary gift in the other. Ayu gleefully shouted *"Leaaaa!"* and ran to hug me unrestrained. My homestay mother coolly accepted the gift, as was customary, but she also made my favorite dish of the season—tsumetai ramen with vegetables—for dinner.

In return, I took pains to hide my underwear from then on. Yet in the time I was gone, there grew a rift between Okaasan and me that was not mendable. Although the woman had taught me to speak, I became deeply aware that she would never be my real mother. The dynamics around the house changed considerably after that first conflict.

From that point on I felt like something was missing in the life I had made for myself in Japan. I got restless, but found myself caught between my adoration of little Ayu and the resentment I was continually building toward Okaasan.

I wanted Ayu for myself. She was a brilliant and insightful little wonder, and I regretted that she was her mother's daughter. "What do you want to be when you grow up?" she asked me one day as I pushed her on a swing. "A nurse or a stewardess?" If Ayu were my little girl we would have attended the theater, modern art exhibits, and feminist film festivals together. We would have adorned ourselves in princess colors and escorted each other to royal banquets where the suitors scrubbed our shoes with toothbrushes.

One night, my little sister tried to color my hair black with her calligraphy pen. "Don't turn around," she ordered, "it's a surprise. I'm turning you Japanese!" Her motivation was apparent: if I became Japanese, I would never have to leave her again. On a few occasions I needed to wash the dark ink out of my blond hair in the shower. I tried to level with her logically about this but her little will was relentless.

6

the crash

The nail that sticks up gets hammered down.

—JAPANESE PROVERB

The road to hell is paved with good intentions.

—WESTERN PROVERB

It was the summer of 2003, and I was terrified of flying. I knew that my sentiment was unreasonable and that it is statistically laughable to fear death in a plane crash; still, reason and terror hardly ever complement each other. Just looking at a plane on the ground made my heart rate race, while a single glimpse of an aircraft soaring above made me short of breath and nauseated. I was never a whiz at physics, so I theorized that with respect to one massive load of metal and fuel suspended in the sky, who is to say that it shouldn't just fall on me?

My dreams were in merciless accord, burning planes plummeted in my sleep nearly every night. I had to watch helplessly as aircraft after aircraft directly above me lost control, went into a tailspin, burst into flames, and plunged right toward me.

My original flight from New York to Japan had been facilitated by a maximum dosage of Xanax, prescribed over a year earlier by the friendly family physician. The time had come to board a plane again, however, for a summer trip to the northern island of Hokkaido to escape the heat. By then, I had been living in my Kanagawa homestay for almost a year.

One morning, I confided in Ito-san that I have an irrational fear of flying in airplanes, and that I usually take sedatives during long flights to ease my anxiety. Because I would be flying to Hokkaido for summer vacation in a matter of weeks, she arranged a psychiatrist appointment for me where I might obtain a similar medication.

I left my first and only psychiatrist appointment in Japan with new insight into why most Japanese decline to talk to professionals about their emotional problems.

"You are not normal," Dr. Kamioka proclaimed.

"Excuse me?" I was in disbelief. I should have skipped my case history and just asked for the meds.

"You are not normal."

"Umm . . . so?"

"The problem is that you are not normal."

"But normal is boring. Is anyone really normal?"

"If you are not normal in Japan this can cause many problems for you."

"I would much rather be abnormal than like all the robotic salary men on the trains every morning."

"I will prescribe you the Xanax you've asked for but I'd also like you to start taking medication called Tegratol. Tegratol is—"

"That's a mood stabilizer," I interrupted. "It will make me stupid and boring. I won't take it. Besides, my last psychiatrist said that it had too many bad side effects."

"I have patients on the drug who are foreign women and they don't feel out of the ordinary taking it. There are no side effects."

"Yes, there are."

"Do you mind if I ask why you came to Japan if you have so many problems?"

"I've always wanted to come live in Japan, since I was a kid. I've studied Japanese for five years."

"Okay, I have one last question," he said, "what would you do if your boss at the school you currently teach at told you that you had to go back to America?"

"He can't do that!" I replied, irritated now as well as confused. "He doesn't have the power to make me leave Japan or revoke my visa. All he can do is fire me, and if that happened I would get another job. Easily."

"Very well, then."

I left his office with a prescription and a headache. The psychiatrist appointment was on a Tuesday, and I had to spend Wednesday and Thursday at an English summer camp sponsored by my school.

On Friday morning, I came in and helped Ito-san with her job taking out the garbage. There was something I had to talk to her about. I finally had had enough of my homestay mother and asked Ito-san if she could change my living arrangement for the remainder of my contract. She told me that she understood, and would make the arrangements as soon as possible. After that I was feeling pleased and very grateful to her for her understanding.

Then she told me that the *kaicho* (president) would like to speak to me later in the day. She had the same nervous smile. I wouldn't call it fake but I wouldn't call it happy, either. A few hours later I casually entered the meeting room and seated there gravely was not only the *kaicho* but also a director and one of my supervisors. The letter was on the table.

"What is going on here?" I tersely asked Ito-san.

"It's not my right to say," she replied. I was furious with her. I was furious with everyone. I picked up the letter.

It was curiously dated July twenty-ninth, three days ago:

Dear Lea Jacobson,

It was reported, for your safety, by the doctor of the hospital you visited today, that due to your mental condition it is not advisable for you to drive a car, and he recommends that you should return to rest in your home country. He also reported that you had been on medication before joining the Happy Learning English School. We were not informed of this fact when we hired you.

In view of the above, we cannot allow you to drive our cars. Therefore we have sadly come to the conclusion that we must terminate the contract immediately.

Sincerely,

Kazuhide Fukuda

President

"This-this-" I struggled to find my voice. "This can't be legal! What about confidentiality? Can't anyone here see that this is wrong?"

There was a deafening silence.

"That doctor was stupid!" I continued, losing more composure with every word. "He got mad at me because I told him so! He said that mood stabilizers have no side effects but that is completely wrong!"

"He is a professional and you are not," Naomi, another administrator, said calmly, quietly. "There's nothing we can do. If anything happens when you drive any of our cars from now on, our company is liable."

"Lea, please," Mr. Fukuda said. "We've tried to do everything we could for you, we really did, now please just sign on the line. We've noticed that you do tend to scratch up your car."

"I tend to scratch the car?" I fumed. "The streets you have us driving down are five feet wide! I don't scratch the car more than anyone else!"

"Just sign." All of the eyes in the room were glaring at me.

Immediately after signing my name I rushed out of the building and ran down the block, where I intended to compose myself in private, only to end up exploding in tears.

There is a famous Japanese proverb that says, "The nail that sticks up gets hammered down." As the Japanese strive to be as "normal" as possible, this saying is fundamental to their way of thinking. But in modern times, the saying is only half true. The Japanese who do not conform get hammered down, yes, but the foreigners who can't fit in get yanked out by the back of the hammer and flung somewhere else. It doesn't matter exactly where, just far enough away from Japan.

To be fair, the culture clash behind the scenes of this drama was extreme. For a Japanese company, the maintenance of a superficial harmony is valued above honesty. This explains why Ito-san withheld this information from me until I read the letter. For the non-Japanese, by contrast, these circumstances seem so deplorable because we value honesty so dearly.

More than that, the psychiatrist betrayed the trust that should have been inherent in his position as a health care provider. There is no clearer essence of betrayal than to be harmed by the hands of one who was entrusted to nurture our emotional needs. In the Western canon, such deception is sentenced to the lowest circle in Dante's

Inferno. That is to say, the psychiatrist would be roasting marshmallows with Judas and Benedict Arnold. Dante's work reminds us that betrayal, in the Western mind-set, is the gravest sin. Worse than murder even.

Having stopped crying, I paced up and down the street of the suburban neighborhood where Happy Learning's office was located, unable to believe what had just transpired. My homestay mother was one for following rules, so it was certain that I would be asked to leave her home in compliance with her affiliation with Happy Learning.

As I continued to ponder my future, which felt bleaker and bleaker every minute, two high school boys in uniform passed by me on the road. *"Gaijin ga se ga takai ne,"* Foreigners are tall, eh, one of the students said to his companion in a loud and confident voice, entirely sure that I wouldn't understand a word he was saying.

For the first time since arriving in Japan, I completely abandoned the public etiquette that my homestay mother had taken such pains to teach me: *"Nihonjin ga manaa ga nai ne,"* The Japanese don't have any manners, eh, I called back almost instantly, without thinking. The boys who had just spoke so confidently turned red and appeared dumbfounded, scurrying away quickly. My words carried a particular sting, seeing as the Japanese happened to pride themselves on their politeness.

Despite the desperation of my current situation, I began to feel curiously pleased with myself after the encounter. The strength of my Japanese skills surprised even me, and my new ability to shock the Japanese felt terrifically satisfying. From that point on, I knew that I wasn't going home despite the advice of basically everyone around me. I had only recently acquired the skill of fluent communication, and if I booked a ticket home that day all my hard work would have been in vain.

I'd done my time in the trenches: graduating from college a year ahead of my class. I hopped practically the first plane to Japan in order to continue my study of the Japanese language informally while earning my own living for the first time. I followed the Commandments (for the most part) and worked loyally for the company that employed me, only to have it end for me in such a demeaning and demoralizing manner.

Still, although Japan more or less instructed me to "go home," my response was a loud and defiant *no. Nobody, not anybody,* I thought to myself, *is going to force me to leave this country before I am ready.* It had come time to screw the Commandments, forget about everyone who had betrayed me, and do Japan *my* way. I couldn't forgive Mr. Fukuda, Ito-san, or Naomi regardless of whether their intentions were valid. There should be an extra clause in that cliché, "It's the thought that counts," about not being a fucking idiot.

I reentered the office, and sang to myself while I packed up all the belongings in my desk. In doing so I most likely assured my employers of my questionable mental state, but by then nothing mattered to me anymore. There is an acute sense of freedom in the abandonment of all pride, and in light of my situation, having had all conceit stripped away, I was overcome by a feeling of liberation. The possibilities suddenly became endless.

An hour later, Naomi and Ito drove me back to my homestay mother's house. Okaasan was home, as always, and Mr. Fukuda had already spoken to her on the phone about the situation earlier. In the kitchen, I perfunctorily helped her prepare tea for our uninvited guests. "*Shokku!*" She expressed the Japanese adaptation of the English word "shock," wondering if perhaps it was the frequency with which I used my asthma inhalers that was making me act so *abnormal.* She was always full of original ideas like that.

"I'm not going home," I told her in Japanese, "I will get another job."

"That is very good." She actually seemed relieved to learn of my resilience. "You will have to come back and visit us often."

From that moment Okaasan and I ceased being rivals and were forced to unite for our common concern: Ayu was not going to take this news well.

"Remember the shark balloon?" Okaasan asked with a nervous smile.

"Of course I do," I replied with a similarly worried expression.

Last winter, Ayu had received a balloon in the shape of a shark from a promotional sale at a children's clothing store. While walking toward the bus stop with Okaasan, the five-year-old lost her grip on the helium balloon and it naturally flew away. There was nothing anyone could do but watch helplessly as the little girl wailed for her wayward balloon.

But this specific event wasn't precisely what my homestay mother was referring to. Ayu had a terrific memory, and she tended to recall the precise happenings of the shark balloon debacle at the most inopportune moments. For months upon months, Ayu would, at seemingly random intervals, begin to cry hysterically at places like the dinner table, the park, and her preschool classroom because she suddenly remembered that "The shark balloon flew away."

Hesitant to become a human "shark balloon" in Ayu's life, I told Ayu that I would be back to see her soon as I left for the airport the next morning. By then, Okaasan had tried to explain to Ayu that after I returned from my trip I would be living in an apartment by myself, because that was what older sisters did when they reached my age. True to my word, I continued to visit the family throughout my stay in Japan.

Hokkaido, I thought to myself on the bus to Narita Airport, *will not be so suffocating and hot.* A friend had been kind enough to let me temporarily store my excess luggage in her mother's garage until I found a new place to live upon returning from my vacation.

Sitting in the terminal the next morning, I wrote in my journal that I probably wouldn't be afraid of flying anymore. It was not because obtaining Xanax proved too risky or because someone finally told me that I'm more likely to drown in my own bathtub than die in a plane crash. Rather, in my life, I've always experienced nightmares about falling airplanes or other large objects whenever I've been feeling anxiety about some sort of failure, either to please someone or to accomplish a lofty goal.

Upon being fired from my job in such a demeaning and dramatic way, the nightmares and the reality had merged. As a teacher I had tried so hard to be the perfect employee, to please everybody and to be the best, but my ambitions had since crashed. I ended up getting fired due to my abnormal "mental condition."

That wasn't all. "I don't think I'll be afraid of airplanes anymore," I wrote in my journal, "because in the past few days I have crashed and survived." And in reality I had more than survived; I was free from my soul-sucking job. I still had a valid working visa and plenty of money in savings. I could forget about everything that happened and start my life over again. In Tokyo.

I would move to Tokyo.

7

city on air

Tokyo has already suffered one of the most devastating earthquakes of modern times. On September 1, 1923, just before noon, the city was hit by what is known as the Great Kanto quake. . . . Two hundred thousand people were killed. Since that time, Tokyo has been eerily quiet, so the strain beneath the surface has been building for eighty years. Eventually it is bound to snap.

— BILL BRYSON, *A Short History of Nearly Everything*

"ʏᴏᴜ ᴡɪʟʟ sᴏᴏɴ be arriving at Shinjuku Station." The same voice always echoed through the cars. "Please transfer here for the JR Sobu Line, the JR Saikyo Line, the JR Chuo Line, the JR Utsunomiya Line, the JR Tokaido Line, the JR Negishi Line, the JR Shonan-Shinjuku Line, the Keio Line, the Keio New Line, the Toei Oedo Line, the Odakyu Line, the Marunouchi Line, and the Seibu Shinjuku Line. This is the JR Yamanote Line bound for Shibuya and

Shinagawa." I sometimes wondered when recorded voices found the time to breathe.

At the start of the twenty-first century in Tokyo, a railway route map of the area looked as if it could have been spun into existence by a workaholic spider. When I arrived in the city I had seen nothing remotely like it before. Unlike many metropolitan systems where the subways tend to advance in straight lines rather than webs, even color-coding on the Tokyo subways was futile due to the sheer volume of mass-transit operations.

That is to say, one could easily mistake the magenta Oedo Line with the more orangish red Keiyō Line, or either of the former with the red Marunouchi Line. Sometimes, the bright blue Mita Line against the slightly paler blue Tozai Line or the teal-colored Nanboku Line could perplex even the locals.

The only constant within the winding matrix was the Yamanote Line. The most boarded commuter train in Tokyo, the JR Yamanote Line was a circular loop that cut across the massive jumble of JR tracks, metropolitan subway lines, as well as a handful of other private railroads around Tokyo. Drawn on most transit maps to be a perfect circle, the JR Yamanote Line crossed through or encircled most major points in the metropolis.

Thinking back, I suppose that the Yamanote could not have been an actual geometric circle to such a scale, still, a circle was how most Tokyo citizens imagined the tracks as we plotted our routes around the city. Like the long hand of a clock, the loop took almost exactly an hour to complete. Due to the mass volume of humans perpetually filling and emptying the cars through the course of the circle, a new train arrived at each station every minute during rush hour.

Luckily, my first Tokyo accommodation was located near the Yamanote. Maddeningly, however, my nearest station was Shinjuku: the largest and busiest train station in the world. During rush hour each day, some two million human beings regularly crawled through the station together. Meeting someone else at Shinjuku Station is near impossible without using a cell phone to call a companion who may be just five feet in front of you. The crowds were that blinding.

Even after I'd lived in Shinjuku Ward for years, I couldn't always find my way from the west exit to the east exit without getting disoriented or outright lost. The west with its wide streets, expensive department stores, skyscrapers, and ritzy business headquarters was in heavy contrast to the east side and its narrow strips of bars and sex clubs known for mafia-related violence. Between the two worlds were diagonally slanted streets that couldn't be classified so easily, and that made following directions all the more difficult.

My first gaijin house was located a ten-minute walk outside of east Shinjuku. It is quite difficult for a non-Japanese to find a nice apartment in Tokyo. More to the point, foreigners in Japan are not allowed to hold leases to most apartments by themselves, so we often live together in special houses. Thus, the typically low-income gaijin house was born. I was happy to have found my own room in a gaijin house, be it the size of a large closet.

A member of the gaijin house crowd could be distinguished by his complete lack of stability. In the time I lived there, the house's character changed every month with the coming and going of tenants. The residents changed while the scenery stayed the same. Generally, though, I found the gaijin house crowd to be, by far, the most interesting group I'd associated with since coming to the island nation. I felt as if I could blend in among them, insofar as I fit in anywhere.

My housemates and I came from different parts of the world, but our collective resentment of Japan brought us all together. "I think that the literal translation of gaijin," Mariano told me, "should be 'foreigner go home.'" He had only been in Japan two weeks then, and was already homesick for Argentina. Kelly, a Frenchman who came to Japan to be with a Japanese girlfriend, was perpetually lost. This led him to curse the intricate and indecipherable transportation system daily. Paul, a British man who taught English for the Nova Corporation, had lived in this house longer than anyone. At the time, Nova was notorious for overworking their foreign employees. I always tried to convince him that if he came home from work at night thinking, "Okay, I'm ready to die now," it could be the time to make some changes.

Carla was Italian and often complained of her employer's incompetence. "Faaack," she said in her thick but confident accent, "I think he smoka da crack or something. Like faack!" It was also amusing to talk with her about earthquakes.

"If the big one comes here like they say, we are totally faacked!"

When I told her I wanted to prepare for such an emergency by keeping bottled water and a first-aid kit in my room, she proposed preparation more along the terms of life insurance policies.

"This building is made of da paper! So faack!"

To Carla's credit, the building did seem to be made of paper. Foreigners are often amazed at how quickly buildings and entire neighborhoods spring up in Japan. We're apt to think that the Japanese possess some innate talent for rapid construction. If we stay for the winter, however, we realize that the reason the buildings here spring up so quickly is because they are built cheaply and with no insulation.

It was not comforting to feel my third-floor apartment swaying in the wind, with the underlying assumption that the building could—at anytime—be destroyed by the next angry earthquake, atomic bomb, tsunami, or volcano. Okay, perhaps not volcano, since the last time Mount Fuji erupted was in 1707, but the fact remains that the lifespan of an average Japanese building is not particularly long.

The Japanese capital's unique vulnerability to major earthquakes is a very real concern. Since the Japanese capital Edo was founded in 1603 (and was renamed Tokyo after the Meiji Restoration of 1868) there have been severely destructive earthquakes—with magnitudes of more than 7.0—directly affecting the capital in 1615, 1649, 1703, 1855, and 1923.

Suffice it to say the Tokugawa shogunate, after winning many a clan war to unite all Japan under its rule, chose for its capital a particularly seismic death trap. Built upon the precise intersection of the Pacific fault, the Eurasian fault, and the Philippine fault, the Tokyo metropolitan area has always been highly susceptible to seismic hazards such as ground shaking, liquefaction, landslides, tsunami, and fires.

During liquefaction, a catastrophic process specific to the region, the stone that holds up Tokyo will actually melt due to such intense underground collisions. The city's foundation will become water. At the same time, the capital's hot summers and strong winds year-round facilitate the spread of fires in the event of quake-prompted gas leaks and explosions.

During the Great Kanto earthquake of 1923 (known in Japanese as *kantō daishinsai* or the great Kanto quake disaster), for example, initial shocks were so violent that the seismographs at the Central Weather Bureau went out of commission, 70 to 80 percent of the metropolis burned to the ground, and 200,000 citizens perished. It was what one American journalist and author called "in all probability, the most serious natural calamity in the long and calamitous history of the human race."

It is not a stretch to say that this international megalopolis is overdue for a seismic event of cataclysmic proportions. Since 1920,

Tokyo's population has increased from two million citizens to twelve million inhabitants by the second millennium. The interim period, perhaps due to the fading of cultural memory, has seen a gradual relaxation of height ordinances imposed on buildings in the most congested regions of the city.

Areas that once contained reservoirs or open parks have been converted into seas of skyscrapers. These towering masses of iron and glass, with their shock-absorbing pillars and posts, are said to be completely earthquake-proof. Then again, so were many of the buildings that toppled over in nearby Kobe more than a decade ago.

The truth is that my fascination with the city of Tokyo is rooted in my own experience. Insofar as a person can relate to a city, I immediately felt—and still feel—an immense bond with Tokyo. I enjoy reading about the history of Tokyo because I am attracted to the city's resilience, her refusal to be crushed, and even to her reckless pride.

There is a famous Japanese proverb that reads, "*Nana korobi ya oki,*" which loosely translates to "fall seven times, stand up eight." It reminds me of an e-mail message I wrote to an old college friend to inform her that I had just been fired from my teaching job for being "mentally unstable," yet had no plans of returning to America yet. "Don't worry about me," I urged, "because I'll bounce back. That is what I do."

In "bouncing back," Tokyo was a great inspiration to me. After all, the city has been completely annihilated twice in the past century, once during the Great Kanto earthquake and then once again in 1945 when its wood and paper structures were obliterated by incendiary bombing raids. In both incidences, however, Tokyo began the process of rebuilding herself only moments after she fell.

As another catastrophic earthquake remains probable, the citizens of Tokyo offer inspiration to the rest of us in their unrelenting will to find beauty in nature's transience and by their resilience in the face of looming terror. And so, with the city of Tokyo as my inspiration, I put my life back together. Still, that's not to say that I didn't remain in a precarious position.

I first heard of the possibility of becoming a bar hostess from my housemate Carla. "You are da type," she told me candidly. "You should really check out da scene in Roppongi."

The task of a hostess, as it was explained to me, was to facilitate fun and flattering conversation with men while consuming alcohol. Originally, I thought she was joking. What madman would really pay me thirty dollars an hour to sit around, drink alcohol, and sing karaoke, plus bonuses for excessive drinking?

However, when I opened the copy of *Tokyo Notice Board,* an English-language publication of classified ads Carla handed to me, to my surprise I discovered that, in fact, there were many such crazy people in this city.

"If you like drinking it's perfect for you," a friend of hers also advised at the time, "they'll basically pay you to look pretty and convince the customers to buy you overpriced cocktails."

Thinking it over, I figured that compared to teaching English, I could make more money as a hostess while I might also be able to shake off the conservative environment that had been suffocating me at my former workplace.

"Well, I do enjoy drinking," I assured them.

a short History of Ukiyo

Living only for the moment, savoring the moon, the snow,
the cherry blossoms and the maple leaves; singing songs, lov-
ing sake, women and poetry, letting oneself drift, bouyant
and carefree, like a gourd floating along the river current.

— RYOI ASAI, *Tales of the Floating World*

It would be inaccurate to describe my transition into the world of bar hostessing without mentioning how captivated I have always been by the uniquely Japanese concept of "the floating world." In fact, throughout my university years, I had studied this aspect of Japanese culture with a passion.

During daylight hours, the modern Japanese dream is one of permanent job security. A far cry from the American dream of striking it rich as an individual, the typical Japanese "salaryman" (or *sarariman*) aspires to enter a successful corporation upon graduation from university and work sixty-hour weeks at the same stable position—adequately providing for his family and serving his country's economy—until he reaches the age of retirement. From an Eastern perspective this is a noble pursuit, in many ways entirely selfless.

Still, even the most diligent of salarymen gets fatigued sometimes. Thus, as the sun goes down each night in certain areas of the capital city, Tokyo's strict daytime culture is completely reversed, giving way to collective dreams and fantasies more centered around personal gratification and a mass catharsis of the overworked. Illusions of stability fade away to illuminate a drastically distinctive entertainment culture known as "the floating world," or *ukiyo*, in Japanese.

The word *ukiyo* was originally a Buddhist expression meaning, "this world of pain." It evolved into "this transient, unreliable world," and finally became "this fleeting, floating world." The fleeting, floating world was an entertainment district where happiness was inextricably linked to a passing moment, and wish fulfillment took precedence over piety.

The old licensed quarters of Tokyo, that is to say the Yoshiwara pleasure district, were enclosed territories, playgrounds for the collective imagination. The district housed three kabuki theaters, countless teahouses frequented by geisha, bars staffed with Japanese hostesses, theatrical parodies of the feudal aristocracy, and thousands of licensed prostitutes.

Art historians regard the woodblock prints that depicted and emerged from these districts as an influential print movement in the history of art, as well as important evidence of a cultural transformation. These prints, called *ukiyo-e*, or "pictures of the floating world," usually depicted natural marvels such as Hokusai's *36 Views of Mt. Fuji* series did, or pornographic spectacles, like the woodblock sex manuals called *shunga*, which emerged despite the sexually repressive norms of the time.

The disparate themes of the *ukiyo-e* remind us that Japan has always been a land of intense extremes, a contrast that is mirrored quite visibly in nature. The celebrated Mount Fuji, which towers more than 12,000 feet high, is only about a hundred miles away from the Tuscorora deep, reaching over 30,000 feet below the ocean. Japan's mountainous terrain is of active volcanic origin and dozens of typhoons sweep through the islands every autumn. Moreover, the nation outclasses the rest of the world in terms of unpredictable seismic activity that has, and will again, reduce modern cities to piles of rubble. In such a light, perhaps the floating world's reverence of transience is due in part to the Japanese archipelago's calamitous geography.

Historically, Tokyo was always known to be a firetrap. As one observer described, it is built of "tinderboxes that could not be more flammable if they were designed expressly for burning." And the Yoshiwara district during its heyday was especially so, due to the prevalence of tightly packed wooden buildings. Historians note that the old Edo was peculiarly proud of her fires, which the commoners admired for their aesthetic appeal and nicknamed *"Edo no hana"* or "the flowers of Edo."

The name seems to suggest a keen perception of aesthetic beauty in otherwise horrific destruction. A similar expression, *"baa no hana"* or "flowers of the bar," refers to another enduring element of *ukiyo* culture: the nightclub hostess, who has enjoyed a privileged place in *ukiyo* culture since its dawn. Perhaps both the raging fire and the bar hostess are similarly compared to flowers because they exhibit a certain transient beauty, one that must be enjoyed before it withers. And similar to the *"edo no hana,"* the *"baa no hana"* can become a destructive force should anyone venture too close to her.

Because the 1923 earthquake and the firebombing of 1945 took their tolls on Yoshiwara, the floating world has gradually become decentralized, wafting to other areas of the city—most notably Roppongi, Asakusa, Kinshichō, Kabukichō, and Ginza—like smoke from an inferno.

Postwar Tokyo has duly inherited the business-pleasure dichotomy that decorates the nation's past, and many Japanese businessmen still manage to party just as hard as they work. This makes for an even more profitable entertainment industry, known by now as the *mizu shobai,* a title signifying the business of ephemeral pleasures.

In the floating world, the normally austere businessman has many options at his fingertips, as the streets of certain quarters transform into strikingly familiar havens of the fleeting pleasures, complete with very, very friendly women.

A presumed hierarchy of the *mizu shobai* rises from the bottom: those establishments where the most sexual services are provided for the least amount of money, toward the most elite establishments—where the fewest sexual services are provided for the most amount of money. The most expensive rung of Tokyo's lucrative sex industry does not deal in sex. Instead it markets simplicity, style, elegance, exclusivity, authenticity, and romantic love.

At the top of the *mizu shobai* remain two classes of women: the traditional geisha and the more economical nightclub hostess. While the geisha continues to dominate the floating world in the cultural capital of Kyoto, Tokyo is gradually giving way to domination by the nightclub hostesses, who are more suited to the capital's post-metropolitan, fast-paced environment.

the Roppongi tour

Roppongi, the "red-light district for foreigners," is a characteristically postwar phenomenon in Tokyo. After the region was flattened by incendiary bombs during World War II, it is said to have risen again around the pizza restaurant of an Italian-American mobster who originally found himself in Tokyo with the occupation forces, then decided to stick around after MacArthur's departure to organize the postwar yakuza, or Japanese mafia.

There is nothing authentically Japanese about Roppongi, just as there is nothing to actually do in the infamous district during the day. At night, however, it becomes heavily populated, largely with drunken foreigners and Japanese women who are looking to meet foreign men in order to improve their English, sample "white meat," or, most likely, both.

As a result, Roppongi is a hybrid mix of world cultures. Yet, on display are not the types of exhibitions you'll find at a world's fair.

I had heard the word *Roppongi* tossed around by my old coworkers in Yokohama, recounting evenings of debauchery in nearby

Tokyo, but I had never actually emerged from the station until the night I showed up in carefully sculpted hair, makeup, and a dress, looking for a job.

the scout from One Eyed Zacks, the largest hostess and cabaret club in Roppongi, had asked me to meet him the following evening on Roppongi Doori, outside station exit A10. Earlier in the week I had sent him an e-mail query that contained my headshot and a full body shot pasted onto the body of the message. Having followed up with a phone call, the man had told me to prepare to meet with the manager of One Eyed Zacks by choosing my clothes and makeup well, since I was to be judged mainly on my appearance.

At first I was taken back by his request, as it began to dawn on me what I might be getting myself into. Then however, I started to wonder if preparing in such a way would be so different from the way I prepared for my interviews all the time, or even my preparation for leaving the house. I firmly believed that most other people judged me by my appearance at least at first, although I didn't admit such things to myself very often. The scout had simply cut the nonsense and gotten straight to the point.

Outside the exit, he was running late. I needed something to do with my hands, so I pulled out a cigarette. In the meantime, another man tapped me on the shoulder to tell me that he knew a great bar down the street looking for a hostess like me. I was about to tell him that I was on my way to interview somewhere else when the first scout showed up behind him. I was afraid for a moment of starting a brawl, but all anxiety was dashed when one said "Hey, man" to the other and the two did one of those secret handshakes that all boys seem to be born knowing how to do.

It turned out that the two were friends, and the second scout arranged to meet me outside of One Eyed Zacks when my first interview was completed.

The manager sat with me at one of the tall round tables for two that surrounded the cabaret stage inside of One Eyed Zacks. Everything that could have been was colored red—the plush carpets, the curtains, the leather on the chairs, the dresses on the other women who were beginning to file in and sit by themselves at designated tables to await the first customers of the night—and done so in a sea of signifiers that could extract hidden passions in even the most lackluster among us.

My first interview did not go so well. The manager did not seem as impressed as I hoped he would be when I confidently told him that I could hold conversations in English, Japanese, French, and Spanish. "The clientele we have here," he replied, "do not require that you speak so many languages. Usually they come to practice English. You are Caucasian," he said, "so if you do not speak English it will just confuse everyone."

"Oh, okay," was all I could think to reply to the manager of One Eyed Zacks. "Do you know of any other establishments where I might be able to use many languages to entertain men?"

"You could look into the upscale clubs in Ginza or Akasaka," he replied, referring me to different sections of Tokyo entirely.

"What about Kabukichō?" I asked, a question so naïve in retrospect that it stings what is left of my pride to recall.

"Americans don't work in Kabukichō," the manager replied, without much explanation.

After my interview, someone must have called the second scout to tell him that I was on my way out because he arrived at the foot of the building within seconds. Everything seemed connected; the degree to which everyone in this neighborhood knew each other so well was almost terrifying.

"So what is your name?" the Japanese man asked me in English, an effort he soon gave up after I continued to respond in Japanese.

"Daisy," I replied, giving him the name of my pet dog, a neurotic but lovable Lhasa apso I'd left with my parents on Long Island before departing across the Pacific.

"And yours?" I asked.

"Hiroki."

"Who do you work for?" I asked blatantly, knowing full well that many recruiters for hostess bars are members or confidants of the yakuza. It was perhaps not the brightest move on my part, but I had downed some shots of tequila before leaving my house that evening.

"I work for pretty girls," he insisted. If he were yakuza, I reasoned, then he was likely to be in the lower rankings, seeing as both of his pinkie fingers were still attached, he had no identifying mafia tattoos visible anywhere upon his body, and he was quite young.

"Sure you do." I shot a sarcastic grin in his direction.

When we entered a club with the characteristically nonsensical title Mayor Venus, the mama-san came out to greet us in the corridor of the establishment. She was a tall, grotesquely thin, blond woman who looked to be in her mid-thirties. Mama-sans, though, as a general rule, tend to appear to be roughly ten to fifteen years younger than their actual age. This is largely because they have the financial resources for plastic surgery, a practice that is quite common, seeing as these women run businesses that value physical beauty over everything else.

"Do you have any tattoos?" the woman asked as she looked me over from head to toe.

"No," I replied with a smile, letting the shawl I was wearing slide off of my back and turning myself around for inspection, playing the part of the piece of meat I was rapidly becoming.

"Do you have a job during the day?" The woman's accent was either Australian or British; later on in my hostess career, I would learn to tell the difference between the two.

"I teach English," I lied, not wanting to appear entirely at her disposal. "I'd really rather work part-time at night."

"I'm sorry," she said coldly with a flat expression that hadn't cracked once since we'd met. "I am not hiring right now."

And just like that, Hiroki and I turned about-face and left the establishment. "If she wasn't hiring anyone anyway," I asked naïvely, "then why ask if I had any tattoos?"

The silence that ensued between us for the next few moments as I followed him back across the busy intersection was thick enough to choke upon.

"There is another club I will take you to on the fourth floor of that building"—Hiroki pointed up at a neon sign that read CLUB DOLL HOUSE, having fully ignored my previous question—"the mama-san here is Japanese."

"Is she nice?" I asked as we entered the building.

"You ask too many questions," Hiroki replied with a sly smile, pushing number four on the elevator.

"An American?" Mama's eyes widened. I later found out this was because there are so very few of us on the scene. "Come sit down over here and I'll be right with you. You are so very cute." She was speaking English with an inviting smile. The Japanese mama-san looked about ten or twenty years older than the mama-san I had met just minutes earlier, which meant that the Japanese woman could have been pushing sixty in mama years.

The club was empty except for a few blond hostesses, all in red dresses, sitting at a table about fifteen feet away. The three women glared over at Hiroki and me without reserve. I knew that I was unwelcome there.

Hiroki and I sat in silence for about five minutes, as the mama never returned. Finally, a waiter emerged from the back room to tell us exactly what we'd just heard at Mayor Venus, "I'm sorry but we are not hiring anyone right now." As we left, I was too confused to even formulate questions for Hiroki anymore, which likely pleased the man.

"Don't worry," Hiroki encouraged, taking a lighter tone with me. "I know of many, many other establishments where you can look for work."

It was my turn to be silent.

"I think you would make a very good hostess," Hiroki continued, unfazed.

"Why's that?" I asked.

"You are very cute and cheerful. That will make your customers very happy to talk to you," he replied. "Also," he continued, "you speak Japanese well, so that makes you very funny."

I was about to ask what was so hilarious about my language abilities when his cell phone rang, echoing the tune of the hit single "Evolution" by the Japanese pop artist Ayumi Hamasaki.

"*Hai . . . hai . . . hai . . . wakarimashita,*" Hiroki said to the caller in an obedient tone, expressing agreement with the speaker on the other end. "I have to go now," he told me as he put his phone back into his pocket. "If you wait here I can come back later tonight and show you around some more hostess bars."

"Wait where?" I asked, anxious about being left on my own resources in the red-light district.

"Why don't you get to know the neighborhood?" he said, pointing to a strip of bars on the other side of Roppongi Crossing.

"Well, when will you be back?" I inquired.

"Maybe by twelve thirty," Hiroki replied, after thinking it over a moment.

"But it's nine fifteen now!" I protested.

"Would you rather I not come back?" he asked.

"I probably won't still be around by then," I sighed, "but thanks anyway."

Hiroki and I bowed to each other before the man turned around and disappeared into the crowd. I never saw him again.

10

propaganda

after being expelled from the Doll House and abandoned by the mysterious Hiroki-san, my confidence was understandably waning some. But the night was far from over. Alone on the corner of the busiest intersection in the district, I noticed a large poster advertising a nightclub called Shot Bar Propaganda. I crossed the street to investigate further.

Looking over Roppongi Crossing was an enlarged image of the American icon Rosie the Riveter pulling up her sleeve to reveal her bicep muscle under the familiar slogan: WE CAN DO IT. It was one of the most prominent images hovering over all of Roppongi Crossing.

"Yeah, whatever," I whispered to myself as I crossed the street, unable to ignore Rosie's hovering presence.

I entered the large building that housed Shot Bar Propaganda, taking with me a copy of *Tokyo Notice Board* from a magazine rack next to the entrance. I was hoping to find an establishment where I could sit down with a cold drink and weigh my employment options.

I poked my head into Propaganda as well as a few other bars in the adjacent building, but nothing looked promising for someone who didn't necessarily want to be bothered by strangers.

As I approached the staircase to explore the basement of the building, I saw a sign marked THE LEMON and an arrow pointing down. About halfway down the staircase I began to overhear a sickeningly bad karaoke rendition of the song "Ai Shiteru" by the Japanese ballad singer Mika Nakashima.

"Hey!" two largely built bouncers greeted me.

"Ladies drink for free all night, sweetheart, come on in!" one of the men said as he extended his arm to lure me into the establishment. I talked to the men for a few moments before deciding to follow them into the Lemon and indulge in free drinks. The men hailed from Nigeria and Ghana, they told me.

I was surprised to find the Lemon empty except for two Japanese businessmen sitting in the corner. One of them had just finished singing the ballad "Ai Shiteru," and a casually dressed waitress with long brown hair was clapping for him enthusiastically.

"What can I get you to drink?" the lone waitress asked me.

"What's good?" I asked.

The young woman told me her name was Eva and that she hailed from Jerusalem. We began a friendly conversation comparing the bright lights and crowds of Tokyo to our respective hometowns.

"What does *'ai shiteru'* mean in English?" I asked her, referring to the chorus of the last song that her customer had sung.

"I think it means 'I love you,'" Eva replied, "but my Japanese is not so great."

"Yeah, that makes sense," I said. "Thanks."

It was incredibly curious that I never learned how to say "I love you" during my six years of prior Japanese studies, or even during my one year with a Japanese family. This was simply because *"ai shiteru"* was never said in any of the environments I'd found myself in before. The Japanese language has a heavily contextual element to it. Words must always be chosen carefully depending upon where one is or to whom he is speaking. As a nonnative speaker, this aspect of the language and culture can be overwhelming at times.

Suddenly Eva's expression became stricken with panic. When I turned around to look at the two men in the corner brushing off their briefcases and putting on their jackets with the obvious intent of leaving the establishment, I realized what was troubling her.

"Please, please, don't go," Eva begged them, "let's all have one more drink together."

"Yeah, don't leave yet, we were just starting to have fun," I chimed in. I hadn't much else to do that evening than give my new acquaintance a hand, since she appeared to be working on commission and it was a slow night for the bar. "I was hoping you would invite us over to drink with you." By then I was speaking a drunken jumble of English and Japanese.

Although the two of us could not confer alone because we were with the customers from that point on, Eva's expression showed me how grateful she was for my help.

"Okay then, what would everyone like to drink?" the older of the two businessmen asked us.

At that, Eva mouthed, "Champagne," to me from behind the man's head.

"Champagne!" I announced, in a gesture of female solidarity.

"Will it be a bottle of Dom Pérignon for all of us to share?" Eva didn't ask so much as tell her customers. Lemon wasn't a hostess bar per se, but the waitress was nonetheless working on commission.

When Eva returned to the table with the bottle of champagne and four glasses, she also had a large lollipop in her hand. She and one of the businessmen partook in the lollipop together, which was dipped into the glasses of champagne as they took turns letting the candy melt away in their mouths. The sheer power of delicate suggestion is far more understood and appreciated in the East than it is in the West.

"My name is Tadashi," the other businessman said to me, "but you can call me Tada-chan." The suffix "chan" is a diminutive variation of the honorific "san." In such a way, he was basically asking me to address him in the same way I would a small child or a beloved pet.

The older man seemed to enjoy being treated like a baby. After some small talk, he asked me to teach him some English the same way I taught my school-age students. He looked like a complete moron singing "Twinkle Twinkle Little Star" with me, hand gestures and all, but I figured since he bought our drinks he had the unwritten license to act like an idiot without consequence.

His head as red as an apple, bobbing along awkwardly with his body—this was an entirely new species of Japanese man I had just come across. He was nothing like my homestay father, whose most defining feature was his general absence and lack of anything to say. Nor did he resemble my strict boss at the English school or the crooked psychiatrist who had tried to expel me from his country for having an attitude.

Later on, however, I'd realize that all three of these men may have acted the same way if put into a similar context. For the typical salaryman there is work, there is play, and there is nothing in between. Any middle ground linking the two is completely hollow.

"Wow, what a great dancer," Eva said, winking at me when the man diverted his gaze. I liked Eva, I decided.

"Why don't you sing something I can dance to?" Tada-chan requested of me.

"Okay," I agreed, plugging a couple of old-school Madonna

songs into the karaoke machine. It was not very challenging for me to sing some Madonna karaoke over champagne. My being a child of the eighties, the woman practically raised me. After I sang the songs "Like a Virgin" and "Like a Prayer," my new friend Tadashi was even more intoxicated.

"What means 'like a'?" Tada-chan asked. The Japanese tend to be much more handy with English vocabulary than they are with grammar. That is likely because English and Japanese grammar patterns could not be any more upside down and backward reflections of each other if they tried.

"It means prayer 'mitai' or virgin 'mitai,' " I explained. The simplest way in Japanese to describe something that resembles something else is to attach the grammatical structure *mitai* to the noun that is being imitated. Curiously, the word *mitai* is likewise a verb conjugation that means "want to see." The phrase is fitting, as people often see what they want to when making comparisons. In my studies I've found that even the most commonplace expressions in the Japanese language tend to sound terrifically poetic to the nonnative ear.

When the Dom Pérignon ran dry I decided that I needed to catch the last train back to my gaijin house while I could still walk in a relatively straight direction. I politely excused myself from the table, bowed deeply to the customers, and thanked them for a pleasant evening. Eva walked me to the door.

"Thank you so much for helping me out," Eva said as we bid farewell. "Come back any time you want and I'll always hook you up with free stuff!"

"No problem," I replied and meant it, "this was a really interesting experience for me.

"Besides," I continued after a pause, "us girls gotta stick together."

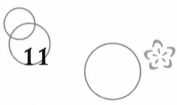

GIRL, OUT OF CONTEXT

The dream: to know a foreign language yet not to understand it: to perceive the difference in it without that difference ever being recuperated by the superficial sociality of discourse, communication or vulgarity . . . to undo our own "reality" under the effect of other formulations, other syntaxes . . . in a word, to descend into the untranslatable.

——ROLAND BARTHES, *Empire of Signs*

BY SEPTEMBER OF 2003 I was still unemployed, although I did stop by the Lemon to help out Eva every now and then. During the third weekend of that month I decided to take a trip to the city of Kyoto with Rachel. My friend's stay in Japan as an English teacher was wrapping up, and she wanted to see the city of Kyoto before returning to North America. She invited me to accompany her that weekend, since the following Monday was a holiday at her school.

Kyoto, or "the western capital" as it is known, is generally agreed upon to be the nation's cultural center. Compared to Tokyo in the east, Kyoto has more greenery, fewer concrete slabs, and is far more pleasing to the eye. There is less "urban jungle" and more "Zen." Unlike Tokyo, the western capital is what most American tourists hope and imagine they'll find in their travels to the Far East.

So with good reason, citizens tend to be highly conscious and proud of their city's rich cultural heritage. My former coworker Naomi once informed me that it is tradition among those in Kyoto to politely refuse an invitation to eat ochazuke (a curiously tasty mixture of green tea and day-old rice) with a neighbor for the first two times the offer is extended. If they are offered ochazuke a third time, however, it becomes okay to partake. The concept is terrifically Japanese.

The holiday weekend marked the coming of the autumnal equinox. Both the vernal equinox and the autumnal equinox are national holidays in Japan. Known respectively as *haru no hikan* and *aki no hikan,* the weeks surrounding each equinox are times that Buddhist monks reserve for meditating on the transience of existence, while average families utilize the vacation to tidy up their household altars and hold memorial services for deceased relatives.

It turns out the monks would have much transience to ponder that year, seeing as there was both an earthquake *and* a typhoon in the Tokyo area that weekend. We knew that the typhoon, called *taifuu juugo* or typhoon fifteen, was about to hit and so we were happy to be leaving the city. Sitting tight on the bullet train to Kyoto at the time of the earthquake, Rachel and I missed out on the apocalyptic spectacle. We didn't even hear about the quake until later that evening.

After settling into our youth hostel late in the afternoon, Rachel and I treated ourselves to dinner at a *kaiten* sushi bar, where we could choose from a conveyer belt of tasty raw fish. There I got a call on my cell phone from my mother.

"I can't really talk now, I'm in a restaurant with someone," I told her before she could really speak.

"Oh," she said, "then I guess you're okay after the earthquake if you're answering your phone."

"There was an earthquake in Tokyo?" I naïvely asked, eyeing Rachel whose expression told me that she was also clueless about the event.

"Yeah," she replied somewhat uneasily, "it was on TV. A few people were injured when the wall of a Buddhist temple collapsed."

"We must have been on the train by then," I said. "I'm in Kyoto for the holiday, like I told you, with my friend Rachel."

"That sounds like fun," she said. "Are you sure you want to stay in Tokyo now instead of coming home to rest? It would be okay for you to stay here for a little while." Her tone was as nurturing as always.

"Nah," I said, "I'm not finished with Japan yet. I'm hoping that my Japanese can get even better. Besides, leaving now would be like letting everyone else win. And I'm tougher than that."

"It's not a contest you know. This isn't *Survivor*," she reminded me.

"What's *Survivor*?" I asked. I had been out of the country a while by then.

After ending the conversation with my mother as quickly as possible, I decided to take another piece of tuna off of the belt; it was the third time the fish had come around past my seat to tempt me, and I finally succumbed to its pull.

"Another earthquake today," I reiterated. "I've never felt so glad to be out of that city!"

"So you finally told your family that you got fired?" Rachel seemed more interested in my relationship with my mother than she was with the weather in Tokyo.

"Yeah," I replied, "I finally got up the courage to tell my mom last week."

"I see." My friend found it odd that I had waited an entire month before managing to tell my mother that I got fired from my teaching job. "Couldn't you have used her support when it happened though?" she asked in earnest.

"Yeah, actually," I admitted, "I could have used it. Still, the idea of telling her scared me to death."

"Why?" she asked, curious.

"I have absolutely no idea"—I looked down at my plate—"but I have been this way for as long as I can remember."

With all the issues I ended up having growing up, many people assume that I come from an unstable home environment. But for the most part, that's not true: my mother and father are good parents. For as long as I can remember, though, I have pushed them away from me like it was my job.

I was in the second grade when I began refusing to cross the street on the way to school, yet I could not dare to tell anyone that the fear was due to my being witness to a minor pedestrian accident at that intersection one morning. My parents sent me to my elementary school's psychologist where I played board games, learned about a purple dragon named Pumsey whose adventures illustrated important lessons about healthy self-esteem, and sang songs like, "I am special, I am special, so are you, so are you," to the tune of "Frère Jacques." In spite of this, I never admitted to anyone why I wouldn't cross the street.

As I got older, this pattern became so severe that I practically created an alternate image of myself to be displayed in the company of my family. I was aggressive and secretive and tried to seem invulnerable. When I could no longer hide from my parents the fact that I was skipping meals, I began to make myself throw up. Later on, when the plumbing in my house began to back up due to my constant purging, and the risk of being found out loomed too high again, I began to cut my arms in order to experience a similar feeling of release.

I cannot stress how meticulously I concealed my weaknesses and shortcomings. The sense of shame I felt was unbearably heavy. Perhaps I was Japanese in a past life.

тhe ѕuѕhi cнeя, a middle-aged man in a white apron who had been standing directly in front of me chopping up fish the entire time, complimented me on my Japanese when he overheard me address one of the waiters. The two of us chatted for a moment; I told him that Rachel and I were Americans living in Tokyo who had just arrived in Kyoto for sightseeing.

"There was a typhoon and an earthquake in Tokyo today," I said in Japanese to the chef as he took a fresh fish out of the tank and lopped off its head without flinching.

"Oh, typhoon fifteen," he replied with interest, "we might get the tail end of that storm over here tomorrow. . . . Is it true that in America you give your storms names?" the man asked as the headless fish's tail still fluttered in panic.

"Yes, of course," I said. "It used to be that hurricanes only took female names, but now the meteorologists alternate between boys' and girls' names."

"Why only female names at first?" he asked, cleaning out the fish's innards.

"Well." I paused a moment before saying, "That's because the women in America are very powerful like hurricanes. Women are actually stronger than the men where I'm from."

"Really?" he asked. The shocked expression on his tired face was priceless. In that short amount of time the fish had been artfully sliced and was already ready to serve.

"No, not really," I responded with a smirk.

He laughed at my joke and refilled my glass of beer on the house. By then I seemed to have already perfected the art of procuring free beer from middle-aged men just about anywhere.

"You may want to call it quits after this one," Rachel, who had been left out of our Japanese conversation, advised. "No sense drinking like there's no tomorrow. We have sightseeing to do in the morning."

"Yeah, I was thinking the same thing," I lied.

The next morning Rachel and I visited Ginkakuji, the famous Silver Temple, which is not really made out of silver. As we learned, the shogun who commissioned the temple's creation had every intention of having it plated with silver. However, he died before the construction was finished and perhaps his predecessors assumed that he was only kidding.

The grounds of Ginkakuji were extremely impressive aesthetically, yet it was a busy weekend at the temple with loud tourists and crying babies, so the ambience was hardly meditative. Rachel hated babies, yet they seemed to follow her everywhere.

At Ginkakuji I took out my digital camera and began taking pictures of the spotted koi, the gigantic goldfish that decorate the ponds surrounding most of the renowned temples of Japan. I patiently waited with my flash turned on for the fish to turn their heads to the camera and strike an artistic pose. My pictures turned out well, as Ginkakuji's gardens were carefully sculpted to be aesthetically pleasing by the expert landscaping artists who trimmed the trees and plowed the sand to perfection daily.

Later in the day, Rachel and I managed to trek across Kyoto on foot (since we couldn't workout regularly while in Kyoto, we were even thankful for the exercise) toward Kinkakuji, or the Golden Temple. The two of us met Tommy, Rachel's old friend from high school, at the gate as we entered the grounds. Half Japanese, bilingual, and a resident of Kyoto at the moment, Tommy proved to be an excellent tour guide.

"It's actually gold," I said. "I thought it was just a name like the other one."

"You know this temple is only an imitation," Rachel, the history buff, informed us when we came to an unobstructed view of the site. "The original one was torched by an insane Buddhist monk who was training there. That was only about fifty years ago, I think."

"Well, a lot of Japan's temples are reconstructions of those destroyed in the war. Even the Great Buddha in Kamakura is a copy of one that was washed away by a tsunami," I, the disaster buff, reminded my friend.

"Yeah," Rachel said, "except this happened more recently. Like 1950."

"So you mean"—I was intrigued—"that Kyoto's most famous landmark survived the 1940s air raids on Japan only to be destroyed from within?"

"Yes," replied my friend, "Kyoto was bypassed by the air raids."

Tommy, who was far more skilled at translating from Japanese to English than I, stopped to read the Japanese inscription by the water. "Yeah, this is the story I think," he said. We let him read in silence as we gazed in awe at the ancient structure's replica; it was gorgeous. Coated entirely with eye-clenching gold, its mirror image could be captured almost without distortion in the bordering pond.

"You're right, Rachel"—Tommy had finished reading—"he loved it so much that he had to burn it down."

"Intense," I thought out loud.

"Yeah, Yukio Mishima wrote a book about that man," Rachel

said, "but he twisted the plot around so that some woman adulteress was fundamentally to blame for the temple's destruction."

"What a dick," I spat satirically.

"Yeah, really," my good friend agreed.

Rachel grinned as the three of us began our walk over to a famous and apparently sacred Zen rock garden in the area. On our arrival the viewing area was crowded yet silent. All the visitors were sitting down to contemplate the large structure, so we assumed the same position.

Sitting in front of the sand so long my feet fell asleep, I quietly shifted my weight, thinking of how much I needed a cigarette. Even the ripples in the sand seemed to resemble flames then. I wondered to myself how magnificent the golden pavilion would have appeared as it burned. There is a most transient form of beauty in destruction, especially in destruction by fire.

on our last night in Kyoto, Rachel and I went to Gion. In Kyoto's floating world district of Gion, Geisha teahouses take precedence over hostess bars. As we passed through Gion, in fact, we almost allowed ourselves to succumb to an overpriced tourist trap when some locals proposed to make our faces up like a geisha or maiko (a geisha in training).

I was about to make a snide remark about how all the geisha were on their cell phones when I saw a geisha who, by some miracle, was not talking on the phone as she passed. Without giving Rachel any explanation, I darted after the unsuspecting woman. I should note that this was during a point in my stay when I first began to feel very comfortable speaking Japanese. At the same time, however, I had not yet learned that I shouldn't use my bilingual powers to annoy other people.

So I used my newfound language ability to ask this geisha how many kimonos she owned, how long she'd been a geisha, whether she liked her job, and if she found it at all difficult to walk in that elaborate costume. With every question her pace sped up, and I increased my walking speed to match hers each time.

"What about those shoes," I asked, nodding toward her traditional geta, "don't they hurt your feet?"

"Not at all." Aside from monosyllabic replies, the woman simply refused to acknowledge me.

"Do they feel good then?"

She didn't respond as she escaped into a teahouse without looking in my direction even once.

If only I could get into a teahouse, I thought to myself. Generally speaking, when I reach a mental state such as the mood that Gion had instilled in me, I tend to feel so driven that nothing can stop me until I either accomplish my mission or slam head-on into a figurative brick wall, whichever comes first.

But this time around there would be no barriers or limits; I was supergirl. I knocked upon the door of the first teahouse we passed, knowing full well that geisha teahouses are strictly off-limits to foreigners as well as everyone else saving the exorbitantly wealthy Japanese elite.

When a middle-aged Japanese woman came to the door, dressed in a traditional kimono, of course, I used my most polite and innocent-sounding Japanese to ask her if I could use the bathroom of her establishment. She said something to another old woman standing behind her to the effect of oh-how-cute-the-little-foreigner-speaks-some-Japanese, then let me in and showed me down the hall.

When I emerged from the rest room, the hallway around me was empty. I was still for a moment and I could hear the sounds of laughing and drunken debauchery coming from the floor above me. My curiosity having already killed my manners much earlier in the evening, I did what any American would do and what no Japanese would ever dare to: I ascended the stairs and interrupted a geisha party.

Inside, some of the men being entertained claimed to be movie stars, but I never verified this. I did manage to take a picture of the party on my digital camera before the house's okaasan dragged me back down the stairs practically by the ear, scolding me the entire way, which of course I deserved.

"That was *so cool*," I told Rachel after getting thrown out of the okiya, relating to her exactly what had happened.

"And what did you say to that geisha on the street anyway?" Rachel asked. My friend shared in my amusement if not my audacity.

"Oh, I don't know, it doesn't translate," I lied, a bit embarrassed at my own behavior.

In retrospect, though, the Japanese didn't translate only because if these conversations in Gion had been in English they never would have taken place at all. I was bothering and deceiving other people in ways that I would have never have dreamed of if I had been speaking English, my mother tongue.

Since all language is coded with norms of modesty and social conditioning that basically all native speakers are brought up to accept, there is a certain freedom that comes with speaking a language so drastically different from one's native tongue. Unlike the French or Spanish I studied, Japanese shares no roots with the English language. So for me, the opportunity to express my thoughts in Japanese basically tore the ground—and by *ground* I mean all the morals I was brought up to observe—right up from under my feet. And when there is no ground to stand upon, this gives the illusion that there is no place to fall. It was a floating world indeed.

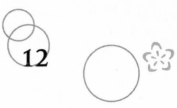

12

the Ginza Bar flowers

People who admire the Japanese traditional arts make much of the "love of nature" that inspired sand gardens, bonsai, ikebana flower arranging, and so forth, but they often fail to realize that . . . these arts were strongly influenced by the military caste that ruled Japan for many centuries, and they demand total control over every branch and twig.

—ALEX KERR, *Dogs and Demons: The Fall of Modern Japan*

Having returned from the weekend in Kyoto, my misadventures in Gion had piqued a new curiosity regarding the relationship between geisha teahouses and hostess bars. Such inquisitiveness was coupled with the realization that, out of context as I was, I could get away with just about anything in this country.

Coincidentally, it was around this time that I received the news that my old friend Lindsey was coming to town. Lindsey's "Tokyo strategy," I was to find out, was to put together some money to pay off her student loans by doing none other than working in a Tokyo hostess bar. I have always had a conviction that degrading activities tend to suck much less when done with a good friend, so I was back in the game.

I drilled Lindsey on the basics of the hostess market and told her all that had transpired during my last tour of Roppongi. Lindsey had higher aspirations, and insisted that we check out the classier international clubs on the Ginza strip.

Ginza is to Tokyo as the Champs-Elysées is to Paris, Rodeo Drive is to Los Angeles, or Fifth Avenue is to New York: expensive. The village is a brand in itself to the Japanese, a people more excited by brand goods than any culture I've ever witnessed, and ritzy shops such as Rolex, Prada, Tiffany, Gucci, Coach, Louis Vuitton (two large stores) are all on the Ginza strip. A step up from basically everywhere else, Ginza is a playground for the very rich, which necessitates the plentiful presence of hostess bars, many of them marketing the classiest international flavor.

To be honest, I never thought we would get hired. After all, I couldn't manage to impress any of the Roppongi mamas enough to take a chance on an inexperienced young American. Ginza was even more daunting.

But having a tour of the Roppongi hostess circuit under my belt, I advised Lindsey of the errors I felt I'd made. For one, I never should have mentioned that I had some interests and hobbies such as studying foreign languages. I thought it was harmless to say that I studied Japanese and looked forward to practicing it with customers at the bar. However, the management does not prefer its girls to do *anything*.

As a result, Lindsey and I decided that playing dumb would be our best prospect.

The night before our first interview with the manager of an

exclusive Ginza club called the Palace, the two of us austerely sat on the floor of my apartment with pen and paper to create fake personalities for ourselves along with a reason why we could only accept the positions if we were hired together.

We decided that Lindsey and I both were from Wilmington, Delaware, Lindsey's actual hometown. I had petitioned that we both be from New York—where I grew up—but Lindsey thought it might make us seem too "street-smart," so Delaware girls we were. As the story went, we had met on our high school cheerleading team. Lindsey and I had truly been teammates on our university cheerleading squad, but under no circumstances could there be any mention of the *u* word.

"Wait," I said as an afterthought, "if I didn't go to college, then how come I can speak Japanese?"

This was an important detail. Almost everyone I spoke to in this country immediately asked me how and why I was so proficient in their language and I usually replied with the truth: that I had studied the language extensively on a university level before moving to Japan.

"You had a Japanese boyfriend once," Lindsey advised without giving much thought to the matter.

At our first interview, we remembered our routine perfectly.

After graduating high school with dual prom queen status, we entered beauty school together in the fall, and dropped out together one month later because it was too challenging. Our interests included shopping, doing each other's hair, and cute puppies.

"We like puppies!" I blurted out, somehow managing to keep a straight face. And finally, we needed to work at the bar together because the two of us were "totally-like-best-friends-in-the-whole-wide-world-and-like-we-just-like-um-like-could-never-stand-to-be-apart!"

The male manager hired us on the spot.

Prior to our first night of work in the upscale district of Tokyo, I guzzled a couple of beers to stomach the version of myself that I was about to unveil. Lindsey chastised me for drinking, warning me not to forget what we'd practiced. She also had me wipe the lipstick off my teeth before we went into the club.

"Do you know who I am?"

The voice came from behind us soon after our entry. We had been standing inside the club together, slightly anxious since the man who had hired us was nowhere to be seen, waiting to be told what to do. We turned around to look at a small built, stunningly beautiful Filipina.

She was decked out in diamond jewelry and a high-end designer dress that I swore I saw in the window of Takashimaya Ginza the week before. After glancing knowingly at each other, then back at the woman—whose relative elegance appeared to be compensating for the fact that she was so much older than most of the Palace girls—one of us said timidly, "Umm . . . Mama?"

"Very good," she replied.

Her posture was impeccable. Mama-sans were generally successful longtime hostesses who were promoted to the high-level position when they began aging. "You are very fortunate to have been hired here, this is a very exclusive club"—she looked us both over carefully from head to toe—"Now I will teach you both how to be the best hostesses."

Just then, however, an unknown voice called out, "Mama Destiny!" from inside the Palace's VIP room. Without so much as excusing herself, Mama Destiny turned her back to us in order to attend to some presumably more important business.

As an afterthought while she sashayed away, she turned around and pointed a petite finger at my feet. "You have to change your shoes," she said firmly, though into what she did not specify. After she turned around the second time, we did not see her again until three nights later. Mama Destiny was in obvious need of better parenting skills.

We ended up standing in the doorway of the club for more than a few moments. Like baby birds abandoned in the nest, we had no idea how to survive without Mama. All we could do was cling to the hope that Mama might return. Standing there awkwardly amid the flurry of activity that would always precede the bar's opening, I felt like a different person. I was dressed up as some other girl who I was supposed to be, one who was a desirable commodity.

When our presence was finally noticed by the manager who had interviewed us earlier, all he did was look the both of us over from head to toe, then leave again in a hurry. The manager then returned almost immediately in the company of another sharply dressed male employee. The two men approached me with their gaze concentrated upon my feet.

"*Kono kutsu wa hidoi ne,*" one man said to the other.

"*Hidoi desu ne,*" the other confirmed.

"They just called my shoes 'horrible'!" I elbowed Lindsey as the men discussed what might be done to rectify my shoe situation.

To my shock, they had just used the word *hidoi,* a Japanese adjective most often used to describe civil wars, natural disasters, or serial killers, and applied it to describe my shoes. The dress shoes I wore weren't high-end or anything, but I'd like to think that *hidoi* was an exaggeration.

The whole dilemma had me feeling like a mismatched mannequin. It was as if I had gotten all dressed up—having stepped into the mold of the pretty girl that the management instructed I become—for the intrinsic purpose of being knocked down.

The men showed me to the box of extra shoes in the locker room, and after profuse complaining to Lindsey of my intense hatred of high-heeled shoes, I finally decided on a pair. It put my five-foot-eight frame at more than six feet tall. I had height insecurities and had always felt too tall, so I'd never actually worn heels before.

"I feel huge in these heels," I told Lindsey. "Can't they see that being a super-tall monster is totally uncute?"

"They look really good," she replied. I had to take her word; she was a far more experienced shoe connoisseur.

Then she left the locker room. "Hey, Lindsey," I called back desperately, "how the hell do I walk in these things?"

There was no answer.

After I managed to put one foot in front of the other enough times to exit the locker room, Rod, the manager, sat us down at the designated table where the hostesses waited to be placed with their clients.

There were about twenty other women sitting at a single round table in silence. Since we all hailed from different regions of the globe, I felt as if I had been placed in a mixed floral bouquet or a Benetton commercial. After all, the Palace was an "international hostess club," and it advertised that inside its doors a customer will behold the most beautiful girls in the world. We sat there upright, like flowers waiting to be picked, and were arranged in the most aesthetically pleasing manner possible as soon as the paying customers came in to behold us.

"Nicolette." Rod singled out one of the white girls. Addressing her in Japanese, Rod asked Nicolette to explain to Lindsey and me what we were supposed to do. The blond strongly built woman with large breasts nodded in agreement, and then winked at the maestro as he walked away. Nicolette then returned to whatever she was accomplishing on the wide screen of her Japanese cell phone, never giving us a second glance. At first we assumed that language barriers prevented her from following Rod's instructions. But that was before we realized that the Russians simply didn't want to talk to us.

"Linz"—I turned to her nervously—"what are we supposed to *do* again?"

"Look over at that table," she said as she directed my glance to a small party of hostesses across the room. They had just begun greeting an entourage of male clients.

"First you give a man a hot towel to wipe his hands and face." Lindsey studied our new coworkers intently. "When making his drink, the ice goes in first, next the whiskey, and then the water."

"They're taking their time with the stirring part," I whispered from the sidelines. "And what are they wiping off the long glasses so tenderly?" I asked.

"Condensation," she replied.

"Is that really necessary?" I questioned.

"Is anything in here necessary?" Lindsey made a subtle nod at another hostess who was meticulously smoothing out the wrinkles on the jacket of a customer who had just entered.

"So what do we do after the drink is made?" I sought her advice.

"Then you be quiet." Lindsey made another gesture toward the women across the room, who came to resemble inanimate decorations while the men they accompanied appeared to be making business negotiations.

"Aren't we supposed to talk to them or something?" I said with a sneer.

"It really depends on the customer," the hostess situated to Lindsey's right leaned over and informed us in a whisper.

Just as we were about to make a new friend, however, the manager came over and shushed us.

"You Americans talk too loudly," he criticized, and then continued his round.

"This job sucks," Lindsey said under her breath.

"Yeah!" I coughed.

The prestige had quickly worn off.

To our surprise and to the resentment of everyone else, Lindsey and I were among the first ladies picked to join the customers who began to flow in steadily at around 10 P.M. Getting chosen early on didn't affect our hourly wages, but it meant that we could finally start drinking and racking in the beer bonuses.

Our job training came largely from the sharply dressed manager, whom we nicknamed Rod on our second night of work, due to the large stick that appeared to be shoved up his ass. Rod's job was to direct each lady to a place at each party, to oversee the interactions among the hostesses and clients to ensure that every man was appropriately catered to, and to see to it that all the rules were strictly obeyed.

Since his attempt to shrug off the new girls onto Nicolette had failed miserably, he needed to constantly remind us when our customer's glass needed filling, to never cross our legs, to sit up straighter, to clap louder after a man finished singing, to fix our makeup, or if there was a blemish on one of our shoes. Hence the nickname.

I don't recall the names or faces of any of my first customers that night. What stands out in my memory, however, was a conversation that occurred a few hours into our first night of work, when Lindsey and I arranged a secret meeting in the bathroom.

"This job totally, totally sucks!" was the first thing she spat, beer on her breath and all.

"Indeed," was all I could reply, "it does."

We complained to each other about having to avoid speaking out of turn, and staying alert to the men's needs at all times. It did, in fact, suck immeasurably.

"You wanna quit?" my friend asked me with a smirk.

"I'm not sure," I replied, feeling tipsy.

"It's a lot of money," she rationalized. "If we can hang on for just two weeks we'll make more than one thousand dollars each."

"That's a lot of money for doing nothing special," I agreed. "So we'll stay two weeks?"

"Two weeks," she concurred.

13

Destiny, Queen of Hearts

"Hold your tongue!" said the Queen, turning purple.
"I won't!" said Alice.
"Off with her head!" the Queen shouted at the top of her
  voice.

—LEWIS CARROLL,

Alice's Adventures in Wonderland

ON MY SECOND night at the Palace, I met Ando, the first customer to show a genuine interest in me.

"I heard you're new here," he told me in impeccable English. His proficiency was uncharacteristic of a Japanese businessman, whose attempts at English are the most unintelligible I've encountered in my world travels.

"Once I heard that there were two new American girls working here," he confessed to me, "I requested to meet one of you right away." I was starting to see why the girls of other nationalities had been relatively unenthusiastic about Lindsey's and my arrival at the

Palace. "American girls are rare," he said, "so all the customers will want to talk to you."

"Why are there so few Americans?" I asked.

"They come and go," he said, "but usually they are not so good at hostessing."

"Why's that?" I asked, remembering to bat my eyelashes.

"Well, they're not so polite," he replied thoughtfully, "not so talented at serving others."

"Oh"—I took in his comment—"so how will I ever learn to be a good hostess?" I flashed my pouty face, which he ate up. By then I'd learned that asking a man to teach me something, anything really, was a good way to make conversation. It was a mutually beneficial arrangement, especially since Mama Destiny and Rod, my virtual parents in this twisted semblance of a family, were failing miserably at teaching me anything about the trade.

"I'll tell you," he said, taking my hand. It was working. "You have to give as much as possible, but at the same time nothing at all. You have to always keep the men panting. You seem to be a natural, though, so don't worry."

Wow, a natural. *"Merci du conseil,"* Thanks for the advice, I replied in French, because French is sexy.

"Can I ask you something personal?" I was drunk enough by then to let it out.

"Of course," he said.

"You're not really Japanese, are you?" I asked, taking a chance. "Your English is too good. Plus, your accent isn't Japanese."

Ando threw up his head in laughter. "You are an astute one! Actually I am ethnically Korean, but my family changed our name to a Japanese one, because Koreans get discriminated against over here.

"You know," he whispered in my ear, "sometimes I hate those fucking Japanese."

"I feel you," I whispered back with a smile. "I hate the Japanese, too." Lying was fun.

On the third night, Lindsey and I finally had private meetings with Mama-san, separately, in a corner of our dressing room that functioned as her office. The list of rules was laminated and chained to the table. I couldn't figure out why I couldn't just take a copy with me, especially since I had earned enough bonuses that night to have become quite intoxicated by the time Mama actually got around to meeting with me. After all, the piece of laminated paper only said things like "stockings must be worn at all times by penalty of salary cuts," and "never discuss your personal problems with customers," but I didn't dare ask her.

I only speculated that perhaps a reporter came in once disguised as a hostess, looking for the secret as to why hostess bars were such lucrative establishments even though they didn't sell sex. Or, more likely, something was illegal. But if anything was certain, it was that Destiny answered to the yakuza bosses far more often than she did to the police.

"I want you to think of me as your big sister, sweetie," Destiny said. "If you have any problems, problems with work or personal problems, I want you to come to me, okay? That is what I'm here for." The compassion in her eyes was mesmerizing.

"Okay, Mama." I smiled, reciprocating her warmth. Upon my meeting with Mama that night, I all but fell in love with her. This was a predictable development, seeing as the tendency to latch onto older maternal-type figures has been so prevalent throughout my life that it's embarrassing.

This fact is not disputable: collecting mothers is one of my favorite hobbies. For as long as I can remember, I have been forming bonds with older females anywhere and everywhere I go. Whether I unwittingly get involved with a teacher, a college professor, an RA in the dorms, an older coworker, a therapist, or a nutrition counselor, these affinities have been maddeningly severe.

Looking back, my fear of appearing vulnerable in front of my own mother had obviously influenced these powerful attachments. Throughout my life I have repeatedly rejected the love and support that was right in front of me in order to seek out my ideal mother elsewhere.

"So you speak French as well," Mama also said that night.

"How did you know?" I asked.

"When you were with Ando, you used French," she said as though it were common knowledge. "I recommend you use French as often as you can. Our clientele will enjoy it. Just try not to seem smarter than they are. That is key. You can be smart, but no smarter than your customer."

"But how did you overhear my conversation with Ando?" I was still a bit creeped out.

"I have my ways," she said, with an air suggesting that this was all she would have to say about the matter.

Mama Destiny, I was discovering, was omnipresent around the Palace. A Big Sister of sorts, she was nowhere and everywhere at the same time.

With Destiny in the role of the Queen of Hearts, the Palace often felt like a house of cards. As the other hostesses and I took turns playing three or four different kinds of women each night, depending upon each consumer's ideal, every new client's arrival necessitated the strategic assembly of another impermanent balance among us. *Ukiyo* culture's emphasis on the transient and fleeting nature of things certainly did penetrate into every aspect of Palace life. Not the least of which turned out to be Mama's Destiny's notoriously unstable demeanor.

Without exception, my fantasies of the "ideal mother," which I projected upon whomever happened to be around at the time, were always foiled eventually. My unsteady experiences with Mama Destiny really brought that point home for me. In retrospect, the only real certainty about any house of cards is that it is destined to fall every time.

It was only a week or so later that my adoration for her predictably crashed. I had arrived at work at 10 P.M. that evening instead of 8 P.M. because I was substituting for a vacationing friend's English class that evening, and I had cleared this with Destiny the evening before.

"Where have you been!" Destiny shouted as I walked through the door. "Ando is waiting for you! We have only been able to supply him with Japanese girls at his table because everyone else is busy, and as you know he hates the Japanese!"

"But, Mama, I already told you that I—" I stopped midsentence when I saw the insanely livid look in Destiny's eyes. Destiny was apparently not used to being answered back to, which likely has something to do with her lack of experience working with Americans.

Samantha, who was also in the dressing room finishing up a bottle of water, probably in a desperate attempt to maintain some semblance of sobriety, made eye contact with me and began to nod her head rapidly, so as to warn me against reasoning with Mama at this point in time.

"Get back out there," Destiny scolded Samantha. "And you"—she turned to a cowering me who had just squeezed into a red dress that was two sizes too small—"hurry up and *gambatte ne*," she said, switching from English to Japanese. Mama Destiny then sashayed out of the room with an aura of self-importance that seemed to be compensating for her small stature. "Just *gambatte!* " she barked at me again from outside.

Gambatte ne is an interesting phrase if only because it is very indicative of the Japanese work ethic, and also because it doesn't translate into English at all. When I was first learning Japanese in school I was taught that the phrase *gambare* (or *gambatte*) meant "good luck." In Japan however, I learned that "good luck" was in fact a very loose translation.

Although *gambare* is used in almost all of the same contexts as "good luck" (such as a parent sending a child off to take an important test, for example), its literal meaning is closest to "try your hardest." And rather than hoping for luck, *gambare* culture asks you to do the best you can even if you are ill, exhausted, bleeding, or becoming clinically insane due to overwork.

For example, if you are climbing a mountain in the snow with heavy luggage on your back, even if the icy wind keeps biting your face and blowing you down, you must continue to push forward. That is *gambare*. "Good luck" would be more along the lines of hitching a ride with a truck driver and hoping that he's not an ax murderer.

I plainly avoided Destiny as much as possible after that incident. Some nights later, however, I witnessed yet another side of Destiny's mysteriously manic personality. I had been dancing wildly to some techno music with two customers when I returned to my chair a bit short of breath. This tended to happen, seeing as I was a regular smoker despite being an asthmatic for my entire life. For that reason I was sure to keep my asthma inhaler, an inhaled medication that possessed the power to clear out my damaged lungs almost immediately, with me at all times.

I excused myself as politely as possible and left for the locker room, where I fetched my bag. I reached inside for my inhaler, first casually, then frantically as I began to realize that it wasn't in there. This was bad. Home was far away. "Okay, Mama is gonna kill me," I said to myself. "Don't panic, don't panic, don't panic. If I panic, then my breath will get even shorter." But all this was moot, and soon I was sitting in her foyer gasping for air.

Suffocation will be an awful way to die, I thought to myself. As my air passages tightened, the sound of my breathing began to resemble a high-pitched scream, the only difference being that the noise was created by drawing air inward instead of pushing it out.

Luckily for me, however, Destiny was in a better mood that night and could recognize that I was suffering from an asthma attack. At that, she signaled for the manager to bring me a glass of water. "My son has asthma," she told me. "I may have one of his extra inhalers in my purse," she mentioned as she dug through her belongings.

"Here we are," Destiny said gratified, handing me the only object that could save my lungs. As soon as I could speak again without gasping, I began thanking her profusely, but Destiny put her finger to my lips to advise me not to speak yet.

"You definitely shouldn't smoke," Mama told me in a motherly manner as she put her hand on my shoulder and squeezed my arm until my condition gradually improved. "You have been working very hard and I am proud of you," she continued, looking me square in the eyes. "You can take the rest of the night off. Go."

On any given night, Destiny could be just as ruthless as she was compassionate. Just a few days later, I was entertaining a customer when the waiter brought me the message that "Mama-san would like to speak with you in the back immediately," and I had to excuse myself for a moment.

"Why hasn't your table ordered anything for the past half hour?" she asked coldly.

"Sorry?" I said.

"Say you want more drinks," she said, "preferably a bottle of wine or some champagne."

"Okay, I understand," I said with my eyes on the floor. "It's just that he's so drunk already." I absolutely hated forcing the intoxicated men to order more.

"That man is extremely rich and he knew what he was getting into when he came here," she snapped, practically reading my doubts.

I nodded.

"Good girl." She gave me her motherly smile again and patted my shoulder. I naturally obeyed her.

It was a most terrifying scene on nights when Mama Destiny would pace back and forth in front of the waiting table looking us over, as if she were a drill sergeant or a prison guard. At times, when she ordered us to change our dresses, shoes, or headpieces, her criticisms were immensely lacking in compassion or tact, employing phrases like, "Those shoes are ugly," "Your dress is dirty," or "Your hair looks like a prostitute's."

Her rules were notoriously strict, yet they had little basis in anything to speak of. For example, she forbade us from ever wearing our hair down. I once heard, though, that at the club across the street, hostesses were forbidden from wearing their hair up. It was if she made it all up as she went along. Regardless, I have never in my life met someone who enjoyed the intrinsic act of "forbidding" so passionately.

She was also notorious for firing her hostesses on impulse, without any apparent provocation or explanation. As time went by, working with Mama Destiny took a larger toll on my self-confidence than my conversations with even the rudest of the male customers.

If not the perfect mother all of the time, Mama-san was nonetheless the perfect hostess. She was extremely intelligent and used her powers strictly for manipulation. She knew exactly where people felt empty inside, and how to fill that void like an addictive drug.

As for all the hostesses working beneath her, she knew that most of us were in our early twenties and were very, very far away from home. She gave us an image of the motherly love we yearned for, but practically required our souls in return. I adored her and despised her at the same time. She was the sharpest double-edged razor I'd ever fallen in love with.

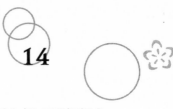

14

ladies in waiting

Nobody would believe what an effort it is to do what little I am able,—to dress and entertain, and order things.
—CHARLOTTE PERKINS GILMAN,
"THE YELLOW WALLPAPER"

TO BE ONE of the flowers in a constantly shifting *ikebana* arrangement may seem like an easy occupation, but this was not the case at the Palace. While my fellow hostesses and I were moving around to different spots of the bar all the time, we could never go anywhere of our own free will. Even if we had to use the bathroom, which occurs quite often in venues where alcohol is served, we usually had to wait until a customer left.

In fact, a great deal of my time at the Palace was spent in various stages of waiting. We had to wait outside the rest room with a hot towel for the duration that our customer spent inside, just so we could make the towel offering precisely when he exited. We had to wait both outside the club and at a designated table inside the Palace for customers to come. Then, when the night was over, we all had to wait again for night transportation to arrive.

The job required that we dress up each night as if we were going to the prom or a wedding. Getting ready to go was the most entertaining part of the job for me, but it usually proved anticlimactic once we clocked into work. We were required to be in Ginza and ready to work at 8 P.M., even though the first customers hardly ever entered the club before 9:30 P.M. So one large table in the corner of the bar was designated as the "waiting area."

From 8 P.M. to 9 or 9:30 P.M., we sat in a circle awaiting the first customers of the evening. With all the nationalities and races represented at the table, I imagine that we must have resembled what the UN might look like if girls ruled the world. Far from solving crises of global diplomacy, however, we couldn't even talk to one another. Even if we were allowed to have conversations while "waiting," the multiple language barriers and the competitive nature of the job severely hindered communication.

And since the ratio of ladies to customers tended to be about four or five to one even on the busiest of nights, a large percentage of us sat waiting even as the bar started to fill with customers. At the waiting table, Rod would purposely sit me as far away from Lindsey as possible, in order to keep us from talking.

Rod would also come over to hush any hostesses who were caught talking to each other too loudly or laughing out loud. He even did this when no one else was inside the bar. It was a place for waiting and only that. We were literally "all dressed up with nowhere to go," and there was a haunting inertia about it all.

After a while I began to view "waiting" as the most unbearable part of the job. I became bored easily, and the whole ritual may have brought back unpleasant memories of standing against the wall during high school dances, hoping that a boy would approach me. It is possible that I just lacked patience, especially seeing as my generation back in America is often associated with an age of "instant gratification." Still, this is not to say that catering to middle-aged men was at all gratifying.

It was a curious way to feel, especially since our hourly salaries remained the same whether we were with a customer or awaiting one. The first 5,000 yen that I usually made within the first hour and a half of each work night was basically just handed to me without my having to make any effort saving to sit still, be silent, and look pretty. In order to avoid death by boredom, I had to constantly remind myself of the money.

On nights when the waiting was most insufferable, I sat calculating my salary in my head, figuring out in the end that I was receiving the rough equivalent of a dollar for every one minute and twenty seconds I sat at that table doing nothing.

Oddly enough, thinking about my salary didn't make the waiting any more tolerable. One night I wondered if such ennui was similar to what Betty Freidan tried to define in *The Feminine Mystique* with respect to all the housewives for whom insufferable boredom was a trade-off for financial stability.

In this, I gained a new appreciation for the allure of sticking one's head into an oven.

In waiting, I felt as lifeless as the paintings on the walls or the statues in the hallway. Only the mama's nod or a man's desire, a paying man's desire, could bring me to life again. If Mama would just move me to a customer's table, I would be allowed to speak and laugh and even sing again, that is so long as it was conducive to his entertainment.

At about eight thirty each night, Rod would approach the waiting table and point to two of us, then make a hand motion toward the door. That meant that the two women he picked out had to go stand

outside and do *bira*. *Bira,* in Japanese, technically means the handing out of flyers to passersby on the street as a way to solicit their attention and give the club publicity. On the Ginza hostess bar circuit,
however, the art of *bira* is a more complicated manner.

We had to be far more subtle about it than the promoters who
handed out free tissues or fans to countless passersby in Shibuya or
Shinjuku, because handing out *bira* for hostess bars—or for any
facet of the *mizu shobai*—is technically illegal. Thus, much like inside
the Palace, we had to stand in a specific space and not move.

One lady would stand outside the Louis Vuitton shop, while another was assigned to the space outside the Rolex store. Both establishments were already closed by that time of night. The reason we
had to stand in specific places outside with no variation was that
those were the spots that the Palace "bought" from the local yakuza,
who truthfully had more jurisdiction over the streets than the police
did.

Doing *bira,* we were strictly forbidden from approaching potential customers and especially from touching them in any way. We
were only supposed to stand there and wait for a man to approach
us, and we weren't allowed to smoke or use our cellular phones.
Once again, this process of waiting was boring as hell.

At the time I began work at the Palace, the rules for doing *bira*
were stricter than they had ever been because of an unfortunate incident that occurred only a few months earlier. Just before Lindsey
and I had arrived at the Palace, an Israeli woman was apparently outside Rolex doing *bira* when it is said that she attempted to drag a man
on the street into the Palace by his arm.

That man turned out to be an undercover police officer and the Israeli woman was actually put in Jail for illegal soliciting, while the Palace
management was made to pay a large fine. Therefore, Mama and Rod
warned us nightly, with wide eyes, to never, ever touch anyone on the

street. I've never met the notorious "Israeli girl," still people in Ginza talk about her disastrous fate to this very day.

I forget exactly how long her prison sentence was, but sometimes when I stood outside Rolex doing *bira,* bored out of my mind, I wondered whether anyone ever visited her in jail.

night transportation

after finishing work each night, there was still more waiting to do. As we waited for the habitually late "night transportation" van to show up outside the door, we were finally permitted to talk or sleep.

The Palace closed at 2 A.M., long after the last trains of the night ran through Tokyo. Taxis in Japan are exorbitantly expensive, so as a result all of the hostesses piled into a large van each night, which would eventually take each of us to our doorsteps. And by eventually, I mean within an hour or two, seeing as Lindsey and I, being the newest additions to the Palace bouquet, were always dropped off last.

Not everyone had to take the club transportation out of Ginza. At the end of the night Mama Destiny would often drive up to the entrance in her Mercedes and personally drive home a couple of her most successful hostesses. Some hostesses got money from customers to take taxicabs, or more often shared cabs with said customers. Others told Rod that they didn't need night transportation and just disappeared. As a result, the large van that Lindsey and I came to affectionately call the hostess mobile housed a different dynamic at the end of each night.

As the newest additions to the Palace staff, Lindsey and I were, after a long night of work and drinking, treated to an hourlong tour of Tokyo and her outskirts before finally getting home. Because we exited last, we always sat together in the rear of the van.

The atmosphere inside the van was very different from that inside the club, if only because all of us were allowed to talk to one another.

On a particular night during our first week on the job, two women sat in front of the van chatting with each other in Russian. Their conversation could have very well been on the topic of Lindsey and me because at that moment we were acting like the stereotypically loud, obnoxious Americans that we were, and it didn't help that we happened to be a bit drunk.

Lindsey was loudly lamenting about how she got stuck talking to a man who insisted he was the reincarnation of Adolf Hitler, and almost knocked over a whiskey bottle to demonstrate his Nazi salute. He was very clear about what he liked. "Iya lika Hitlaa," he repeated often in his heavily accented English, "Iya lika Bushi! Iya lika Rasputin!"

"Rasputin?" I asked.

"Whatever," said Lindsey, "the point is that I just had to smile and be polite the entire time."

"The rules say that we have to agree with everything they say"—I smirked—"so were you like, 'Yeah, white power'?"

"I couldn't even remind this Japanese guy that he wasn't white!" she further complained. "I was like, more alcohol, please!" At that the two of us burst out in loud laughter, visibly irritating the Russians again, especially one named Svetlana. Catching the negative vibes and lowering her voice a bit, Lindsey went on to explain about how she had begged Rod to switch her to another table. This proved difficult because the man would only sit with another white girl but the Russians and I were already occupied at the time.

"I'm starting to see why these men will pay so much just for conversation," I said thoughtfully. "Who else but a hostess would ever put up with a guy like that?"

Svetlana was dropped off first. Svetlana had a teased mop of frizzy red hair, piercing hazel eyes, seemingly permanent bloodred lipstick decorating her large lips, and generously ample breasts. I had yet to see her smile. Upon exiting the van she quietly bid good-bye to Cristina, a Russian woman with long blond hair, painted-on eyebrows, and noticeably fake eyelashes with whom Svetlana had been conversing earlier, to the driver, and to no one else. Svetlana's demeanor shot a blast of cold air through the vehicle when she slammed the van's sliding door behind her.

Next to escape the hostess mobile was Cristina. Cristina woke up from the light sleep she'd fallen into and barely said a word to anyone as she stumbled from the van to the door of her apartment.

"I'm going on a picnic"—it was Lindsey's turn to continue our boredom game—"and I'm going to bring: apples, blueberry schnapps, cute boys, Dom Pérignon, egg creams, Fruit Roll-Ups, grape soda . . . and . . . and . . . Hennessey!"

"Grape soda and Hennessey?"—a woman with short dark hair, large doe eyes, perfect skin, and a most ridiculously waiflike build, turned to face us in the backseat disapprovingly—"Now that's just gross!"

"Sorry, are we bothering you?" Lindsey asked apologetically.

"Nah, it's okay," she said. Lynn, we would find out, was from South Africa. "You two are funny."

"Hey, can we play your game, too?" Samantha and Linda took

this opportunity to switch their conversation from their native Tagalog to English. "We don't get to practice English so often."

"Sure," I said, "just think of something to bring on a picnic that starts with *I* . . ."

The next two to get dropped off were Lynn and her Brazilian sidekick, Desiree, at Roppongi Crossing. Roppongi was the bustling center of young Tokyo's nightlife, especially for the city's foreign population. "Do you guys live *here?*" I asked Lynn in disbelief as she gathered her belongings to exit the van. "No," she said, "we're going out partying."

"I know the manager at Club Womb," she continued. "You two wanna come along?" Lindsey and I could only laugh at the idea and say that we were too tired. After all, it was almost 3 A.M. on a Tuesday night.

"Thanks for the invite, though," Lindsey said, bidding them farewell, "maybe we'll come out with you some other time, like Friday night."

"Yeah, Friday," I agreed.

The next girl to get dropped off was Anastasia, the silent model. No one had ever heard her speak any language other than Russian, and it was presumed that she couldn't. Anastasia, one could tell at a glance, had come to Japan as a model and was working at the Palace between modeling shoots. Or so we heard through the grapevine. Anastasia's lack of verbal skills just went to show that if a girl was pretty enough, she didn't have to do anything else to make it in the Palace's world, not even speak.

From there the van drove to Kabukichō, to drop off Aika. Aika, the club's only Japanese national, smiled and politely bowed in everyone's general direction before leaving, although she didn't care to speak to any of us while we sat beside her. Her behavior was typically Japanese.

"She doesn't live there, does she?" I asked Samantha as I nodded toward the busy intersection where Aika exited. I assumed as much because there were no residences amid the onslaught of red lights.

"No," Samantha said knowingly.

"God," I said, "she doesn't work there after-hours, does she?"

I had realized by then that Kabukichō, aside from its many blow job bars, soap lands, and strip clubs in which audience participation is encouraged, specialized in establishments known as *imekura* or "image clubs." An image club is a brothel of sorts where customers enjoy sexual role-play with prostitutes dressed-up as doctors, nurses, policewomen, and most popularly schoolgirls.

To varying degrees, Tokyo's entertainment districts really do test the limits of the human imagination. The raunchiest red-light district in the city, the name Kabukichō is derived from the traditional Japanese kabuki theater, evoking the memory of an era in Japanese history when theater performers were synonymous with prostitutes.

"No, no." Samantha laughed. "Aika doesn't work there."

"Then I don't get it," I said, perplexed.

"Word on the street," Samantha sighed, "is that Aika is in love with a host. Kabukichō is also where most of the host bars are, you know."

A nightclub host was the male equivalent of the hostess, and a constantly growing phenomenon in Tokyo. The host's livelihood depended on entertaining and flirting with the middle-aged Japanese housewives who were left at home while their husbands ran after hostesses. There was also the occasional hostess herself, who had become caught in the cycle of spending her nightly earnings on a preferred male, who in turn received a salary to massage her spirit and restore the self-confidence she had lost at her nightly job.

"I don't understand why so many Japanese hostesses are spending all their money at host bars these days," said Samantha. "It's so stupid. I mean, whoever this guy is, Aika is just his customer. Why doesn't she get that? It's not like she's not familiar with the business!"

"Bizarre," Lindsey reflected.

I dozed off in the van sometime after Linda got dropped off in Ikebukuro, and didn't get a chance to bid farewell to my new acquaintance Samantha.

Lindsey roused me from sleep some time later, when I had to provide the driver of the van with specific directions—in Japanese—from the main road to the door of our apartment. A simple address could never suffice in Tokyo, seeing as there were hardly any streets with actual names. And locating an address by number was no relief considering that the buildings in Tokyo were given numbers in accordance to the order in which they're built, rather than any remotely consecutive arrangement.

After getting dropped off I thanked the driver and made a blind rush for my bed. We fell onto our futons and stared at the ceiling of the closet-sized room Lindsey and I were sharing for the time being.

"I can't believe Desiree, Lynn, and Aika are still out partying right now," I mumbled.

"While you were sleeping," Lindsey responded, "Samantha told me that Lynn has two kids at home who she leaves in her apartment while she goes out and does coke every night."

"No way," I said in disbelief as I rolled over to fall asleep facing the wall.

"Come brush your teeth before falling asleep," Lindsey bossed.

"Can't. Do. Anything. But. Sleep," I grumbled.

"Well, I'm gonna try." Lindsey lifted her body and moved toward the bathroom. Lindsey had always been the more motivated and sensible one between the two of us. My friend came back into the room a few minutes later and shut off the light.

"Ah, my teeth feel so nice and clean!" She roused me from my partial sleep.

"Shut the fuck up, Linz."

"Love you too, Lea."

"Has it been two weeks yet?" she asked me.

"I've lost track of time already." I honestly couldn't recall anything in the state I was in.

"We're not gonna get out after two weeks, are we?" she sighed.

"Not likely," I admitted.

"No, not likely," she agreed.

"Night, babe."

"Night."

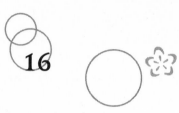

16

the eastern bloc

the Russian, Ukranian, and Belarussian young women at our particular club generally kept to themselves in a tight clique, which Lindsey and I came to refer to as the Eastern Bloc. Even without understanding their language, it was easy to recognize that their leader was the seemingly older (that is to say late twenties) woman named Svetlana. Svetlana had the biggest, reddest hair I had ever seen and she always teased it out in all of its frizzy glory before coming to work. Lindsey and I called her "Big Red."

Mama knew that Svetlana hated me, still she seemed to place us opposite each other rather frequently. By that, I mean that Mama would order us to share the same table with a single customer, where we would have to compete for his attention. It was as if Mama Destiny wanted there to be competition between us, perhaps to keep us on our toes.

The intentionally orchestrated duel between Svetlana and me often proceeded as follows: if Svetlana and I were both sitting at the waiting table and a customer came inside the club by himself, and he had no specific request for a girl, Mama-san would first point to Svetlana and escort her over to the man's table.

"This is Svetlana," Mama would tell him, "a very exotic beauty from Russia. Is she to your liking?" The customer would almost always nod in agreement, in the same manner one would to a waiter after tasting a fine wine. The first girl to meet the customer usually handed him a hot towel, which he used to wipe off his hands and face.

Then Mama would return to the waiting table and look over all of her girls thoroughly before pointing to me.

"And this is Daisy," Mama would say as she escorted me to his other side. "She is from America but she can speak fluent Japanese. Very unusual, yes?" The customer then nodded for the second time, and I would begin to show him the variety of whiskeys we served before delicately pouring the brand he chose. Svetlana and I would then take turns refilling his glass with ice or wiping the condensation off of his oblong glass.

The game was on, and its rules were complex. Our interactions were under almost constant observation in order to determine which one of us would win the man's attention. In one drink's time, Rod or Mama would tap Svetlana or me on the shoulder and point back to a specific seat at the waiting table. Whichever one of us was less successful would be replaced by another girl in the same ritualistic fashion. It always happened like this; the flower arrangement was in perpetual flux.

In retrospect, Mama's covert efforts to increase our working potential by pitting Svetlana and I against each other were highly successful. Because of the rivalry I had with Svetlana, gaining the affections of men two or three times my age became more and more of a priority. I came to dread the waiting table as a symbol of failure, and to anticipate being chosen as if it were actually important, a token of my success.

On nights when Svetlana was victorious, it was due to immense efforts on her part. She would immediately take the customer's hands in her own and begin massaging his arm or whispering in his ear. It was a truly nauseating spectacle from my end of the table.

In the incidences when Svetlana was escorted back to waiting, however, the customer usually showed more interest in me only because I was American. I would distract him from Svetlana's grasp by fostering discussion about his recent trip to New York City, or some topic of that nature.

As an "authentic American girl," I was a rare and exotic specimen inside the Palace. There are a few main reasons why American women do not typically work in Japanese hostess bars. First of all, it is hard for us to believe that there is actually no sex or touching involved in this kind of work, since our culture has rather puritanical roots.

And, in contrast to the Confucian-influenced societies of the East, ours is not a culture of obedience, which makes processing direct orders and obeying rigid social codes all the more unbearable. On top of that, most of the women working in hostess bars today were born after 1980, well after the feminist movement of the 1970s. As a result, most young American women are not used to playing such subservient roles, a fact to which Ando had first alerted me. We are not very good at catering to a man's needs in word and gesture, even when doing so for a salary. It's also true that we get progressively worse at acting "ladylike" as the alcohol keeps flowing.

Still, perhaps the main reason that there are so few of us working in hostess bars has to do with immigration issues. Hostesses from Korea, Australia, France, Canada, New Zealand, the United Kingdom, and Germany can come to Japan with a "working holiday" visa, a reciprocal agreement between Japan and these nations that allows nationals to find work abroad for a period of twelve months. No such agreement exists between Japan and America.

The most serious hostesses in the game, who in my experience have come from countries such as Russia, China, Romania, and the Philippines, practically all have "visa marriages." But paper marriages are only popular among nationals of countries whose standard of living is far, far lower than that of Japan's, so this trend does not exist among Americans, either.

It used to be possible for hostesses to acquire six-month "entertainment visas," but the government has put serious limits on the granting of such visas in recent years, and basically no hostess bars can provide them anymore.

In order to work legally in Japan, all Americans (saving those with spousal visas, who do not fit into the hostess demographic anyway), must possess a university degree and have a qualified sponsor who can testify to the fact that the American can provide a unique skill that can benefit Japanese society.

Thus, the few Americans who do hostess in Japan tend to be ex-English teachers who are overqualified for the position, curiosities that are unique to the hostessing realm of the *mizu shobai*. I assumed that this was why Svetlana detested my presence so much. On top of that, there was the issue of my being far more educated than she was.

By then, I had learned to speak grammatically correct Japanese that reflected many years of intensive study, so my manner of speaking heavily contrasted the vulgar Japanese that the Russians had acquired from years on the job. I could write the customer's names in kanji, the most difficult of the Japanese's three writing systems, which contains thousands of characters derived from classical Chinese.

Lindsey spoke only English and hardly ever knew what was going on, a fact that the Eastern Bloc could revel in and look down upon her for. Because I could hold conversations in four languages, however, the Russians held a special hatred for me.

"Where did you learn to speak Japanese?" Elena, a member of the Russian clique, who spoke some English, asked me one night in the hostess mobile.

"College," I replied.

"Zen . . . vat are you doing here?" she asked in a slightly threatening manner.

"Good question," I said as I flashed my fake smile and turned away, pretending to respond to a text message on my cell phone.

Although Svetlana was clearly my first real archenemy, I made an effort to be friendly to her regardless, if only because my fake smiles pissed her off all the more. When the clients went to the bathroom or were otherwise distracted, I repeatedly tried to break the ice with Svetlana. Since I didn't speak Russian and she didn't or wouldn't speak English, I'd try to say something in Japanese.

"So where are you from?" I asked her once, as if I didn't already know.

"Russia." It seemed a painful effort for her to turn and face me.

"Where in Russia?" I persisted.

"You wouldn't know where it is," she said in an attempt to brush me off.

"Try me." The wide smile I flashed in her direction was a plain act of aggression.

"St. Petersburg," she said blandly.

"Of course I know where that is," I said, having already learned how to hide the fact that I was offended. "I know someone from St. Petersburg and his name is Petr, isn't that funny?"

Nothing.

But I wasn't going to stop. Flattering others and *acting* nice was suddenly a specialty.

"I think you're very beautiful," I lied.

"*Urusai!*" she snapped back.

Did she really just call me annoying? I thought to myself, in a quiet declaration of war. I had tried to be very nice to Svetlana. I ignored her evil stares daily and sometimes even smiled back. I looked aside when she blatantly stole my clients, reasoning that she seemed to need the money more anyway. In spite of all this, I had tried to be very nice.

But Svetlana had succeeded in pissing me off.

"How do you say 'fuck you' in Russian?" I asked politely, quietly congratulating myself on the subtlety of my insult. At that, our client suddenly returned to the table from the rest room, where he had likely been masturbating.

"Be quiet," she said.

"No, Svetlana, I really want to know," I said, feigning innocence.

Unfortunately the mama-san had caught wind of our quiet confrontation and escorted me away from the table to be replaced by Linda.

But that wasn't all. I hadn't even a minute to make myself comfortable at the waiting table before Rod approached to inform me that Mama would like to meet with me in the hallway outside of the club. Then in the hallway, Mama lectured me that I had been creating tension at the table, and that my actions were the precise opposite of what she was paying me for.

"But Svetlan—" I started to protest.

"If you don't like what I say you can go home." It was the first of many times I would hear her say that exact phrase. It had become obvious to me by then that Destiny was completely full of herself.

"I'm gonna quit," I told Samantha as we drank and smoked Sheeshah that night at a bar in Roppongi that specialized in flavored tobacco for Middle Eastern hookahs. "I can't deal with Svetlana. She is just such a bitch!"

"You know why the Russians don't like you and Lindsey, right?" she asked.

"I don't know," I replied. "I didn't fucking do anything to them and I'm totally sick of it."

"The men treat you Americans differently," she said knowingly.

"Why?" I asked in disbelief.

"Probably because of America's place in the world," she replied.

"That's stupid, everyone hates America, right?" I countered.

"Don't you notice the men trying to touch the Russian girls all the time? It is officially a no-touch bar, but the clients feel like they can get away with more if the girl is from a poorer country."

"But Svetlana's always touching *them!*"

"No," Samantha lectured me, "Svetlana is always grabbing on to her customers' arms and hands, so she knows where they are at all times."

"Oh, wow," I acknowledged, "I never even considered that before."

I thought of Svetlana differently after the enlightening discussion I had with Samantha that night. Svetlana and I would never be friends, that was for sure, but I stopped deliberately trying to anger her from then on. Sometimes, I even began to covertly feel as if the two of us were actually on the same team, or at least that we should be.

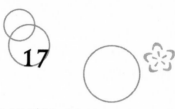

the Regular Game

There's a tendency with some to think that all foreign women are pushovers, but familiarity can breed respect, and most foreign hostesses concede that regular customers are the best behaved.

—NICHOLAS BORNOFF, *Pink Samurai: Love, Marriage and Sex in Contemporary Japan*

MOST HOSTESS BARS have two-week trial periods for a new recruit, during which she simply has to decorate the tables of first-time clients or other women's customers. If a hostess reaches the end of her two-week trial period and still hasn't acquired a handful of regular customers, she either gets fired or her salary drops dramatically. That said, the difficulty of the job is not so much in looking good, serving drinks, and sitting still, as it is in attracting regulars. Every working girl had a different strategy in this regard.

For me, I used to sit at the small desk in my room at around six thirty—the time when most *salarimen* finish work and begin to make their drinking plans for the evening—with my cellular phone, a stack of business cards, and a glass of straight vodka on ice. The purpose of the vodka was to make the somewhat humiliating process of calling each man—someone who had given me his business card at one time or another—and inviting him to the Palace that evening tolerable.

Sometimes the men I called didn't remember me to the same degree that I couldn't remember them, but other times they were excited to hear my voice and were flattered by the invitation. At the same time, however, I had to make about twenty calls for every one customer I could convince to come see me at the Palace. Because hostess bars are so astronomically expensive, it is most often the hostess herself who has to initiate the relationships. Still most women, young and modern as we are, are not very used to the process of asking men out on many dates. Hence the vodka, my liquid confidence.

On Sundays, however, the only day when the Palace was closed, my cell phone would ring constantly. And constantly, I would have to turn down dinner invitations from middle-aged men, most likely the same ones who refused to answer my calls on nights I was working. Under the deluded impression that the two of us were actually dating, they really thought that I might want to go out with them without getting paid for it.

One such Sunday morning, Lindsey and I were eating eggs for breakfast in our kitchen when her phone rang. After she hung up, Lindsey barely had the time to tell me it had been a man from the Palace named Tonkawa before the ringing of my cell interrupted her.

"Hurro?" a man's voice said in broken English.

"Yes?" I said.

"This is Tonkawa."

"Yes?"

"Do you remember me? We were together at the Palace last week. We very enjoyed. You are so very sweet."

"Thank you very much, how are you today, Mr. Tonkawa?" Lindsey burst out laughing and had to leave the room.

"I'm very good. Would you like to go to Disneyland with me today?" he asked.

"I'm sorry but I have to clean my room," I said without thinking.

"Okay, no problem, see you next time!" He didn't give me a chance to bid him farewell before hanging up; he was likely in a hurry to make another call.

It was a trying process, but once a regular customer is acquired, it is like he belongs to you. Ando was my first regular, and every time he came to the Palace, I would get a cut of all the money he spent. Even if he bought a drink for every girl working besides me, his check had my name, "Daisy," written on the top.

We had to attract regular customers by pretending to have relationships with them, to be in love with them. Though I had accepted the job under the impression that I would only be working nights, it turned out that I had to answer the client's calls on our off-hours and pretend to care what they had to say. It was truly bizarre, like playing a game of make-believe with grown men.

There were various aspects of the hostess's profession that I did not realize were in my job description when I first signed on. Most customers of hostess bars will continue to patronize the same bar because of a vested interest in a specific girl, and it is her job entirely to keep him coming back for more. And although all hostesses must have a variety of regular customers, it is entirely our responsibility to methodically arrange our schedules so that our respective regulars never, ever showed up on the same night.

If this happened by accident, a hostess not only risked losing her customer, but became a target of animosity among the other hostesses.

That's because there is nothing worse than having to entertain a man whose preferred hostess is busy with another gentleman, usually in plain sight.

In rare cases, a hostess can grow fond of one of her regular customers, sometimes due to the sheer amount of time they spend together, especially if he is a gentleman who treats the lady with respect. While the hostess remains a platonic girlfriend in practice, it is entirely possible to get lost in the ritual and lose track of age differences. At the same time, intoxication tends to blur the lines between acting talent and genuine emotions.

There was one regular customer in particular whose companionship I could swear that I sincerely enjoyed, although I second-guessed my own sentiments often.

The evening I first met Hideo, it was nearing the end of the night and everyone was a bit drunk. I had entertained two customers before him. The first was a balding plastic surgeon who'd come in alone and signaled to Rod to switch me with another girl after our third toast. From there it was off to decorate the side of a company outing to celebrate a manager's birthday. When the party ended, each man was personally escorted out the door by a hostess or two. We smiled, waved, and blew kisses as we saw them into the elevator. As the elevator door closed, however, our fake smiles were all erased at once as if mechanically, and we marched back into the club, back to waiting.

Hideo was a round-faced heavyset man sitting between two colleagues. He looked me over from head to toe when I was escorted to his side by Rod, and I found him creepy at first. Yet like a true Japanese, I hid my feelings well.

I don't remember what we talked about, but I must have been doing something right, because an hour later his colleagues had gone home while the two of us were still sitting close at the table, arms around each other's shoulders, as if the night were young and he were, too. We got drunk enough to think that we should sing "Bohemian Rhapsody" by Queen on the karaoke machine, which took a lot of abuse from bad singers by that time of evening.

After we finished singing and were showered with applause from many pretty girls whose job it was to clap for us, Hideo went to use the bathroom. Mama Destiny took this opportunity to come over to my table and give me a hot towel, which I would routinely present to Hideo upon his return.

"I've been watching you two." She peered up at me.

"Sorry about the bad karaoke." I tried to beat her to any criticism she was about to express.

"No, that's not important," she said. "He's drunk enough to think that the two of you sounded good together.

"Now listen to me," Mama said firmly after a pause. "When he comes out of the bathroom I want you to ask him for a *dōhan* tomorrow night. The two of you can meet at eight o'clock in front of the club, go out to dinner, and then get back here at ten sharp. I'll explain the rest to you tonight before you go home."

Now that I had clientele, Mama was paying me even more attention.

Hideo, like so many customers, took forever in the bathroom. When he returned I did exactly what Destiny told me to do, knowing that she was watching us. I couldn't guess how Mama Destiny did it but she was right, and Hideo was unable to resist my request for a dōhan.

I felt guilty about doing what I did, about seemingly taking advantage of this drunken guy. At the same time, however, I became full of this bizarre and insatiable yearning to please Mama. *Destiny knows men so well,* I thought silently to myself, *but she uses all her power for evil.*

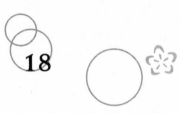

18

tea ceremony and pepper spray

a dōhan is basically a paid date, the really expensive kind, in which regular hostess bar customers show off their buying power around town, in female form, for a couple of hours before reentering the closed doors of the Palace. When the hostess and her client arrive at the club together, the man must pay a special dōhan fee along with the hourly rate and everything else. Most hostess bars have monthly dōhan quotas, which the girls must meet in order to stay employed.

If the boundary between a client and an unlikely love interest is blurred by the process of attracting regulars, in soliciting dōhans it is all but erased. The only saving grace in such a scenario is that everyone knows the rules of the game, although such guidelines are never specifically mentioned or spelled out between hostess and customer. So rather, the boundary is basically invisible. Yet, in the vast majority of cases, it is still there.

Walking to the restaurant on the following night, Hideo and I held hands. As we waited for our food at the restaurant the following night, Hideo complimented me on my Japanese skills. When I shared with him how interested I was in Japanese language and culture, he beamed, and began to share with me his family's history. I was genuinely fascinated, and there was a rare spark between the two of us.

Hideo was thirty-six years old and unmarried. He had recently taken over his family's clothing company, which had been in existence since the Edo period. It was unusual for the average family business to have made it through the war, during which time Japan exhausted all of its material resources in their fight to the death. However, his company had earned an extraordinary amount of money with their hat business in the Meiji period.

The Meiji Restoration had abolished the rigid class structure of the Tokugawa shogunate. This rendered the role of the samurai warriors obsolete, even outlawing the samurai warrior's traditional topknot hairstyle. Hideo's family, coming from the samurai class themselves, sympathized with the plight of their people and developed a style of hat designed to camouflage a samurai's topknot so that the new order might not force him to remove it.

As a student of Japanese culture, I was most interested in hearing his family's success story.

Lindsey was at the club when we arrived, and was sent over to accompany us briefly. After Hideo left the Palace that night, my friend and I agreed that my customer bore some facial resemblances to a famed Japanese cartoon character and action figure called Anpanman, or Sweet Bread Man in English. Anpanman was basically a piece of round bread with a body and a cape who, along with his sidekicks White Bread Man, Melon Bread Girl, and Curry Bread Man, flew about fighting their archenemy: an evil piece of germ. Because Hideo was also my first dōhan, the nickname "Dōhanman" became appropriate, and stuck very well.

After Dōhanman and I had been "dating" for three weeks, he

invited me to take the Shinkansen to Nagano with him to meet some of his extended family. Basically, I was not allowed to go. Leaving city limits with a customer was off-limits, period. The night he asked me, however, the offer had been so tempting that I couldn't refuse.

Looking back, my self-preservation instincts could have been more intact. Maybe it was the very thrill of disobeying Mama Destiny, to be able to tactfully court Dōhanman's affections without her ever-present watchful eye.

At the same time, however, I wasn't a *complete* idiot. "Do you know where I can find pepper spray or mace?" I asked Lindsey the next day. "I'm going to Nagano on Sunday to meet dōhan family."

"Try Don Quixote," she said, suggesting a miscellaneous discount store located around the corner in east Shinjuku. Thirty minutes later I came back from Don Quixote, pissed off. "The guy at the desk said that mace is illegal in Japan."

"What?" Lindsey looked up from her magazine in disbelief.

"Yeah," I continued. "This country is totally fucked-up."

"Are you sure you should go?" my friend asked.

"I know I shouldn't go," I said, "but I want to. I want to see Nagano, and his family's estate in the country. Apparently it goes back hundreds of years, like from before Meiji. Besides"—I rationalized with myself—"I have a good feeling about him. Dōhanman is harmless. He's like a big teddy bear."

"Hope you're right," Lindsey said as she returned to her article.

"I know!" I blurted out. "I can *make* pepper spray, right?"

"Go for it," replied Lindsey, who was probably reading the same sentence over and over again. "All my spices are on the top shelf."

And so I concocted a most heinous mix of every hot pepper imaginable and loaded the violent mixture into a perfume bottle. To see if it worked, I sprayed it into the air above me. Within seconds some of the particles landed on my face and eyes, causing me to shriek in pain.

"I can't believe you just tested your homemade pepper spray on yourself!" Lindsey scolded as she walked into the kitchen to find me flushing my eyes in the sink. "Now what are you going to tell Dōhanman tomorrow when your eyes are bloodshot all through your date?"

"At least I know it works now," I whined. I put the perfume bottle in a Ziploc bag and sealed it in my pocketbook, so I wouldn't forget to bring it later.

As it turned out, I was the only human to ever feel the wrath of Lea's homemade pepper spray. The Nagano estate was amazing. The family seemed to live in a series of ancient temples along the countryside. Hideo's brother's wife was a certified teacher of the traditional Japanese tea ceremony, so I participated in a tea ceremony with the family. She tried to teach me about conducting the ritual, but I only understood about 75 percent of all the Japanese spoken due to their regional dialect.

Throughout all this, I couldn't get over the fact that Hideo was introducing me to his family as his girlfriend. They had to know I was a hostess, and I worried that they thought I was a gold digger. Basically, I had no idea what type of behavior would be acceptable in this type of situation. I didn't even know what the situation was, as much of their Japanese invariably went over my head when I wasn't focused enough to apply 100 percent of my listening skills. Still, something about the cultural fuzziness made it all bearable, and I peacefully accepted the fact that I had no idea what was going on.

Afterward, Dōhanman, his brother, his brother's wife, and I went out for sushi. I knew that it was an expensive restaurant because it was the kind of establishment where they killed the fish right in front of you. I was gradually learning that one of the most amusing activities for the average Japanese in the company of a foreigner is to take his guest to a sushi shop and see how many things on the menu the foreigner could eat without getting grossed-out. The dōhanman clan was no exception.

After we ordered the most expensive dish on the menu, the sushi chef presented us each with an individual plate of lobster. Then he placed the bottom half of the lobster, itself halved and turned upside down, at the center of the table with an array of sauce surrounding it.

"How will we eat that part?" I naïvely asked Hideo.

"We don't"—everyone at my table chuckled a bit—"it's only for decoration, to show how fresh the fish is."

"*Imi ga wakaranai,*" I don't get it, I said.

"Look closer," he said. "The lobster's legs are still moving."

I did, and the shriek I let out was once again of great entertainment value for the group. After dinner I slept on Dōhanman's shoulder on the Shinkansen ride back into Tokyo, which was the extent of our intimacy throughout the entire adventure.

"you met his *family?*" Samantha exclaimed in disbelief on Monday night at work. "We're never supposed to do that at this job."

"Yeah, so what?" I replied casually.

"In Japanese culture," she informed me, "introducing you to his family means that he wants to marry you!"

"What?" I asked. "No way. You've got it wrong. Besides, I've only known Dōhanman a few weeks."

"It doesn't matter," Samantha replied with disapproval.

"Wait," I said after a long pause. "Seriously?"

"Yeah," said Samantha, cracking a smile to appreciate the humor in my cultural illiteracy, "and didn't you say you had a boyfriend to boot?"

"Well, a sort-of boyfriend," I corrected.

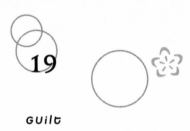

19

Guilt

The fear of being out of control—in relation to food and money as well as sex—is characteristic of contemporary women. We understand loss of control to be inappropriate—and that it could turn a woman into a monster.

—NAOMI WOLF, *Promiscuities*

Mako was the sort-of boyfriend whom I'd been seeing on and off since getting kicked out of my homestay. Mako, in retrospect, was basically a loser. Many a girlfriend of mine has remarked on my less-than-stellar taste in men, and Mako was no exception. He was a high school dropout who lived with his mother. Still, somehow, there was a certain chemistry between us.

I had met him some months earlier in front of Shibuya Crossing, where he asked me for an extra cigarette and then propositioned me to go out for a beer. I accepted his offer, although my real date was with the beer. I slept with him on our second date because I couldn't think of a good-enough reason not to. Although I found something adorably damaged about him, Makoto was always more of a cultural experience than a lover, so our relationship never became serious.

I find it impossible to compare his company to that of my past boyfriends in America, if only because the context was so different and I could only comprehend what Mako was saying to me about 60 percent of the time. Japanese spoken by men was slurred, throaty, and took me a lot longer to learn than the relatively clearer female speech.

Getting picked up in Mako's car—or more accurately his mother's car—was infinitely preferable to the hostess mobile any night. *"Konban dareka ga kimi o sawachatta no?"* Did any customers try to touch you tonight? he asked.

"Iie," No, I replied. It was one of the very few contexts in Japanese conversation in which saying the word *no* was acceptable.

"Hoteru wa dō desu ka?" How about going to a hotel, he asked expectedly.

"Haaaai," I agreed, feigning shyness, since he found shyness attractive.

Soon we were in Shibuya, passing a strip of hotels with English names such as Hotel Sexe, Hotel Casanova, Venus Lounge, Hotel XOXO, and Hotel Artemis. Mako pulled into the Venus Lounge without asking my opinion on the matter, which was perfectly okay with me since he was the one who would be paying. Not having to pay for anything, I was learning, came at the cost of having no voice in making decisions. But since the relationship wasn't very serious, I didn't care. We were just having fun.

The Japanese "love hotel" is an interesting contraption. Upon entering a love hotel, there are no breathing humans at the counter. That would be too embarrassing, given that the typical Japanese male in such a situation is about as timid as the average junior high school student watching a video about menstruation in sex education class.

There is only a vending machine. One button specifies the number of hours one wants to stay, spanning from one hour to two nights. The other button is slightly more complicated. The couple, or rather the man, who usually pays, looks at photographs of different bedrooms and chooses the ambience he likes best. When the proper amount of money enters the machine, the key dispenses.

Some say that one day the machine might display pictures of potential sex partners as well. This is not science fiction, my readers; mechanical sex is the logical result when the human condition mates with advanced capitalism.

Once you bought the key you earned your way into a different world, one where nothing was embarrassing and everything revolved around instant gratification. In a love hotel, that was called love. However, one must emerge before his money runs out or his coach could turn into a pumpkin and be towed from the parking lot by the management.

Makoto picked a room that had a karaoke machine. Ah, karaoke, the drunken Japanese pastime. More forgiving than the typical American karaoke bar, the authentic Japanese karaoke establishment rents out private rooms, allowing customers to showcase their lack of singing talent in front of their loved ones exclusively. Karaoke is a brilliant invention, and many Japanese rent the soundproof rooms to sing by themselves as a method of coping in times of stress. Inside hotel rooms, naked karaoke is a popular variation.

One of the things one has to notice in a love hotel is the porn. Japanese porn is, generally speaking, not very good. All the important parts, of the film and otherwise, are blurred over with a fuzzy TV blob, leaving the onlooker to actually notice how bad and unrealistic the story line actually is. Luckily there were a few different porn channels, allowing me to skip around frequently. I stopped on one of the channels because the woman in the film looked like someone I knew, someone I'd met once, whose identity I couldn't quite place. Then I noticed how tired and drugged the porn star's face looked, taking note of the dark circles under her eyes, and suddenly my memory clicked.

She looked like a girl I'd met once, a topless dancer in Roppongi with similar circles under her eyes. I would get taken out many places after work by certain regular customers who had long-standing relationships with the mama-san, and once a group of us went to a strip bar after-hours. When it was time for my customer to go home and send a tired me home in a taxi with a 10,000-yen bill to pay my way, the dancer working at the bar kept persuading this inebriated man to stay. She held his arm. When I asked her to please let up, she practically lunged at me. Still, it was hard to take another chick seriously in battle when she was half-naked, so I used my own physical strength to drag the nearly unconscious man out of the bar myself.

That girl, the dancer, she had eyes like that.

mako had to leave early the next morning to work construction. Checkout time wasn't until 12 P.M., which meant that I had some time to myself in the hotel room. So I decided to pace myself while I prepared to leave the enchanted Venus Lounge to face the outside world again.

I tried watching porn on the big-screen TV, but became bored after about five minutes and changed the channel to the NHK news. A train attendant got shot right in front of Shibuya Station a week earlier, killed at point-blank range in broad daylight, and there weren't any suspects yet in the case. The fact was so mind-boggling because of the sheer crowd of people hovering outside Shibuya at any time of day or night, none had seen a thing.

It must be gang-related, I thought to myself. I flipped the channel back to the porn, only to find that the scenario had changed to that of a schoolgirl being raped. I switched it off altogether.

At that, I crawled back into the unmade bed, rested on my back, and greeted my own reflection in the ceiling mirror. Though I assured myself that I didn't look half bad for having been out all night, I slipped into a more melancholy mood.

My thoughts turned to Hideo, the dōhanman. I was fond of him as a friend, but as much as I lied about being attracted to him, I couldn't force chemistry where there wasn't any. I hated myself for lying to him, for doing the work Mama had given me so well. And what if he really did want to marry me as Samantha said? The very fact that I had allowed a small part of myself to grow fond of the man was sabotaging my effectiveness at my job, which at times felt as simple as persuading drunken old men to spend obscene amounts of money. Hideo would have been better off if he'd never met me.

At the same time, however, I didn't understand why I had to feel so ashamed of myself. None of the other girls at the club ever seemed to express remorse about stringing along their customers and lying to them. It was merely our job description, and everyone involved knew it. The men, as well, came in knowing exactly what they were getting into.

So why should I feel guilty? I wondered. I was no stranger to guilt: a serious eating disorder consumed four years of my adolescence, a time in my life that consisted of ritualistic self-punishments that I still have the scars to prove.

Even in American society, I feel like I've been made to feel guilty about everything I've touched or experienced: first kisses, close dancing, hand jobs, pizza. I felt guilty for the rashness of my behavior, even as I threw up the pizza. I felt guilty for trying to starve to death the part of myself that was feeling guilty. Everything was somehow my fault. Everything. And at twenty-two, I was already sick of feeling that way.

So I got up from the still unmade bed, determined to escape the relentless shame I bore in the best way I knew how. I made my way over to the minifridge to insert some yen and make a purchase.

Then, at nine thirty on a Saturday morning, I opened my first beer of the day.

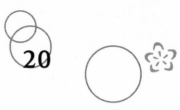

20

the thrill of the fall

waking up one evening, I found the sky was already dark.

"*Eimi!*" I suddenly thought out loud. My eyes widened with worry as the first coherent thought that came to my mind concerned the dubious whereabouts of my new friend. I had to call Eimi.

"*Moshi-moshi.*" She picked up the phone, a good sign.

"*Ohayo gozaimasu,*" Good morning, I said.

"*Ohayo,*" she grumbled, apparently roused from her sleep.

"*Daijoubu desu ka?*" I asked her if she was okay. It seemed a most appropriate inquiry, seeing as Eimi was last seen in the corner of Shot Bar 911 making out with some guy who wasn't her boyfriend.

"*Daijobu da yo,*" she answered affirmatively. Eimi was always okay, even when she wasn't. "*Futsukayooi kedo . . .*" she continued. This meant "I'm hungover, but . . ." It was commonplace to end sentences with a conjunction followed by a pause in her native tongue. In this respect the Japanese language lent itself entirely to the elaborate guessing game that is dealing with Japanese people.

"*Hai—yoku yasunde ne.*" I encouraged her to rest well before flipping my phone shut.

The previous night, a Thursday, had been "ladies' night" at a club called Shot Bar 911 in Roppongi. This meant that women could drink all of the cheap champagne their bodies could endure for free, while the alcoholic beverages for the men cost double their usual price. If hostessing taught me anything, it was that meeting drunk girls was a far more costly commodity than associating with sober ones.

In all honesty, the Palace was a safer environment for women, if only for all the no-touch rules. Despite the fact that I associated with men closer to my own age at this time of night, and did so entirely of my own accord, anything was more wholesome than the likes of Shot Bar 911 on a Thursday night.

When Eimi and I met each other in there some weeks earlier, I could tell that Eimi (pronounced like "Amy") was also a hostess almost immediately. Only a professional drinker could drink the way this girl did. Through gulps of liquor, she told me that she worked as a hostess in the neighborhood of Kinshichō, which I hadn't heard of yet. Still, our common profession gave us lots to talk about. Eimi's English was on about the same level as my Japanese, which made for a fragmented yet perfectly functional means of communication between us when we were together.

And much like me, Eimi was a self-inflicted hostess. By that I mean that we both had the option of making our respective livings in Tokyo during the day, yet we willingly chose to work nights instead. We began partying together regularly immediately after becoming acquainted, if only because we were the only people we knew who could keep up with each other's drinking.

Watching our clients socialize and enjoy themselves freely although we weren't permitted to do so ourselves planted a certain frustration in many a bar flower. It was a malady that could only be relieved by excessive partying. On many nights, Eimi and I met up after work to hit Tokyo's bar and club scene until the first trains of the morning passed through at 6 A.M. Since we usually slept all day long, in the real world we barely existed. We were creatures of the night: the stuff of other people's dreams.

In the bars, we shared a table and let off steam about how lame and boring our straightjacketed customers were. In the clubs, we fiercely competed for all the attention on any given dance floor, taking turns in recruiting some stranger to buy us our next round of drinks. In the evening twilight, we woke up in whomever's apartment we'd crashed, surrounded by the various loot we had shoplifted from convenience stores on the way home.

As I gradually learned about her personal life, Eimi's case struck me as an agonizing waste of potential. The girl was basically brilliant. She worked her way through the unspeakably rigorous Japanese high school system, studying dutifully and getting an average of three or four hours of sleep each night in order to pass the entrance exam for Tokyo University, Japan's most prestigious four-year college.

After passing the notorious examination, however, Eimi suffered a mental breakdown and was unable to attend. Her story was particularly wrenching, seeing as compared to the stresses of high school, university life in Japan more or less amounts to a four-year vacation.

I sometimes wondered if I would have been fated for a similar end had I been born in Tokyo rather than in New York. And if so, if Eimi might be the Japanese version of me.

It was hard to tell whether we showed up for the first interview this way, or if the long nights on the job did it to us, yet the fact remained that hostessing is not a profession that emotionally stable young women tend to find themselves involved in very often.

My friend Lindsey, however, seemed an exception to the rule. Lindsey didn't click with Eimi to the same extent that I did, largely because she didn't share our penchant for shoplifting and general excess. Adding to this, Lindsey couldn't follow the Japanese portions of our dialogue. And after Lindsey found herself a love interest with a posh loft in the exclusive neighborhood of Roppongi Hills, the most we saw of each other was at work.

Without having Lindsey around as often, I sometimes visited Eimi at her apartment share in Odaiba. Odaiba, an artificial island that was built in Tokyo Bay as a defense fortress against intruders, was constructed in the same year that Commodore Perry arrived with his Black Boats. Fittingly, its name is derived from the Japanese word for "cannon batteries." Presently, however, the island had been converted into a theme park for tourists, with a hot spring, a futuristic shopping mall, and a record-breaking Ferris wheel.

There were still a few housing compounds left over on Odaiba from the bubble period, when developers foresaw the island as a self-sufficient and highly populated future city. This was a ten-billion-dollar project that tanked when the bubble burst. Eimi lived in one such residence.

On a typical Saturday we would meet up at her apartment, and although it was our day off of work we would nonetheless begin drinking in the morning. Then we would go to Venus Fort, a shopping mall that is modeled upon an eighteenth-century Italian city, and spend all the cash we could muster on clothes, makeup, and more alcohol. I would never have allowed myself to waste so much of my earnings on such frivolous expenses had I been sober.

One evening after a typical day of extravagance and debauchery, Eimi had the idea to buy some more liquor at the convenience store and drink it as we rode on the famed Giant Sky Wheel that put Odaiba on the map.

She was not aware, however, that the high incidence of earthquakes in Japan had instilled in me a new fear of heights since I moved over. For my first six months in the country I would not enter an elevator, for fear of being trapped or falling in a strong tremor. To make matters worse, my curious obsession with earthquake research had informed me that Odaiba was built on the same type of reclaimed land that utterly collapsed from liquefaction in the Kobe earthquake more than ten years earlier.

But I was drunk, so that changed everything.

"Let's do it," I declared.

Being so intoxicated, I was not afraid of anything. The rush I felt at the top of the wheel as we overlooked the entire metropolitan area on a clear Saturday night was both breathtaking and liberating.

"To your right you will see the Hyper Shoot and Hyper Drop," the phantom voice inside the gondola told us in English as we rounded the wheel, "where you can experience the thrill of a fifty-eight-meter drop to the ground!"

We both looked over at the free-fall ride and then simultaneously glanced at each other. "We'll get sick if we go on that ride," Eimi and I warned each other at nearly the same moment. So instead, we decided to hit another bar upon our return to the earth.

21

mirror play

All the world's a stage, and all the men and women merely players.

——SHAKESPEARE, *As You Like It*

soon it was November, and hostessing, alcohol, and I were experiencing a honeymoon period as a threesome.

Autumn is a beautiful season in Tokyo. In those months, there is finally a reprieve to the stifling heat and indescribable humidity of the Tokyo summer. Autumn in Tokyo reminded me of the spring season when I lived in Montreal, when the snows finally melted. In both cases, the change in seasons meant that going outside was no longer a painful experience, and the natural air became tolerable again.

I liked my new job. Well, I at least enjoyed getting ready for work each night.

Depression doesn't generally lend itself to personal hygiene, so I had forgotten how much fun it could be to fuss over my own appearance before entering the world of hostessing. Preparing to go to the Palace felt like a childishly amusing game of dress up, through the course of which I tried on various evening dresses and applied so much makeup on my face that I resembled a China doll. In this, a part of my spirit felt renewed, as if I had been given the chance to act like a kid again.

I treated myself to manicures and pedicures for the first time in my life, and I let Eimi convince me to have my hair professionally highlighted from strawberry blond to platinum. These were vanities that I would have never allowed myself to enjoy if I hadn't been able to rationalize the expenses as work-related. Acquiring an actual sense of fashion and getting noticed in that way was all very novel to me.

And most of all, I realized that when one gets all dolled up each night, it becomes more and more fun to look in the mirror.

Some evenings, I practiced serving drinks and lighting cigarettes in front of the mirror. Young women of my generation in America are no longer groomed for servitude, so it was something I had to learn from scratch.

I practiced pouring whiskey, mixing it with ice and water, stirring it delicately, and finally wiping the condensation off of the sides of the long, phallic-shaped glass with a napkin. Only as I performed the spectacle in front of the mirror did I realize how erotic it all was. The Japanese understand the inherent power of suggestion like no other culture.

Once I mastered the art of evocative drink mixing, I began experimenting with different methods of smiling and winking at my reflection. I even taught myself how to lift one eyebrow and pucker my lips without looking silly. I realized that if I leaned over at a thirty-five-degree angle as I lit a cigarette, it would give a customer only the slightest glimpse of cleavage.

When I received a 1920s-style cigarette holder from a customer,

I also started smoking in the mirror so that I might look like a classical movie star. In doing so, I raised my eyebrows, tilted my chin down, and glanced up at my reflection with the most confidently erotic gaze I could muster.

It was around that time when I realized that the Russian and Filipina hostesses did not possess a natural aptitude for singing Japanese pop music on the karaoke machine: they practiced. This was how I came to spend my waking daytime hours, as sparse as they were, downloading J-pop on the Internet and memorizing lyrics.

The first song I taught myself was a lively and upbeat dance tune called "Trauma" by the overexposed young artist Ayumi Hamasaki. Ayumi's singing voice strongly resembled that of a chipmunk, but that was okay, since the secret to performing karaoke well was to select artists with the least vocal talent.

After getting ready for work, I would play "Trauma" loudly on my laptop and rehearse singing it to myself in the mirror. Unable to look away from my reflection, I was a great audience for myself. Many of the other hostesses must have practiced in the same way, even though no one would admit to making so much of an effort. Even the most innately talented foreign singer could not make it through the Japanese lettering on the karaoke screen without practice.

The lyrics to "Trauma" raced by especially quickly. I let the upbeat nature of the song overshadow the chorus's rather insipid lines.

One of Ayumi Hamasaki's many trademarks is to christen her songs with titles in English that in no way reflect the Japanese content of her lyrics. The more unfortunately titled of these include: "Are You Wake Up?" "My Name's Women," "Step You," and "Kiss o' Kill."

Despite the fact that Hamasaki doesn't appear to have any English-speaking friends or advisers, her incoherence is less than irrelevant within a pop culture where English words exist only for decoration.

Further, the less than traumatic Japanese lyrics of the song "Trauma" have inspired a specific line dance, consisting of synchronized gestures that Ayumi fans will typically act out whenever the J-pop superstar performs the song in concert.

So of course, I danced in the mirror while I sang, alone in my apartment with my headphones on. Performing for my reflection as such, I was able to harness an extroverted and even exhibitionist version of myself that I never knew existed. It satisfied this aspect of my personality, letting out a desire to perform that had previously lain latent inside of me.

I danced my most sexy and suggestive dances. Like the geisha, a hostess is seen as a "work of art" before she is seen as a human. Still, there is something to be said for being an untouchable piece of art, and only that.

After "learning my lines," it was curiously fun for me to play the role of a temptress. This was especially so seeing as the act took place within the controlled environment of a hostess bar, where I would never be expected to actually put out.

At seven each evening I would leave my gaijin house in east Shinjuku and take the Marunouchi subway line over to Ginza. The ride lasted sixteen minutes, but sometimes I wished that my commute lasted longer because I absolutely loved, as I got on and off the train and emerged onto the streets of Ginza, how everyone I passed knew that I was a hostess.

I was treated with far more respect than I have ever been on the streets of New York, and in the rare event that I was accosted by an inappropriately flirtatious man, I simply gave him my business card. Once he saw that I was a hostess in the most expensive district of Tokyo he would usually gasp and run away. It is well known that pretty hostesses have amounted to economic ruin for a broad spectrum of lonely Japanese men.

Men and women on the street looked at me like they eyed the district's remaining geisha. "Yes, yes, it's true," I wanted to tell them, "I get a salary to do hardly anything but receive free cocktails." The aging geisha who walked along the same path reminded the Japanese of their past traditions; I, on the other hand, the Japanese-speaking blond girl from the internationally themed bar, symbolized the future. Oddly enough, the other hostesses and I were cultural artifacts of a society that wasn't even our own.

The rush that I experienced as I walked through the posh streets of this foreign city was nothing less than theatrical. Feeling as if I were living inside a play or a movie made me think of Ayu again, and the tea party we had on the night we first met more than a year ago. But it was becoming progressively harder to relate to my old self anymore. I was an entirely different person now. And it was time for work.

"Hey, Lolita." Samantha could only have been addressing me, as I was sitting by myself at a table after some customers had just departed, catching my breath.

Samantha had taken to calling me "Lolita" due to my penchant for wearing short schoolgirl-type skirts to work in order to show off my longer than average legs. Skin equaled yen, I was learning.

"Do you know that song 'Waterfalls' by TLC?" she asked.

"Sure," I replied, happy to talk to someone, however briefly, whom I wasn't expected to entertain.

"I put it in to sing for my customer and it's next on line to play on the karaoke machine," she continued.

"Cool," I encouraged her. "I'm learning Ayumi Hamasaki myself." Samantha had a showstopping singing voice, much like so many of the other Filipinas at the Palace. It must have been something in their genes.

"Do you know that rap part in the middle of 'Waterfalls'?" she asked.

"Yeah." I began to wonder, between monosyllabic replies, exactly what Samantha was getting at.

"Well, can you sing that part for me?" I noticed just then that she was holding two microphones in her hands, one of which she was pushing my way. "The English is too fast for me to read."

"Me?" I panicked, Asian-style, with a nervous smile on my face. "But I can't rap! I've never rapped before! Just look at me, I'm white!"

"Sure you can." Samantha was unfazed by my protests. "You *are* an American, right?"

"Of course." My eyes widened in fear as I gave in and took the microphone she relentlessly shoved at me.

"Then you can rap," she said. "Come here, we're on!" She rushed me over to her customer's table, introduced me quickly, and began singing.

I tried to absorb the beat of the song despite my tipsiness, and soon it was my turn. I found it hard to believe myself, but I was almost staying on beat. Maybe Samantha was right after all about all Americans being able to rap. I went on.

Performing karaoke while drunk, for an intoxicated audience who did not speak English and would never notice when I made mistakes, was a lot like that dream many people have about becoming a famous rock star with adoring fans.

In academic circles, a karaoke machine is spoken of as an "electric geisha," since the traditional role of a geisha has always involved playing the background music for a man's song. Since the advent of karaoke machines, however, such electronics not only accomplish half of the hostesses job for her, the machine allows her to have a free hand to do some of the singing herself as well.

Because of their very modernity, hostess bars have always depended upon more technology than geisha houses do. These modern advances include voice-enhancing microphones, strobe lighting, and surround sound, among other devices. If the electricity should ever go out I presume that most hostesses would have a great deal of trouble entertaining their clients.

"Thanks, Samantha," I whispered to my friend after I had been officially invited to her customers' table to partake in the wine and conversation. The night was especially enjoyable, seeing as the table's conversation largely amounted to what a great rapper I was and how I should make a record.

"No problem," she said.

"This is the best job I've ever had," I expressed under my breath. We exchanged knowing grins, the both of us aware that, by no liberal stretch of the truth, could I actually rap.

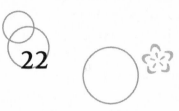

22

the art of conversation

conversation dominated the early-evening hours of a work night, and it lasted until the customers were drunk enough to start singing or try flirting. Such conversation was incredibly predictable. At least two or three times a week I would be asked whether I liked Japanese food. Another four or five times per week I was asked whether I've ever had a Japanese boyfriend. Just as often, customers inquired as to which aspects of Japanese culture I found most interesting.

We had to keep smiles on the faces of our clients at all times, because Destiny was perpetually watching. Sometimes I honestly wished that I could just reach over and give one of the men a backrub instead, but the Palace was a no-touch bar. Touching would have been easier; keeping the smile going without any physical contact, now that was a challenge.

For many of my customers who were not comfortable speaking English, meeting me was the first opportunity they had to speak with an American woman about her impressions of Japanese culture. The Japanese have a very strong sense of national identity, so I had to remember that anything I said about their country I might just as well be saying about them individually. Although I had to remember never to criticize Japanese culture in any way, I was well aware that complimenting his culture was an indirect method of flattering the customer as a man.

"I like to practice calligraphy," I told one such customer.

"Ah," he replied, interested, "what sorts of things do you write?"

"Well," I said, "I'm still working on *ei*. My homestay mom said that once I can write *ei* perfectly, then I will be able to write all the other characters as well."

"That's what everyone says," he replied.

"Oh, really?" I asked, even though I already knew that all students of both Chinese and Japanese calligraphy begin with the character *ei*, the pictograph meaning eternity, and usually practice writing the same character countless times until it is flawless.

"But I will never write a perfect *ei*," I lamented. "I will be writing *ei* for all eternity I think!" The man laughed, appreciating my pun, which I took as a sign to continue along the same line of discussion.

"Another thing I love about Japan is the *sakura*," I went on. "I can't wait until cherry blossom season comes again." I figured that this was a safe topic, seeing as I have never met a Japanese national who didn't enjoy the cherry blossoms.

Cherry blossoms, known as *sakura* in Japanese, mark a huge occasion in Japan. For a week or two in April when the *sakura* blooms, friends, families, and companies have many picnics where participants drink copious amounts of sake while admiring the country's many flowering cherry trees. Everyone is in high spirits and businessmen even smile. Therefore, any reference to *sakura* would usually make my companion feel happy.

"Cherry blossoms remind me of Japanese people because the petals are crowded so closely together," I reflected. "I mean that some trees are planted so closely together that the clouds of pink blossoms make distinctions between trees indiscernible. It reminds me of all the people crowded together on the streets and on the trains in Shinjuku and Shibuya."

"So you think that all Japanese people are pink?" he jested.

"Well, your face is right now!" I retorted, referring to the fact that his face had grown rather red due to his consumption of alcohol. This made him laugh again. Customers who liked to laugh were my favorite kind to entertain.

In 2003, there were many goings-on in popular culture and life that were worth discussing from a cross-cultural perspective as well. The Japanese baseball hero Hideki Matsui had just completed his first season with the New York Yankees, Tom Cruise came to Tokyo to promote his new film *The Last Samurai,* and the film *Lost in Translation* was nominated for Best Picture at the Oscars.

I knew that Japan had an extremely collectivist culture, yet I was still shocked by the consensus on issues of both global importance and popular culture. This made my job easier, however, since it allowed me to have basically the same conversations over and over again, sometimes with two or three customers per night.

As far as popular movies were concerned, the Japanese loved *The Last Samurai* while their response to *Lost in Translation* was rather tepid. Therefore I had to rack my brain for the aspects of *The Last Samurai* that were the most moving while I would point out the more irritating points in *Lost in Translation.*

"Okay, first of all," I commented to a group of businessmen once, "*Lost in Translation* opens with a lengthy close-up shot of Scarlett Johansson's ass."

"That is my favorite part!" said one of the men, his comment sending the group of three or four male companions into a fit of uproarious laughter. The four or five hostesses at the table pretended to find this funny as well, although at least half of us could not follow the Japanese conversation at all.

"But really," I continued along the same lines, "what if the movie had opened with a big picture of Bill Murray's ass?" I joked, "I think that the whole audience would scream and run out of the theater."

"Yes, that would be more like a horror movie!" another of the businessmen exclaimed, which resulted in another stream of continuous laughter.

I naturally enjoy entertaining others and making people laugh. I suppose I had the personality of a performer, the actress-comedian type who is always striving for approval in all situations because deep down she feels inadequate or something. Still, saying witty things is not always enough; the best hostesses know how to manipulate conversations in such a way that the most amusing comments are uttered by the customers themselves, thus increasing their enjoyment and pride in themselves.

Around the same time, I went to see *The Last Samurai* in the movie theater by myself. I had to do so as a form of homework, since various customers were constantly asking me what I thought of the film. I would not have gone out of my way to see the movie otherwise. In fact, I remember thinking that Tom Cruise looked rather foolish as he lectured the Japanese on "the way of the samurai" during a televised press conference to promote the film in Tokyo.

"It will be good for you to watch *The Last Samurai*," one customer said to me over shots of tequila, "so you can learn a little about Japanese culture."

Having studied East Asia in college and having lived with a Japanese family for the previous year, I liked to think that I already knew more than a little about Japanese culture. Still, that fact was more than completely irrelevant in the given context.

"I thought the ending of *The Last Samurai* was so moving," I remember telling yet another inquiring customer after seeing the film. "It taught me so very much about Japanese culture!" I almost gagged on my own tongue while I somehow managed to keep smiling throughout.

Customers also prompted me to speak about Japanese animation; I was most familiar with the full-length movies by the well-known director Hayao Miyazaki.

"You should also see *Laputa*," a client advised me when I brought up the subject of the animated film *Spirited Away*, and its subsequent success in America. "*Laputa* is an older Miyazaki film, so you haven't seen it."

"Really?" I feigned ignorance. "What is *Laputa* about?" In reality, I had written a term paper about *Laputa* in college. My thesis was that the animated film lost basically all of its critical meaning in the English version, when translation rights were sold to Disney.

"It is about a floating castle and a girl who falls from the sky," he replied.

"Hmm," I reflected thoughtfully. "Maybe the floating castle is something like this club, since we are called the Palace and this type of business is part of the floating world in Japanese culture!" I was noticeably proud of my insight, and this was a conversational error.

"No, not really." He didn't share my sentiment.

"Okay, dear," I told the old man, "I will promise to rent *Laputa* from the video store over the weekend if you promise to come back next week and discuss it with me." I rectified my position.

"I think I'll have the time to come by after work one night," he replied with a soapy smile.

" 'First request,' right?" I made sure. If I received a first request from the new acquaintance during his next visit, he would be added to my growing list of regulars.

"Sure!" He'd fallen for my trap.

With the more intelligent customers I was permitted to discuss politics as well. I would happily join in any criticism of American policy, if my customer was so inclined, and that particular topic hardly ever spawned a dull moment. I knew a few things about Asian politics as well.

Although in the real world my favorite topic concerning Japan tended to be my morbid fascination with Japanese war crimes and the nation's subsequent reluctance to apologize to the rest of Asia for their imperialistic actions during World War II, the subject was off-limits for obvious reasons.

Instead I brought up the subject of Japan's postwar economic miracle, which often made my clients nostalgic, seeing as they had actually been alive back then. The men also enjoyed reminiscing about Japan's "bubble days," when 10,000-yen bills flew out of everyone's pockets and practically flooded the streets. Such conversation was inevitably followed up by a market analysis describing how and why the Japanese economy was gradually but steadily on its way back up.

No matter what the topic, however, it was my job to ensure that the tone of our conversations was overwhelmingly positive and made the customers feel good about themselves in one way or another.

The Japanese are taught from a young age that self-pride is among the most abominable of vices. When they grow old, however, they become willing to pay out their ears for another person to stroke their egos extensively. In such a way, hostess bars are the curious by-product of a culture that discourages self-esteem.

Through conversation, I was expected to make the men feel proud of their own culture's place in the global hierarchy, and to in turn feel proud of themselves. After all, proud men spend money, and proud men who spent money increased my bonuses.

23

Geishas Interrupted

It was as if my stomach thought of itself as a heart. And no matter how I filled it—with men, with books, with food . . . it refused to be still. Unfillable—that's what I was. Nymphomania of the brain. Starvation of the heart.

—ERICA JONG, *Fear of Flying*

When I came to, I was surrounded by rice fields. As I lifted my head, some of the glittery eye shadow I had applied the night before rubbed off on the jacket of the stranger upon whose shoulder I had been sleeping. Luckily, he pretended not to notice me while he flipped through the morning paper.

Not again, I thought to myself.

At the train's next stop I lifted myself up and pushed past the sea of straightjacketed salarymen on their way into work. I then exited the car, determined to ascertain wherever the fuck I had ended up this time. From what I gather, falling asleep on the train and subsequently waking up in the Japanese countryside is a strikingly common experience for the average Tokyo drunk.

I hadn't even been working the evening prior, so I couldn't blame my blackout on the job this time. On those nights when I wasn't working and went out partying instead, I always promised myself—before I took the first drink—that I would catch the last train back home to Shinjuku at midnight. Before every night, I actually believed that I could maintain my willpower. Yet over and over again, like a delinquent version of Cinderella, I missed the train because I was having far too much fun.

It was on the first train that morning, the gray-colored Hibiya Line from Roppongi, that I subsequently lost consciousness and found myself all the way out in the Saitama Prefecture, northwest of Tokyo. In order to head for home, I needed to cross the platform to the Tokyo-bound train and sit tight for upward of two more hours until I reentered the city.

On the train back into Tokyo, I fell asleep again. This time I woke up at Jiyugaoka, five stations past where I lived in the other direction. So I had to switch platforms to change directions a second time. Looking back, I should have taken this as a warning sign that I was losing control of my direction in life.

It was only when I reached my bed in the gaijin house that I began to attempt to reconstruct the events of the night before. My memory was basically a pile of detached events and images, and putting the events together into a coherent narrative was less than possible.

Eimi and I had found ourselves in Propaganda, a bar at Roppongi Crossing. I had first inquired about Eva's whereabouts downstairs at the Lemon, but my waitress friend from Jerusalem was nowhere to be found that evening, so Eimi and I ventured upstairs. Early in the night, I suggested that I call Makoto to inquire about his plans.

"Dame, dame!" No, don't, Eimi exclaimed. She was not a fan of Makoto, who would occasionally join us on our nights out.

"Mako just dates foreign women because he is too socially awkward to deal with women within his own culture," Eimi said.

"He's not awkward with me," I replied.

"That's just it," she said, "because he's not intimidated by you."

"You're one to talk," I said, challenging her. "Ryo is a total ass-hole." I changed the subject to that of Eimi's lust interest, whose company I similarly opposed.

"So?" she asked with a smirk.

After it was decided that the boys were uninvited, we nonetheless had no intention of paying for our own cocktails that night. Eimi lost at "rock-paper-scissors," so it was her duty to swindle in the first round.

"Who wants to buy us a drink?" Eimi approached the bar with the confidence and expectations of a true hostess.

"If I get you some shots of tequila," an unmemorable Japanese man called out, "will you both kiss me?"

"No way," Eimi affirmed.

"Will you kiss each other then?" asked his companion.

Eimi and I looked at each other. Actually, there had always been a curious sexual tension between us. Although we both preferred men, she and I were always doting on each other's more attractive attributes. I saw the challenge as an exciting opportunity, but wasn't about to let my enthusiasm show.

"Why not?" I mumbled as if unaffected.

Eimi shrugged her shoulders.

From the moment we first kissed to receive our first shots, my memory starts to blur. Our adoring public apparently had a fetish for white girl on Asian girl action, so the cocktails must have kept coming. I have a fleeting memory of hooking up with her later in the night, except this time we were in the corner of a different bar, making out of our own accord.

It was the first time I had ever kissed a girl, but the events weren't so surprising to me. Whenever I drank lately, I had a growing tendency to become sexually involved with whomever happened to be around at the moment. Drinking not only freed me of the intense inhibition, self-doubt, and guilt that I often felt while sober, but it also enhanced a certain emptiness I felt inside. This made for a vicious combination. With sex rather than food this time around, I restricted my own desires only to eventually snap and overflow with sexual energy in a characteristically bulimic cycle.

I don't remember how I got myself onto the Hibiya Line that morning.

The following evening and for days after that night, Eimi refused to answer any of my calls or e-mail messages. This irritated me, since I didn't see what the big deal was about our hook up. Couldn't she just drink more to kill the embarrassment that inevitably surfaces when one accidentally makes out with her best friend? That's what I was doing, and it seemed to work fine.

It was beginning to occur to me that Eimi, for lack of a better description, might be even crazier than I was. The girl had a definite pattern of snapping back violently after becoming intensely obsessed with a given person or thing. Thus, she was treating me just as she had treated her beloved studies when she abruptly quit school. Although I was concerned for Eimi's well-being, I let my pride get the best of me and gave up trying to contact her after a week had passed.

Eimi pursued her desires in excess until she reached a breaking point, at which instant she abruptly constrained herself. I, on the other hand, took to restricting my own will until it inevitably overflowed. It took Eimi's sudden absence from my life for me to realize that Eimi's behavior patterns were like an inverted reflection of my own.

So it followed that I would replace Eimi's presence in my life with men: lots and lots of different men. And this time, adding to the toxic mixture of alcohol and emptiness, I had developed a fetish for strangers—for sleeping with handfuls of mysterious men who would fuck me and then leave me, until the pain of abandonment felt good.

Among the more memorable of my few hour flings was Rico, a dark and handsome man whom I'd met on the street walking home. Sooner than not, I agreed to accompany him to a small yet posh pub in Azabu-Juban. He bought me a Yebisu beer.

"You like green?" he asked.

"You mean pot?" I responded, a bit surprised.

"Yeah," he replied, checking his back.

"I do." I tried to hide my excitement. "But are you sure it's safe?" Penalties for drug possession in Japan were close to medieval. (One joint in your possession gets you three years in jail. Such severity is likely why the Japanese are so partial to alcohol.)

"It's okay," he said. "I can hook it up for you and we can smoke it at a hotel later. First I have to run an errand though. Is that cool?"

"Sweet," I said, taking his hand.

Somewhere in the middle of our taxi ride there and back, I realized far later than I should have that Rico was the party selling the drugs rather than the one buying them.

"Is your name really Rico?" I asked him when we exited the cab and had some privacy.

"No," he said, "but that's what my Italian passport says, so please play along."

"What's your real name?"

"You'll call me Rico." His tone both frightened me and turned me on at the same time. "You won't be able to pronounce my real name anyway."

"And where are you from?" I inquired.

"Iran," he said flatly.

"What's it like there?" I asked naïvely.

"It's very beautiful," he replied more tenderly, "but girls like you don't want to go. Trust me.

"Whatever my job is, it has nothing to do with you," he said after we entered the hotel. "If I get caught at this hotel, nothing will happen to you, so don't worry." He had noticed my unease after he had spread out of some lines of cocaine on the coffee table. "You're a pretty blond girl with an American passport. You'll walk out of here. That's the way things are."

It was the first time I had seen real cocaine. I once made a pact with myself that I would never go near coke since I so obviously had an addictive personality. Still, I didn't hesitate to try it that night, seeing as I was so far gone already. Luckily, I don't remember feeling anything great or distinct about the high, saving that I suddenly felt like staying up and having sex all night.

"What the hell is that?" Rico was visibly disturbed by the scars on my left wrist as we lay in bed after sex.

"I don't wanna talk about it," I mumbled as I thrust my exposed left arm back underneath the sheets.

"You did that yourself, didn't you"—he leered at me disapprovingly. I couldn't figure out why he was taking such offense to my own personal fuckups. He was the coke fiend after all.

"Mmm," I mumbled as I racked my mind for a change of topic.

"All this violent shit is stupid!" he blurted out before I could think of anything.

Rico didn't seem so much angry with me as he was with the vacant space straight in front of him. "I was in the Iran-Iraq War," he said as he continued to stare away from me, "and I saw my best friend blown to bits right in front of me." My eyes widened at the revelation. "So I don't wanna look at any violent shit. None of it makes sense!"

"Oh, my god," I gasped, and our room was quiet for a while after that.

"So how old are you anyway?" I eventually broke the silence.

"Twenty-nine," he replied, though I remember thinking that he looked even younger.

ᴀғᴛᴇʀ ᴡᴇ ᴘᴀʀᴛᴇᴅ the following day, I lay in bed pondering what he told me the night before. *Twenty-nine,* I thought to myself. Could he have been lying about his age? I could have sworn that the Iran-Iraq War went down in the eighties. Since the war he'd spoken of predated my ability to read, I pulled my laptop up to my chin and performed an Internet search to ascertain the exact dates of the conflict.

I quickly ascertained that the war lasted eight years between 1980 and 1988. The current year being 2003, Rico could not have been more than thirteen when the conflict ended. Rico must have been lying to me about something, because he was far too young—even at the war's end—to have fought.

Or was he? Two clicks upon a link to a human rights resource page proved my assumption incorrect. As it turned out, child soldiers were used by Iran during the end of the conflict to clear minefields by running through them or riding across on bicycles. The mental image of Rico's friend getting killed in one such minefield made me sick to my stomach, so I put my computer away so as not to become sick upon the keyboard.

Rolling over on my futon, I stared at my scars with an acute and more globally aware sense of shame in the pit of my gut. I was so incredibly fortunate that I hadn't lived through the hell that Rico experienced. Still, I had insisted on abusing myself anyway. *None of it makes sense,* as he'd said.

As I drifted in and out of a disturbed sleep that day, likely still wired from my first experience with cocaine, I had a familiar recurring dream that I was the passenger in a car with a mysterious person who abruptly abandoned the driver's seat and insisted that I drive the rest of the distance by myself. The only problem was that I was sitting in the backseat of the car, where I could barely touch the steering wheel and couldn't find the pedals at all.

Some say that you are all the characters in your dreams, and I would have to agree. In this dream I played two roles simultaneously. I was just as much the merciless phantom who abandoned someone in a fast-moving vehicle as I was the girl in the backseat who struggled but could not seem to reach the brakes.

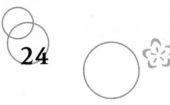

24

the art of reflection

Now of course a mirror image is always darker and distorted. Convex and concave swap places, falsehood wins out over reality, light and shadow play tricks.

—HARUKI MURAKAMI, *Underground*

"I need to reinvent myself," I declared over a casual Sunday dinner with Hideo and his sister. "I want to change my hostess name, too many Japanese people have trouble saying 'Daisy.'

"Think of one for me," I ordered Hideo, with the same tone of voice I use when I tell him to order for me in restaurants. Although I was having dinner with him in my free time, I was secretly hoping that, by allowing him to choose my new hostess name, he would feel inclined to patronize me at the Palace even more often. I had chosen to completely ignore Samantha's warning that Hideo might want to marry me.

"What about Meiree?" Hideo suggested. "That is a cute name."

"Mary?" I asked. "No, I don't think so"—I hesitated—"in America that is more of an old-fashioned name."

"What about Misheru," his sister Akiko suggested, "like the Beatles song."

"Everyone is named Michelle," I countered.

"Or Guroria"—Hideo took a turn to advise—"like Guroria Estutefanu."

"Nah," I said, "too many *r*'s and *l*'s. When the Japanese try to say Gloria I can't even understand it anymore." I could be more blunt with Hideo than with most customers.

"Then how about Shindee." Hideo was wearing his thoughtful face. I could tell that he enjoyed the concept of creating a name for me. "Because you are very good at singing karaoke by Shindee Ropaa."

"Cindy, Cindy, Cindy," I repeated to myself, unable to find anything wrong with the name for the moment.

"But, wait," said Akiko, "Shindee starts with a *shi*, is that not inauspicious?" She was referring to the fact that the word *shi*, in Japanese, also means "death." *Shi* also means "four" in Japanese, so many buildings in Japan do not have fourth floors for this very reason.

"But *shi* is in so many words anyway," Hideo corrected his sister. "Besides it is a foreign word anyway, so the *shi* doesn't carry over so much."

"So it is decided," I said, "from Monday night I will be Shindee."

"Just remember never to say it like *shinde*," Hideo joked, pronouncing it as shinday, *shinde* being the command form of the verb "to die."

From the following Monday, however, my new hostess name proved quite auspicious.

"This is destiny, Shindee-chan!" Calvin said that night. "Our meeting is truly a miracle."

"Yes." I smiled and nodded. The two of us had only met about thirty minutes earlier, yet Calvin was quickly transforming into "regular" material.

"If I hadn't passed by your club by chance," he said with a passion in his eyes that could have easily been mistaken for sincerity if not for the context, "we would never have been able to meet."

"Yes." I repeated the gesture of agreement.

"Our coming together," he continued, "it is an act of fate."

"May I order another beer?" I asked politely.

"Of course," he said, summoning Rod.

Calvin, whose name was not really Calvin, was the eccentric type. He appeared to be in his late forties, with overstyled Elvis hair, wire-rimmed glasses, and a hopelessly feminine pink Windbreaker. He seemed the sort who had likely been teased in high school. I nicknamed him Calvin right away because he reeked of Calvin Klein cologne.

Calvin was rather tolerable company that evening. He was polite, had a gentle demeanor, and bought me all of the drinks I requested even though they were ridiculously overpriced. In turn I conditioned myself, as much as possible, to find his dorkiness and eccentricities adorable.

The only real drawback of our meetings was his incessant declaration of undying love for me. Had I met him earlier in my hostess career I would have been more frightened by his apparent obsession, but by then I knew the rules of the game well enough to play along.

He often said that I reminded him of his first love, who was a foreign girl from Europe. It's amazing how many "first loves" I've reminded my customers of over the years. Perhaps, I've often thought to myself, all women in their twenties start to look the same after a man reaches a certain age.

For Calvin, however, I symbolized much more to him than his dwindling youth. The man was also obsessed with the idea of

"America." And in that, I represented an ideal of "freedom." There is an entire subculture of Japanese men with a large propensity to "fall in love" with foreign women because they feel terribly constrained by the rigid social codes that govern relationships within their own culture, and thus they pursue foreign women in a figurative attempt to escape.

So I played his game, answering each of his questions about my home country in the most positive light possible, in order to tell him precisely what he wanted to hear.

In his largely unintelligible English, he told me many stories— and many of the same anecdotes over and over again—about his experiences as an exchange student at a university in Kentucky when he was in his prime. Listening to his humorous tales, I laughed so hard and continuously my belly ached.

All this was despite the fact that when the conversation ended I still had no idea what was so funny due to the man's slurred speech. My job certainly involved learning to read subtle social cues and body language to determine whether a client's next remark was intended to be funny.

After about the third time he repeated the same anecdote (as drunk people are apt to do), I finally realized that he was trying to tell me that he named his only son Kenta because it sounded like Kentucky. When I finally realized the meaning I would have liked to laugh for real, but my belly hurt too much from laughing before, so I let out a fake girlish giggle instead.

By the end of the evening Calvin's elation was visibly wearing off, and he looked tired. It was then that he confessed to me all about how he hated his job as a computer programmer, and wished he had become a musician instead.

In this, I came to see that my face alone was Calvin's temporary ticket out of Japan, and by extension, out of reality. "Falling in love"

with someone you don't know can be a lot less complicated than lov-
ing somebody that you do, and this may explain why so many Japanese men prefer to pay for it. They paid to fall in love with their own
fantasies of who we were.

Calvin reminded me of a customer Samantha had, who would
come to see her at least twice a week. Samantha would brag that this
man knew absolutely nothing about her personal life at all. Instead,
he was hopelessly infatuated with her manners, with the exotic and
mysterious character she played so well at the bar. I often wondered
what they could possibly talk about. Yet having met Calvin, I began
to understand. If Samantha and her customer were anything like
Calvin and me, then it sufficed for them to speak of "love," "dreams,"
"fate," and other such illusions.

Calvin's case helped me to understand why so many men spent
such obscene amounts of money simply for our conversation. The
majority of Japanese men, especially the aging ones, are hopelessly
awkward with respect to interpersonal relations. As a result, they
take refuge in an environment where the conversation is facilitated
for them, where their opinions are never questioned, and where our
flattering remarks help them to feel loved and accepted.

If the men wanted sex they could go elsewhere, and there were
lots of cheaper places to go. The Japanese certainly do not lack creativity in these respects. Yet instead of seeking such physical stimulation, the men who frequented places like the Palace sought to fill an
emptiness of a more emotional nature.

At the Palace, our jobs were to be as lacking in our own personalities as possible. The ideal hostess resembles a blow-up doll: flawlessly plastic on the outside, hollow on the inside. Such hollowness
is essential in order to become a vessel for her client's fantasies. She's
a blank screen upon which others' dreams are projected.

The more mysterious our airs, the better it was for business.

Mystery breeds creativity, and mystery awakens the imagination. And the imagination is a powerful force. It keeps the economy turning, and the *mizu shobai* flowing. It is likely one of the top grossing industries in Tokyo.

the following night, I was not surprised at all when Hideo returned to the Palace to visit his very own Shindee, for the first time.

manic girls buy puppies

you will be my new friend. You will be my new life.

I thought this to myself when I first laid eyes on the abnormally tiny two-month-old long-haired, blond miniature dachshund as I passed by the twenty-four-hour pet shop in Roppongi. I was in desperate need of a new life, seeing as it had reached late morning by then, and I was still feeling very intoxicated from the night before.

Her tiny eyes alert, the puppy's long nose protruded through the metal grid of her crate. She seemed to already know that it had been a long, long ass night for me.

To say the least, the night before I met Pika had been one to forget. That evening, as most of them had, started off at work. At the Palace I had gotten enough drinks in my system to persuade myself that going out partying after-hours—where I would invariably put even more chemicals into my body than I was being paid to consume—was a most grand idea, as per usual.

This time I was accompanied by a girl named Tsunami whom I'd met on duty at the Palace. Tsunami was full Japanese, a rarity among international bar staffers in Ginza, although it didn't make much of a difference since most of our clientele lately was Japanese speaking.

I doubted whether Tsunami was her real name. Most likely she had chosen her hostess name after the popular J-pop hit song of the same name. We liked to name ourselves after songs on the radio; it gave us something to talk—or perhaps even sing—about with our clients.

And everyone was singing "Tsunami" on the karaoke machines that year. In fact, I wouldn't have been much of a hostess if I didn't know all the words to the hit song, a catchy ballad about an emotion so powerful it drew comparison to a tidal wave.

By contrast, Tsunami herself was a flighty waif of a young woman. Her slight frame rose just over five feet tall.

I was trying to stay away from Roppongi already by then, because Roppongi is evil, so we bypassed the hostess mobile's nightly stop at Roppongi Crossing and I convinced Tsunami to accompany me that night to a British pub in the Ebisu where I knew a few of the bartenders.

There, Tsunami met a boy, and the two seemed quite enthralled with each other. I don't recall his name; what I remember is that he was a youngish attractive tax lawyer for a very well-known international bank. Visiting Tokyo on business, he was staying at the luxurious Ebisu Westin.

At 3 A.M. the bars closed, and Tsunami took the yuppie on a tour of all the temples and shrines in the Ebisu area. However, the lawyer didn't speak any Japanese and Tsunami's English was not so understandable, which was basically why I was still around, as the third-wheel translator.

Predictably, the tour reached its conclusion in a hotel room at the Ebisu Westin. Tsunami insisted on having room service cart up a bottle of Dom Pérignon at four in the morning. And then another bottle after the first one emptied itself.

Sometime during the second bottle, Tsunami and I started to kiss.

"I like where this is going!" the man said, with the permanent grin he had been wearing since the two of us agreed to accompany him up to his room. I had taken to kissing girls when I was drunk beyond recognition; it seemed a much safer alternative to kissing a man. The three of us fooled around in the hotel room until about sunrise, when a very unfortunate event took place: Tsunami's boyfriend called.

"Damn it, Tsunami, you can't just leave *now!*" I was furious. I was the one who was supposed to bail out on *her*. The boy and the two bottles of Dom were her idea, after all!

Needless to say, Tsunami and I were no longer friends after that morning.

I didn't want to have intercourse with the lawyer after Tsunami left me alone with him. But he was already excited and I felt obligated to, keeping in mind all the luxuries we'd enjoyed on his dime that evening. It was entirely consensual sex, which gave me even more reason to be livid with myself when I woke up alone in the hotel late that afternoon.

A thought entered my head that would tease me over and over again throughout my stay in Tokyo: *If I am just fucking anyone anyway, why not get paid for it? Why not just take the bridge over to prostitution?* The marijuana of the *mizu shobai,* bar hostessing is basically a gateway drug. More than once I've seen it take formerly shy girls into careers as strippers, if not outright prostitutes.

Fortunately, though, such thoughts eventually gave way to an aching feeling in my gut; it lectured me that my current lifestyle wasn't working. *Something's gotta give*, I thought to myself over and over again on my way to get some lunch at the Freshness Burger chain restaurant in Roppongi.

And at that point I came upon Pika. She and I looked at each other steadily for about five minutes as her long nose protruded out of a space between the metal bars of her crate in an unspeakably adorable fashion.

Then, after stopping at an ATM to withdraw some hostessing wages I had earned in the past few months, I bought a two-thousand-dollar puppy on impulse, with cash, knowing full well that my gaijin house didn't allow pets. That was okay, though, because I would move (I ultimately ended up moving three times because of this dog), and I desperately needed a lifestyle change. Most important, I needed a good reason to come home after work—an alternative to the nocturnal world of unmemorable after-parties I had become accustomed to.

Truth be told, I hadn't worked very hard for that money, which may have been why I didn't feel so guilty about spending it all. At the time, I was living like a rich girl without ever really having the cash. *Mizu shobai* really is a terrifically descriptive phrase. As soon as I got paid I would just start giving the yen back to the man, as if the salary were never really mine to begin with.

Pika was named after a piece of calligraphy I had recently admired at an art museum. The character for star, the majority of its strokes extend outward like infinite rays of light. The kanji is pronounced *hikari* (star) or *hikaru* (the verb to glitter), both of which are popular girls' names in the Japanese language. Pika is an affectionate shortening of either name. At the same time, Japan has one of the few languages in which flashing lights make a noise worthy of an onomatopoeia: *pikapika.*

And Pika really was a little flicker of light for me. There is a popular phrase in Japanese that is pronounced "oya-baka." *Oya* is Japanese for *parent,* while *baka* is the commonly used word for *idiot.* Thus, the Japanese expression *oya-baka* refers to a parent who believes his or her own child to be the greatest thing since white rice.

Pika, however, actually was the cutest puppy in the world. And the Japanese knew cute like no one else.

I took my dog for walks when I would have otherwise been persuaded to go to one bar or the other. When Pika was a puppy she and I would go on outings to Harajuku, where people gathered around my dog like she was a celebrity. It was terrifically amusing to see how many times the word *"Kawaii!"* could be squealed by school-age Japanese girls as Pika trotted from one street corner to the next.

Harajuku is generally where you bought your prefaded jeans for five hundred dollars, your prefringed and torn cutoffs (just fifty dollars), weathered leather in all colors, and anything else you might need to look like a tough British rock star who sold out in the eighties. A pricey shop on the end of the street even specialized in USED AMERICAN CLOTHING, or so it advertised.

Schoolgirls practically went into convulsions upon laying eyes on my tiny dog. I remember one in particular who stooped over to pet Pika and began to jump up and down orgasmically squealing: *"Tabetai! Tabetai!"* (I want to eat it!) *"Tabenakute ii,"* It would be okay if you didn't, I recall responding.

Truth be told, Pika was far fonder of the opposite side of Harajuku Station, which hosted the Meiji-Jingu shrine and its surrounding park, known as Yoyogi Koen. One of the larger and more impressive Shinto shrines in the area, the Meiji-Jingu shrine was built to commemorate the Meiji emperor, with whose restoration Edo became Tokyo in 1868. By Meiji-Jingu, Pika enjoyed chasing pigeons, because it made her—all five pounds of her—feel very, very big.

Unlike the streetwalkers of Harajuku, I've never been one for designer goods or expensive brand names. Instead it was Pika who basically cost me my savings. This was ultimately due to multiple apartment moves, lost security deposits, and the costly I'm sorry presents that ensue when tatami mats are urinated upon.

Suddenly I was living from paycheck to paycheck again.

I became dependent upon dinner dates for sustenance. As a result I enjoyed a brief renaissance as the "dōhan queen" at the Palace. At my height I was raking in three dōhans per week. To put this in context, hostesses at even the most exclusive hostess bars have to fill a quota of only two dōhans per month.

I also managed to maintain my alcoholism solely upon drinks that were bought for me by men. Tall men, short men, ugly men, pretty men—the beer always tasted the same.

I made it known among my customers that while I wouldn't accept gifts for myself, I would gladly accept gifts for my dog. Thus, it got to the point where Pika practically needed her own closet for all of her dog kimonos and dresses and sweaters and that coat with little angel wings that would flutter when she walked.

One summer evening I attended a crowded fireworks spectacle with Hideo. Again, I had chosen to spend my free time with this customer. Hideo took a great liking to Pika, and had just purchased for her a silk kimono to suit the occasion.

"Everyone is staring at us," he said to me with a smirk.

"Well," I replied, "have you ever seen a foreigner with a dog in a kimono before?" We laughed.

26

Jishin

because i was out of money, I decided to register for a modeling agency in hopes that I might be able to support Pika better if I got some modeling gigs.

Monika, my new modeling agent, and I were alone in her apartment one afternoon. I had never seen so spacious a flat since moving to Tokyo. Usually in the space-choked capital, rooms tended to resemble coffins. But Monika's apartment had breathing room for numerous Persian rugs, exotic wall hangings, and an array of plant life extending out onto her balcony. There was even a walk-in closet for me to change into the variously garish outfits she had me pose in for the portfolio she was creating for potential clients.

Monika put down her camera to adjust my pose, moving my shoulders slightly forward and my head a nudge back. I was feeling slightly naked in what little fabric comprised what she defined as "cute."

"*Hone ga mieta hō ga ii*," Monika assured me confidently.

Monika's words rang through my head, translating from Japanese to English, then back to Japanese, the language in which I had been thinking and speaking at the moment: *Hone ga mieta hō ga ii.* Her assertion shocked my train of thought entirely back to English, where I assured myself that I'd translated properly: *It's better if your bones stick out,* Monika had said.

Better to see my bones, I thought to myself. As the translated words seeped into my head, their heroin-chic implications of ideal waiflike bodies put me into a trance. Perhaps I was briefly possessed, obsessing over possible crash diets that could make each bone of my body gradually more visible to Monika, more attractive.

"No!" My carefully posed body practically convulsed, gripped with the sudden urge to panic and run for cover. I had to get out of there. I could not relapse into anorexia: I had too much to lose this time around, plus, home was halfway across the world. I had no safety net.

"Dō shita no?" What happened, Monika asked, disheveled.

"Nanka ne, ano ano, etto ne . . . " I filled my speech with words of the Japanese language that have no meanings whatsoever, but function only as delayers of speech, allowing the speaker to think over what she is about to say and avoid an awkward silence. *"Jishin o kanjimashita ka?"* Did you just feel an earthquake, I finally asked as I put myself back in order.

"Jishin?" Monika's eyes, already stapled open by plastic surgery, became even more impossibly wide.

"Oh, never mind"—I felt guilty for scaring her—"sometimes I feel earthquakes when there aren't any."

"Jishin," Monika thought aloud. "That reminds me, Lea, I heard that you didn't get the Godiva job in Harajuku because the director thought you didn't have any self-confidence."

In the Japanese language, the word *earthquake* is a homonym for the word *self-confidence:* both are called *jishin.*

"Whatever!" I mocked. Monika was bilingual, so we were now

conversing in English. "But I *do* have self-confidence!" I replied. "I just pretended not to because I thought that all Japanese men love shy girls and feel threatened by assertive females. After all," I continued, "I get a lot more accomplished at the Palace by pretending to be shy than by ever speaking my mind."

"A modeling audition is not a hostess bar." Monika was unimpressed. "Just exude more confidence next time."

"Well, it certainly seemed a lot like a hostess bar," I continued unnecessarily. "All the important decisions are being made by middle-aged men!"

"I know, dear," she replied. "Better luck next time. There is a Juice Inc. audition I can send you on this weekend if you promise to act more confident. Your performance is a reflection on me, too, you know."

"Fine," I sighed. "I promise to have more *jishin* next time."

At that, I changed back into my own clothes, politely refused a second round of tea, and left Monika's apartment as soon as I possibly could. I had to get home to Shinjuku, shower, and head to Ginza on the Marunouchi subway line.

At the Juice Inc. audition on Saturday afternoon, all the men and women who were called to audition sat together at some white tables in a large room. It was there that we all found out, at the same time, that the photo shoot we would have to prepare for involved sticking out our tongues and curling them across the sides of our faces in a most unnatural position.

Immediately after hearing this, many of the more professional model types took out their portable mirrors and began to exercise their tongue muscles, contorting their mouths in various positions. At the same moment, my eyes met those of a young woman seated next to me. On both of our faces was a similar expression, as if to say "This is just too ridiculous," or "I don't know what I'm doing here."

"This is kind of stupid," I whispered over in her direction.

"I know," the short brunette replied with a warm smile.

"What agency are you with?" I began to make conversation to combat my boredom.

"Design Japan Studios," she said.

"Me, too!" I related. "With Monika?"

"Yes, with Monika," she said knowingly, which led to some inevitable small talk on the subject of our rather eccentric modeling agent.

"By the way I'm Lea," I said, introducing myself.

"I'm Jade," she replied, "but most of my friends call me Jadie."

"Nice to meet you."

Across from us, a clean-cut blond-haired blue-eyed young man with a thick Russian accent was discussing a previous television gig. "It was so silly," he revealed. "They had me dress up like an American soldier, hustle into a fake cave, and capture this actor who pretended to be Saddam Hussein."

Jadie and I were forced to join the conversation when we couldn't help but giggle at what we had just overheard.

"They didn't care that you're not American?" I asked him.

"Well," he replied, "I wasn't allowed to open my mouth to say anything at all, obviously, because I can't speak English."

"Your English is just fine," Jadie assured him, "but what about the guy who played Saddam Hussein? What was his nationality?"

"He was a fat Japanese guy with a huge amount of makeup and a big, fake beard," he replied to our immense amusement.

"What was this TV program for?" someone else inquired.

"It was a reenactment for network news." He smiled.

Jadie and I basically bombed the Juice Inc. audition because neither one of us could stop laughing when the team of judges carefully examined our tongues from different angles. Monika would later stop calling me to auditions for this very reason, but at the moment I didn't care.

"All of those skinny models make me hungry," I mumbled as Jadie and I took the elevator down to the ground floor of the building.

"Me, too," she admitted. And so it was we ate lunch together.

Jadie was half Japanese and half American, and having been raised in both worlds, it was pretty safe to say that she knew everything. She was what the Japanese called *hafu*, a word recently deemed politically incorrect seeing as it's the Japanese connotation of half-a-person. Aside from the occasional modeling gig, Jadie worked for a transla- tion company part-time as well.

"That's so cool!" I exclaimed when she told me about her day job. "I'd like to work in translation too but my reading and writing is only on a third- or fourth-grade level. I'll have to study more. So what kind of jobs have you done for Monika?"

"Well, I do parties sometimes," she responded.

"What's that?" I inquired.

"It's really dumb," she said. "You have to stand up and stay still during these big corporate events at hotels or whatever. You just have to bow whenever a man passes you or have a polite conversa- tion if a man initiates one."

"So you're basically just there for decoration?" I assumed.

"Basically."

"Wow," I thought out loud, "that sounds a lot like my job."

"Then last week I had to pass out champagne for this promotion outside the big Godiva shop—"

"You got the Godiva job!?" I exclaimed, interrupting her. "I au- ditioned for that but didn't get it because they said I had no *jishin*."

"You seem to have plenty of *jishin*," she told me between bites of her meal.

"I suppose." I processed her words as I swallowed my food. "I guess I just don't show it sometimes."

the way of the dōhanman

People think [Japan's] run by men but that's a myth. The women are in charge. . . . They stay behind the scenes because they're smart. The men die from overwork and the women do the decorating.

—CATHERINE HANRAHAN, *Lost Girls and Love Hotels*

In three months' time, Lindsey and I had made up our own language to describe various aspects of our environment at the Palace. Old words didn't exactly fit our new experiences so well, so making up our own names for everyone and everything was somewhat of a survival tactic. After Lindsey's tourist visa expired, however, and my friend returned to Delaware with a fat pile of yen, our language died.

When Lindsey left Tokyo, I instantly felt as if a spell had been broken. Rod wasn't called Rod anymore, but instead he became *Tenchō-san* (Mr. Manager). The Eastern Bloc was only a clique of

Russian hostesses who hated me, and their leader, Big Red, returned to being called Svetlana.

Dōhanman lived on, however, largely due to the presence of my new friend Jade.

"Do you wanna go to a rich people party?" I asked Jadie one night as we watched the TV show *Friends* as it appeared dubbed over in Japanese on network television.

"One of my clients is having it at his beach house in Hayama," I informed her. "It might be good for networking."

"Will the emperor be there?" Jadie jested. After all, Hayama was an elite waterfront town where the emperor kept his vacation house.

"My client's name is Hideo Marui," I explained, "but I always call him 'Dōhanman' because he was my first dōhan and he looks like Anpanman."

"I used to love Anpanman!" Jadie exclaimed. "I had the action figures and everything." Having been raised in both America and Japan, Jadie was very familiar with the superhero composed of sweet bread.

"What did Bread man *do*, anyway?" I inquired.

"Anpanman was famous for finding lost children in the forest and giving them the energy they needed to find their way home," she informed me.

"How did he do that?" I asked.

"He let them take a bite out of his head, and it gave them energy," she replied.

"Naturally." I smirked.

"I always envied those children because they had a stable home to return to," she reflected more seriously. "My parents were always moving back and forth across the ocean."

"Well, at least your upbringing helped you become a kick-ass translator," I said with admiration. "I could work at Japanese my entire life and probably never be as good as you."

Jadie did end up joining me at the rich people party held on Dōhanman's beach estate. When I first received the invite, I assumed it would be a ballroom-style event with wine, cheese, and snobbery. I was surprised, however, when Hideo told me that dress would be casual since the event was being held at his private beach. And casual it was. So much so that I was able to bring Pika, who happily sprinted back and forth across the tides, making a slew of new friends.

While Jadie bobbed about the party in a hopeful search for some high-paying translation work, I sat on the sand watching the waves, sometimes engaging in polite small talk with strangers. I didn't have to stand up often, since Dōhanman brought anything I might need—be it food, drink, or blanket—to my feet. And every time he brought me something I patted him affectionately or complimented his food, service, or attire. It was bizarre to act as if I were his girlfriend in such a casual setting. Especially considering that, due to our age difference to say the least, everyone in the crowd could guess the sort of establishment where Hideo and I had become acquainted, by category if not outright by name.

Although everyone at the party seemed to be in on the joke, nobody laughed. It was not out of the ordinary for male members of the Japanese elite—even the married ones—to keep a preferred hostess or geisha in their rankings at even the most casual events such as beach parties or golf outings. It was making Hideo seem incredibly influential to have a hostess would attend his party at her own accord, and even bring with her an attractive friend. So people noticed not who I was, but what I symbolized. I felt pampered and catered to, if not genuinely cared for, and that would have to do for the time being.

I stopped letting Pika mingle at will when I spotted one of the more intoxicated partygoers feeding her a banana, which Pika gleefully gobbled down. Upon witnessing this, I rushed over and reattached her leash, thereby ending Pika's run as the social butterfly that she was. Having my dog to take care of, I couldn't drink as much as I would have liked to in order to numb the experience of being perceived as a symbol rather than a person. My relative sobriety, however, gave me the opportunity to more aptly observe my environment.

I found that when Japanese men drink, society no longer expects them to act in an orderly fashion. This was fitting, since by nightfall many of the partygoers could hardly walk in a straight line. One memorable character, who was wearing a green hat in the shape of a frog, had approached me to practice the English phrase, "Aii ammu aaa flog," before falling over in the sand.

Once they got the right amount of alcohol in them, Japan's elite were just as silly and stupid as the homeless congregation in Shinjuku who often threw makeshift drinking parties as they gathered around common tables made from cardboard boxes. The sake at the center of their cardboard tables was considerably cheaper than that served in excess at the dōhanman estate, still, the slurred speech and erratic behavior was remarkably similar.

After the party ended, Hideo cordially drove Jadie, Pika, and me back to central Tokyo. And with another kiss on the cheek and a promise from him to visit me at the Palace sometime soon, we said good-bye.

Still, I ended up in Dōhanman's company again sooner than expected.

As it turned out, since Lindsey left Japan it was no longer possible to keep Pika a secret anymore in my gaijin house. Lindsey's departure caused me to realize how much I had been relying upon her to help me take care of Pika. Pika basically fit into my purse and traveled about the city with me out of necessity, still, there were some ventures upon which the dog could not accompany me.

When left alone, Pika would cry loudly and incessantly. Before working at the Palace each night, I would take her running around the block a few times before I left for Ginza, seeing to it that she would feel exhausted enough to fall asleep in my absence. The last thing I would do before locking her in her crate for the evening was put a CD that contained mood music by the Japanese New Age musician named Kitaro on shuffle. Of all the composers I've tried, Kitaro was best at putting Pika to sleep. All this had to be done in order to keep Pika from waking up the entire guesthouse neighborhood in my absence. I could not go out partying with my fellow hostesses after work anymore, ever. The newfound responsibility was a turn for the best that I had refused to take the easy way.

When I heard from a real estate agent that a room in one of her apartments would be opening, and that pets were allowed in the building, I started packing right away. Crisis struck, however, when Makoto chose the night before he promised to help me move apartments to tell me, not in person but by e-mail of all methods, that he needed to break up with me because he felt that I was spending too much time with Pika. Truth be told, I was indifferent to Mako's general existence by then so his breaking off relations with me did not bother me as much as his going back on his promise to help me move.

Professional movers are extremely expensive in Tokyo, and far out of my budget range. So Pika and I, sitting atop a pile of baggage that had increased two- or threefold since I moved to Japan a year and a half prior, were hit by a wave of desperation. I racked my brain for possible solutions to this conundrum as Pika sat upon my lap feeling confused. I went through the list of phone numbers programmed into the address book of my cellular phone, looking for a friend who might be able to give me advice. As I passed the number of one Hideo Marui, a red light went on in my head and the scrolling stopped.

Since I felt like I had nothing left to lose anyway, I gave Marui-san a call and told him that my movers canceled at the last minute. I once read that as soon as a person passes a certain age, it is no longer appropriate to ask your friends to help you move. While I had ruled some of my friends out of the picture some minutes earlier if only because I wanted them to remain my friends, Hideo couldn't quite be called a friend. In fact he couldn't really be classified at all, he was a dōhan. And Dōhanman, without the slightest hesitation, asked me where and when he should show up at my doorstep with his van.

If Hideo had only provided me with the use of his car to take my belongings across Tokyo, as Mako had promised, I would have still been immensely grateful. But in reality, Hideo did so much more than that. When he arrived promptly at my gaijin house the next morning, Marui-san did not even let me do any of the heavy lifting. In fact, I may have just as well been sitting on a lawn chair eating popcorn and drinking beer as I watched him lug my bags down three flights of stairs and into his van. Then, en route to my new apartment, we stopped at a department store where he purchased for me various housewarming accessories that included a carpet, linens, a new futon, and some flowerpots.

After all of my things were safely transported from Shinjuku to Shibuya, he took me out to dinner to celebrate having completed the move, even though he had done all of the work himself. Pika snuck along inside of my purse, as per usual, and enjoyed ample helpings of sushi under the table as a reward for keeping quiet. Pika loved sushi. She likewise enjoyed eating out, and the tiny dog seemed to have taken a curiously strong liking to Dōhanman.

"I had to ask Marui-san to help me move last weekend," I confessed to Mama Destiny one night the following week, during our weekly one-on-one meeting. "You don't think he'll expect anything in return for the favor, do you?"

"Marui is a gentleman," Destiny replied. "He has too much pride to request anything from you in return. He probably just enjoys doing nice things for you."

"Okay, I understand." I nodded.

"But, Cindy"—Destiny's voice became scarily stern with the afterthought—"the next time Marui helps you move, you must bring him back to the club afterward. You know it is forbidden for you to meet customers outside of the club unless it is a dōhan." She was actually serious.

"Yes, Mama," I replied obediently.

28

myth

A bad earthquake at once destroys the oldest associations; the world, the very emblem of all that is solid, has moved beneath our feet like a crust over fluid; one second of time has created in the mind a strong idea of insecurity, which hours of reflection would not have produced.

—CHARLES DARWIN, *Journal of Researches into the Geology and Natural History of the Various Countries Visited by HMS Beagle from 1832 to 1836*

SHORTLY AFTER MIDNIGHT, the Palace began to sway back and forth. The tremor was strong enough to make all of the wineglasses and whiskey bottles brush against each other, yet so weak that nothing actually broke. The effect gave way to an eerie clinking noise that echoed through the Palace like a wayward wind chime. It was the type of earthquake we were all used to.

Regardless, at the first shock Samantha jumped into her customer's arms in apparent fear. Following suit, I grabbed the Professor's collar for stability as my client wrapped his hands around me tightly, taking full advantage of this momentary lapse of the Palace's no-touch policy. The club trembled like that for twenty or thirty seconds, during which time many of the other girls and I pretended to be afraid in such a manner that our male counterparts could feel more masculine as they comforted us.

That I was able to improvise such an unrehearsed display of fake emotions just as well as any of the other hostesses both surprised me and creeped me out. If anything, though, the other hostesses and I were relieved that a new topic for conversation had come out of nowhere to assist us with our task of keeping the social talk flowing.

"I knew it," said Kiriko as soon as the ground began to shake. "I spotted an earthquake cloud in the sky on the way to work today!" I happened to be working opposite a hostess named Kiriko at the moment, who was otherwise known as the Palace mystic. She then took out the astrological chart that she always kept on her person. "Earthquakes always occur during or around eclipses of the sun or moon," she told us.

Kiriko was a tiny woman with jet-black hair and long fingernails to match. Approaching thirty, Kiriko was a bit older than most hostesses at the Palace. Kiriko told customers that she hailed from some exotic island off the coast of Malta, although I'm pretty sure she was Japanese and Brazilian. The name she chose, "Kiriko," literally translates as "child of the mist," and always fit her well, or it at least fit the personality she projected at the Palace.

While entertaining her male clients, Kiriko claimed the ability to see ghosts and channel spirits. She read her customers' palms, made their astrological charts, and told the men's fortunes. It's important to understand that in a facet of the sex industry in which no actual sex occurs, the provider of services must be extremely interesting in other ways. Most hostesses at the Palace agreed that Kiriko stuck to magic and fortune-telling because she couldn't sing or dance, so we took her premonitions with a perpetual grain of salt.

Kiriko's ramblings tended to freak me out, so I was exceedingly relieved when I noticed one of my regulars, the sharply dressed Daisuke-san, enter the bar soon after the earthquake. He told me to call him Dai-chan, a nickname that juxtaposed the diminuitive suffix *chan* against the kanji character meaning *large*. And true to his (nick)namesake, Dai-chan was a human exercise in irony.

He was always dressed impeccably, in freshly pressed designer three-piece suits, and clean-shaven without exception. I assumed that he was high in the rankings at some important corporation, but never asked him about it since so much was obvious. The moment he entered the Palace, his behavior turned as erratic and slapstick as the typically eccentric Japanese comedian. He knocked bottles off of tables, lost his footing on the dance floor, and bumped into walls at regular intervals.

In his absence, I took to calling him the Drunken Penguin.

When the Drunken Penguin calmed himself on occasion, his favorite discussion topic was literature. It was a topic in which I took a sincere interest, which is probably why I became his preferred hostess.

"When do earthquakes appear in old Japanese literature?" Dai-chan quizzed me, as he was apt to do.

"I don't really know." I feigned shame at my lack of knowledge on the subject. "I've heard the story of Kashima and Namazu though," I added as an afterthought. "You know," I continued, "from all the old *ukio-e* prints?"

"That's an interesting topic," he said approvingly. "Do you know the entire story?"

"Not really," I lied.

"Under ancient Japan"—the Drunken Penguin put on his storyteller face—"a giant catfish lived in the mud. The fish had a twisted sense of humor, so it enjoyed playing many pranks on the inhabitants of Japan. A mighty god named Kashima usually restrained the fish," he continued, "but whenever Kashima relaxed his guard, the catfish caused an earthquake."

"That's fascinating," I said. I remember thinking it characteristic of Japan's workaholic culture to attribute disaster to relaxation or laziness, even in ancient times.

"Are you familiar with any other earthquake mythology?" he asked.

"No." I nodded my head and bent my gaze toward the red carpet.

At that, he took a few minutes to explain to me some such myths. For example, he told me that the Native Americans in Southern California believed that giant turtles carried the earth on their backs, so tremors occurred when they argued about which way to swim. On the Indian subcontinent, one of the twelve mighty elephants who held up the land would occasionally cause an earthquake when he grew weary and shook his head. Those in Siberia assumed the ground was held up by a sled pulled by flea-infested dogs who shook the earth when they stopped to scratch. Mongolia, on the other hand, had the misfortune of being built upon a gigantic twitch-prone frog.

"All these ancient myths are about trapped animals," I observed. "What about humans?" I asked. "Did anyone believe earthquakes could be caused by humans?"

"Not that I know of," he said, "but I can make one up for you."

"Oh, yeah?" I raised my eyebrows.

"Once upon a time," he began, "a man and a woman lived in a love hotel buried far under the ground." He smirked. "Whenever the sex was so amazing that they both achieved orgasm at the same moment, the effect was so awesome that the ground above them shook as a result."

"Wow," I said, "you should write this stuff down." I was used to customers who would go to any lengths to bring the subject of sex into our conversations.

"How about you?" he asked me. "If you could make up an earthquake myth, what would it be?"

"You probably won't like it"—I brushed him off—"for I am not nearly as creative as you are."

"Just go for it," he encouraged me.

"Okay . . . well." I paused. "The Earth Goddess lived underground with her husband, three children, and two dogs"—my myth began—"when her husband and kids didn't help her with the housework, the woman became so hot with anger that she liquefied and swallowed her family whole. And that was how the process of liquefaction came to be." I finished with a mischievous smile, waiting for his response.

"That's ghastly!" Dai-chan exclaimed, both disgusted and impressed at the same time.

29

Liquefaction

"can you come see me at the Palace tonight?" I sent a text message the next evening to a client whom I called the Professor. "I have a science question for you." The man's nickname evolved quickly, seeing as he was a very important researcher at a leading university in the city.

"I'm interested in the process of soil liquefaction during earthquakes," I declared after he showed up to join me at a table. "What makes it happen?"

"My field is molecular biology"—he grimaced as he took his first sip of Henessey—"so I'm not sure how well I can answer that question."

"I'm sure you know more than I do," I insisted.

"It's when soil behaves as a liquid because of intense pressure. It's extremely destructive in urban areas, as you may imagine," he answered.

"How does it work?" I asked. "I'm no good at science."

"I believe that liquefaction only occurs during cyclical ground shaking, when pore water pressure increases and the strength of the soil decreases as a result."

"Like quicksand?" I asked.

"Sometimes," he replied.

"Thanks so much!" I beamed.

"I'm happy to be of service. Is that all you really want to know?" the man questioned.

"Actually"—I batted my eyelashes and tried to blush—"I have a confession to make."

"What's that?" he asked, suddenly more interested.

"I'm not really that interested in liquefaction," I lied. "I just made that up because I really wanted to see you again."

At that, it became his turn to blush.

"Everything in this world"—he took my hand as his face became ruddy from the whiskey—"is a process that involves the giving and taking of energy. You should remember that."

"Okay," I agreed, my silence inviting him to elaborate further.

"I have to leave here early tonight," he said apologetically. "I have a date with another girl at Club Kingdom across the street." He actually called the costly encounter "a date."

"Is she prettier than me?" I jested.

"No," he said, "but she is younger."

"Oh." I looked at the floor.

"You may wonder why somebody of my social standing chooses to frequent hostess bars so often," he said, the alcohol in his system making him more sure of himself.

"Actually"—I looked him in the eye—"I do."

"At clubs like this I can unload my problems, and then absorb the youthful energy of the young women who listen to me. It's another process of exchange, you see?"

"I see," I said.

After seeing the Professor out, I couldn't help wondering whether this process of "exchange" he spoke of was part of the reason why I was feeling so tired lately. After all, each night I was carrying the burdens of several men-children upon my back. Then, in exchange, they stole my energy. Or more accurately, they were buying it in a perfectly legal arrangement.

At this, my aggression turned to the management at the Palace. They were in on this secret, for sure. As my anger opened up, I began to feel a distinct bitterness toward Destiny and Tenchō-san in particular. They were always talking down to the other hostesses and me, tactlessly insulting our clothing, conduct, and the like. All this was despite the fact that it was our life energy, and it could only be ours, which fueled their precarious ikebana arrangement, and made it all go around.

as it would happen, the next night I arrived at work having forgotten my stockings, and Tenchō-san scolded me.

"You have to go out and buy stockings before you can start work," he said, matter-of-factly.

"But where?" I asked. "All the shops in this area are closed already. Why don't *you* go out and buy me some stockings, then, if you know where they're sold."

"She can work without stockings just for tonight." The disembodied voice of Mama Destiny echoed from behind the curtain-bordered area that was her office, effectively ending the debate although she remained out of our vision.

About ten minutes later, I was sitting at the waiting table, bored to death as usual. Tenchō approached the group of us and after looking us over he pointed at me, pointed toward the door, and made a slight bow, indicating that I would have to go outside the club to do *bira*.

It's hard to describe what happened next. I am reminded of a passage in Marya Hornbacher's autobiography *Wasted: A Memoir of Anorexia and Bulimia*, where the author discusses a curious phenomenon that occurs where the body is starving to an extreme extent because the brain is instructing it not to eat. That is to say, there is a point when one's body stops listening to her brain and, in a spirit of mutiny, begins gorging itself with food by its own accord.

I think that this is similar to what happened to me that night, because I can't think of any other explanation for why I just couldn't stand up. My body was so exhausted it took on a life of its own, and refused to move. In retrospect, the realization of how tired I was likely intensified the feeling itself.

"*Iya da,*" I said to Tenchō. In a language that does not even tolerate the use of the word *no, iya da* is an extremely strong form of refusal and the phrase is typically used only by children and drunks. I'd learned the phrase from Ayu, back at my homestay.

Tenchō-san just stared at me in disbelief and repeated the gesture as if it were the first time.

"*Iya da,*" I replied again. It was the only thing I could open my mouth to say.

He pointed a third time and was met with the same response. The Japanese, especially in employment situations, have basically no idea what to do when a subordinate refuses to follow orders. It simply doesn't happen often enough.

"You will have to go meet with Mama," Tenchō told me in a surprised and irritated tone of voice. "Wait one moment, please."

In five minutes' time, I was summoned to Mama's office. I didn't even stop to sit down. I only poked my head through the curtain and said something along the lines of, "I'm sorry, I can't do this anymore," before taking my belongings and leaving.

It was well known that Destiny often fired her hostesses without any explanation at all, and with that in mind I didn't feel like I owed her any more than those few words.

I never went back to the Palace to pick up my remaining salary. I figured that Destiny would probably deduct it as a penalty for my sudden departure anyway, and I didn't want to give her the satisfaction of telling me so.

This was how, in a sudden, unexpected, and somewhat quake-like chain of events, Cindy and Shindee perished forever.

30

my so·called Hiatus

Determined to return to a more legitimate lifestyle in Japan, in the weeks to come I landed myself a teaching job at an elite international preschool in the neighborhood of Shirokanedai, Tokyo. Shirokane is Japanese for "white money," and most of the students I taught were the children of foreign ambassadors, or the offspring of Japanese zaibatsu families with intimidating surnames such as "Honda," or "Toyoda."

I was not, by any stretch of the imagination, qualified for the position. My coworkers all had graduate degrees in early childhood education, while I only possessed a B.A. in English and Japanese. In retrospect, I suppose that I must have been hired for my looks.

Truth be told, the preschool gig wasn't so different from hostessing. Children learn best while they are having fun, so I was cast in a similar role of entertainer at work. I found there to be many similarities between the two- and three-year-olds I taught every day and the drunken men I entertained at the Palace. For example, both occasionally made attempts to grab at my breasts.

I was asked to resign from the job after only three months, when my supervisor cited that I was not dedicated enough. This was a fair estimate. My official working hours were from 8 A.M. to 3:30 P.M., without a lunch break (the same hours that I had spent sleeping when I had been a Ginza hostess), and I left the job every day at three thirty sharp, while my coworkers often stayed at the office planning lessons until 5 or 6 P.M. of their own accord.

I adored my students. Still I was more engulfed in a series of (unpublished) short stories that I was writing, all of which were set in Tokyo's floating world. One involved a series of futuristic sex robots in Kabukichō's pleasure district that came to life during the Shinto festival of Obon, a time when the spirits of the dead are said to roam the earth. Literally fucking all of their customers to death, the robotic prostitutes ravaged the pleasure quarters in a manner that may be imagined as what might occur if Carrie met Godzilla. My other stories were likewise science fiction–oriented revenge fantasies that involved Tokyo sex workers in one way or another.

After being fired from my second teaching job, I had resigned myself to playing my violin for change on Tokyo street corners, and living off of my savings from the preschool gig. I was also drinking every night, at a famous British sports bar in the Ebisu district called the Footnik. It turned out that the alcoholism I had acquired at the Palace could not be discarded quite as easily as the job itself had been.

It was during this time, one night in early autumn, that I met Nigel. Jadie and I were enjoying a beer over at Footnik, but there wasn't much time before we had to clear out in order to catch the last train. Still by twelve forty-five, I still had half a pint of Yebisu beer left in my glass. Not about to let the fine ale go to waste, I did what any drunk girl would do: I took the glass with me to the train station.

The last train that runs through Tokyo each night really is a cultural spectacle to behold. Especially so with respect to the Yamanote Line, the loop that stops at most of Tokyo's busiest stations, the loop Jadie and I were about to board. That night the train was packed with drunk people in their most highly concentrated form, many of whom—including myself—were still drinking.

"You stole that glass from Footnik." Nigel brazenly approached me once the train started moving.

"Go away," I told the stranger flatly.

"I saw you in Footnik drinking out of that same glass." He didn't give up.

"I'm serious, get the fuck away from me!" I exclaimed, drawing more attention to myself than there was already, being a tall blond gaijin and all.

"You really should leave her alone," Jadie warned. "She's dangerous when she's this drunk."

"Where are you from?" Jadie asked Nigel, probably to get him to stop bugging me; she was a good friend like that.

"Ireland," he replied with the same unending grin.

"Ireland?'" My ears perked up. My great-grandparents came over to America from Ireland during the potato famine. "Where in Ireland?" I inquired.

"Belfast," he replied.

"Oh," Jadie and I replied in unison, almost interested, as the train came to a halt at Harajuku Station.

"Are you in the NRA?" I asked with a straight face, as the train began moving again, my speech slurred. I am acutely aware of some of the dumber statements I've made while intoxicated, largely because my companions derive humor from reminding me after the fact.

"She means the IRA," Jadie corrected.

"That's what I said," I slurred. "So are you?"

"Why, yes!" he replied.

"Really?" we exclaimed in unison.

"No, of course not." His tone forced a laugh out of me. Nigel was this evasive about everything, and for some reason I found it charming. Maybe it was the mystery of it all, though alcohol likely had the most to do with it.

So we got off the train, the three of us, busting through the gates again.

"I'm hungry," I declared as we emerged onto the streets of east Shinjuku, a good walking distance from both Jadie and my apartments.

"What should we eat?" Nigel interjected, assuming he would be included in our late-night munchie fest.

"Ramen," Jadie and I said almost at the same time.

"Let's eat at one of those fresh noodle stands outside the station," I said, deciding for us. "Nigel, you can pick which one, since you'll be the one paying for all of us," I continued with the same aura of confidence that Nigel had exuded when he approached us on the train.

And ramen it was. I ordered my usual shoyu (soy sauce) flavored ramen noodles, Nigel ate a bowl of spicy ramen with a plate of gyoza, and Jadie had a large bowl of kimchi ramen (east Shinjuku borders on Korean town), passing me the large slab of pork floating in her bowl. As Jade and Lindsey often said, being a vegetarian in Tokyo is basically reduced—for practical reasons—to picking the meat out of your dishes and putting them onto someone else's plate.

"Hey, Jadie-chan," I said in Japanese, correctly assuming that Nigel wouldn't understand me, "he's kinda cute."

"*Zenzen kawaikunai,*" He is not cute at all, Jadie responded between loud slurps of her noodles. Slurping of noodles is not only acceptable in Japan, but the loudness of one's eating is supposed to connote how delicious the dish is.

"*Demo me o miru to chotto kawaii,*" But when you look into his eyes he's kinda cute.

"*Zenzen kawaikunai.*" Jadie repeated herself, nodding her head in disapproval. Jadie and I had notoriously different tastes in guys.

"*Me ga aoi yo,*" His eyes are bright blue. I was relentless.

"*Ojii-san da yo.*" Jadie retorted by using the Japanese word for "grandfather" to describe Nigel, meaning, in this context, that he was way too old for me.

"Nigel, show Jadie your eyes for a sec?" I asked and he obeyed.

"*Mada kawaikunai yo,*" He's still not cute. She laughed. Nigel smiled then, too, though he had little idea what we were saying.

"Let's go do karaoke now," I exclaimed after Nigel picked up the check for our Ramen.

"I gotta get back. Ren's waiting," Jadie lamented, referring to her boyfriend. "He's been all pissed off lately."

"There is karaoke by my apartment," Nigel volunteered. This idea logically turned into there being karaoke *inside* Nigel's apartment, where I eventually agreed to visit even though it was understood that he didn't actually have a karaoke machine.

The two of us settled down as Nigel busted a fresh six-pack out of the fridge and carefully chose a CD to play. I was familiar with the record by the first note; it was *Jagged Little Pill,* Alanis Morissette's debut album, a CD almost everyone in my generation is familiar with in one way or another. We used our beer bottles as microphones as we belted out her lyrics. I made him play the sixth song on the album repeatedly, a song called "Forgiven."

After sleeping with Nigel at six in the morning, I took the first train home that next day. Nigel and I ended up dating for seven months, a time when Pika and I practically moved into his apartment. He and I also took on the joint venture of selling fake designer handbags on the streets of Shibuya, Harajuku, Kabukichō, and Kichijoji. When we were approached by the police, which always happened eventually, I just pretended not to speak any Japanese and we moved along to the next location.

Looking back, Nigel was basically my drinking buddy and my partner in crime. We shoplifted copious amounts of beer and stole other useful items when we saw fit, such as the time we took the SAY NO TO DRUGS poster right off the wall of a vacant police box and hung it up in Nigel's apartment as a symbol of our accomplishment. I admired his rebelliousness and refusal to sell out. We could certainly make each other laugh, although we did spend a disproportionately large amount of our time together making fun of each other's accents.

When Jadie broke up with Ren, she began to supplement her day job by working as a hostess in Ginza on some nights, in a bar called Club Heaven, in order to foot the rent all by herself at the Shinjuku apartment that the couple had formerly shared. She often invited me to come work with her, but I was not so interested at the time.

Many people assumed that I didn't work as a hostess while Nigel and I were dating because he wouldn't have approved of my line of work. But that is not the case. In fact, it was more because hostessing took away all of my emotional energy, so that the last person I would want to relate to after coming home each night was a man I cared about. Hostessing made me so sick of smiling and caring for my appearance that it left me no remaining desire for real men at the end of the night.

Nigel and I visited my house on Long Island one Christmas, and I introduced Nigel and Pika to my parents. Sadly for me, but happily for Pika, my dog took a strong liking to my parent's house, which contained another dog to play with and a large backyard she could run around in. So she stayed in New York and became an immigrant dog. Although the sudden decision was best for everyone involved, I cried nonstop atop Nigel's shoulder on the flight back to Tokyo.

A month later, my life took another sharp turn for the worse. Around the time that Nigel and I had nearly gotten arrested in almost every ward of Tokyo, after we had watched every downloadable episode of *South Park* on the Internet, and I was wondering what we might be up for next, the bomb dropped. It was a type of bomb that is otherwise known as "the truth." I was unprepared when it exploded, and this made the effects even more disastrous.

You see Nigel had a confession to make: he wasn't really thirty-four years old as he had told me he was when we met. He was actually forty-six. I almost threw up.

"Get away from me," I told him.

"But I'm the same person. Come on, Lea," he whined.

"I'm getting the fuck out of here," I exclaimed, not having taken the news as well as he might have hoped.

The Nigel debacle gave me new insight into the way humans tend to fall in love with fantasies rather than with other people. And it's amazing how blind humans can be when we don't want to see something, when we'd rather be in love or just keep having fun.

Since we can never really know what another person is truly thinking or feeling in a relationship, sometimes we have to imagine that we know. There is a leap of faith, so to speak. But sometimes we can let our imaginations get the best of us. Such was the case with Nigel. I had been as dumb-witted as my customers at the Palace.

I suppose there is a point in time when all fantasies crash. Nigel was what I'd imagined him to be, I realized that night, and nothing more than that. I had no wish to associate anymore with the man he really was.

So many thoughts were going through my head that night when suddenly I knew what I was going to do. I showered, carefully put on more makeup than usual, then put on a fancy dress. When I looked at Nigel's face as I emerged from the bathroom, it was as if he didn't even recognize me.

"Wow, you look amazing," Nigel said to me, not realizing that I had gotten dressed up to go to work.

"Screw you"—I looked him in the eye—"I'm going to go get paid to talk to old men."

At that I walked out of Nigel's apartment, took the train over to Ginza, and showed up at Heaven unannounced.

"I want to work," I told the mama-san who greeted me at the door. "Can I start tonight?"

"What is your name and nationality?" she asked.

"Ellie," I told her, quickly choosing the name of a popular karaoke song at the time, a Japanese rendition of a Ray Charles classic, "from America. And I am a friend of Jewel's." Jewel was the name that Jadie had decided to call herself at work.

"Did you bring a change of clothes?" Mama Mari asked.

"I can borrow one of Jewel's gowns just for tonight."

"Okay," Mari replied, "but we will have to discuss the salary system later. It is a Friday night and the club is already becoming crowded. So hurry up and change your clothes," she said with a quick, expressionless aura that I would soon be accustomed to.

"Thank you, Mama-san!" I was beaming.

31

Blood, Sushi, Showtime

тнат nіднт іn Heaven, I began to come to terms with the fact that the men who frequented hostess bars were a lot like the ones I dated anyway: they were liars. But at least in Ginza we all understood it to be a game, so no one ever got as burned as I felt after the breakup with Nigel. At least in Heaven everyone knew the rules to the game, so there would be no devastating twists in the plot.

Heaven suited me well that night. It gave me a brand-new realm for my fantasies to dwell within.

For six hours at work that night, I drank like a blowfish, flirted incessantly with middle-aged men, and forgot Nigel ever existed. I sang and danced along to every song that anyone put into the karaoke box, encouraging everyone else to be merry along with me. I smiled and laughed with vigor throughout the entire time, as was my job description, until I could almost feel as happy as my customers looked.

As a result of my efforts that Friday night, I met two separate men who would become my long-term customers, and by the time working hours were over, the mama-san was practically begging me to return to her club the following Monday.

I had missed hostessing, and was glad to be back. Working as a nightclub hostess undeniably satisfied a certain aspect of my personality. It was a need that I had to perform, to somehow garner the approval of others, and to be the center of attention.

Yet there are many different types of performances in life, and not all of them entertain.

It's difficult for me to explain what happened after Jadie and I stumbled back to her apartment, unspeakably smashed, and fell into bed. Nothing I can write will be entirely accurate anyway, given my state at the time, and how the vicious consumption of alcohol adversely affects the human memory. Suffice to say that what goes up, must come down.

It is a terrific shame that I chose such an inopportune time, place, and technique to come to terms with my rage, with the livid anger I felt toward Nigel for deceiving me all that time. I am not the slightest bit proud of this behavior.

That said, I remember waiting for Jadie to fall asleep, then locking myself in the bathroom with her sushi knife. The top edge of the knife was too dull, however, to put any significant marks on the skin of my left arm, where I was accustomed to cutting since I was in high school. It had been more than a year since I'd done it last.

Frustrated that it wasn't working, I held the knife up and thrust it into the tiny room's wooden door. I then withdrew the knife in a fury and hurled it against the adjoining wall that boxed me inside.

This time, however, my grip on the knife's handle was not as strong. As the sushi knife pierced the wall for the second time, I lost my grip. My hand slipped onto the sharp edge and was terribly gouged by the bottom corner of the blade.

My shocked scream woke Jadie up.

"What have you done now?" she asked as she turned the light on, fixed her glasses upon her face, and witnessed my blood pouring onto her floor as I clumsily tried to catch it with a roll of toilet paper.

All attempts to explain that I hadn't made this particular wound on purpose were for naught.

"What the fuck is this about?" Jadie inquired, visibly annoyed.

"I don't want to live anymore," I mumbled drunkenly, not knowing what else to tell her, as blood continued to drip from my palm, crossing my wrist, and staining my friend's carpet.

"That's such a retarded thing to say!" She was angry. Jadie hated blood with a passion, but she dressed my wound as well as she could anyway, and put me to bed again, as if I were a child.

"When are you going to grow up, Lea?" she said to me once we were settled in bed again. "I don't understand it. You are so pretty, so smart, and so fun. What is it you have against life anyway?"

"I'm so sorry, Jade," was all I managed to say, before falling into a disturbed, dream-filled sleep.

ᴛʜᴇ ɴᴇxᴛ ᴍᴏʀɴɪɴɢ, as I scrubbed the blood from her carpet with the only hand I would be able to use for two weeks, Jadie convinced me that I should not go back to Nigel's apartment, even to retrieve my belongings. Instead, she insisted that I send him a text message requesting that my belongings at Nigel's apartment be packed up and delivered to Jadie's doorstep, stressing that this was the least that he could do for me after having lied about his age for seven months.

She and I were sitting in front of her TV drinking smoothies I had made for us when a knock came on her door. We looked at each other fearfully.

"Fuck, he wants to come in!" I exclaimed.

"Go in there and lock the door." Jadie practically shoved me into her bathroom. "I'll tell him you're not home. Just be good this time!" she urged.

"Of course I will," I assured her with all the sincerity I could muster.

At that Jadie went outside her apartment's door and remained in the hallway for about five minutes, where she was presumably speaking to Nigel.

As I remained motionless in the bathroom, which felt small and stuffy as a coffin, there was nothing to do but stare at the two knife wounds on my friend's walls and contemplate how I would have to repair them in the coming week.

Soon, however, I began to hear his voice as my belongings were being hauled into the apartment by the two of them. My heart sank into my stomach.

"Are you sure she is convinced that we can't work things out?" I overheard Nigel say.

"Absolutely," Jadie told him firmly.

At that, I thought I heard him begin to sob from the other side of the door. Even though Nigel was so undeserving of my compassion, in that moment I desperately wanted to unlock the door of the bathroom and run to him anyway, to tell him that I loved him despite everything and that we could work it out and be together forever.

But I didn't do any such thing, if only because I knew that Jadie would have been disappointed in me, so I remained perfectly still as I allowed the others to carry in my belongings.

Some minutes later, Jadie assured me that the coast was clear. I unlocked the door of the bathroom, took a few feeble steps out the door, and then fell onto the futon she set up for me on the floor, where I began hysterically crying.

For a while after Nigel's departure, Jadie joined me on the ground. She didn't tell me, "It's okay, Lea," because it so obviously wasn't. Nor did she tell me to "Cheer up," because she knew that I didn't want to.

Instead, despite how I had angered her the night before, Jadie lay down on the futon beside me and steadied my feverous shaking with a hug, simply saying: "I love you, I love you, I love you."

And that was the best thing for me that anyone could have done.

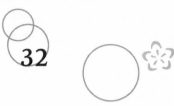

32

the Destiny Hatred Society

after my first week in Heaven, I fell in love with the job again. To boot, the environment in Heaven was light-years more enjoyable than that of the Palace. Heaven was started by three former hostesses at the Palace, all from the Philippines, who eventually collected enough money to pool their earnings together and buy their own club, which was ironically located just around the corner from the Palace on the Ginza.

Of the three women, one of them, Mama Mari, was the head mama-san, whose duties were similar to those of Mama Destiny in Heaven. Mari had a serious face and a businesslike demeanor, so I spent my first few weeks in Heaven in fear of her. Under Mama Mari were the two chi-mamas, Angela and Jackie.

Chi-mama is the term that is used for the mama-in-training at a hostess bar who has been chosen to become the reigning mama's successor. It was somewhat irrational that Heaven should have two chi-mamas rather than one, but it was necessary given that the three women had started the club together. Before I could remember all the mamas' names, in my mind I referred to Angela as "the elegant one," Jackie as "the little cute one," and Mama-Mari as "the Mama one," because Mama could be nothing other than Mama.

And to my delight, there was no male Tenchō-san at the bar. There was a man named Kento, the bartender, but his duties consisted mainly of fixing cocktails or food rather than giving the hostesses strict instructions in a Rod-like manner. And since there was no Rod to ensure our silence, the other hostesses and I were allowed to talk to one another during the first hour or so each night while the bar was empty. This simple leniency changed the environment remarkably.

For one, this was how I found out that most of the ladies working in Heaven, including the mamas, had once worked at the Palace. Mama Destiny was known to fire hostesses regularly without notice or explanation, while the intolerable environment at the club caused many more of us to quit abruptly, so one could say that Heaven functioned as a sanctuary for many a Palace refugee.

Aside from the mamas, there was one other woman from the Philippines, a gentle-faced and friendly young woman named Cheri. Cheri was petite, quiet, and had perfect skin. She was not at all like my Filipina acquaintance Samantha, who was tall, outspoken, and loved karaoke. Unfortunately, I hadn't heard from Samantha since quitting my job at the Palace the year before.

Saki was an extroverted aspiring model from Ethiopia. During my first week in Heaven, she showed me beautiful pictures of her home country, images that more often than not exhibited shots of her beautiful boyfriend as well. Some time later, Saki would accompany a customer and me on a double-dōhan at an Ethiopian restaurant in Nakameguro, where she would teach us to eat curry with our hands and recommend that we sample the alligator meat. (It tasted like chicken.)

There was an eastern European contingent in Heaven as well, but it was nothing so chillingly cliquish as the Eastern Bloc at the Palace, likely because there were only two of them. Katria and Anica were friends. At first, I assumed that they were so close because they shared a common language, but was surprised to hear them constantly communicating in Japanese.

This was because Anica was Romanian and Katria was from Russia. I was surprised to learn that the Romanian language is not similar to Russian at all, despite the proximity of the two countries. I did not have the opportunity to learn so much at the Palace, seeing as the hostesses usually weren't allowed to converse.

Katria possessed a model's stature, platinum blond hair, and the porcelain white complexion that drove the typical Japanese grandfather dumb with lust. The garden-variety Russian hostess at a high-class establishment, Katria often behaved as if she had taken a class on hostessing technique before her arrival in Tokyo. Her mannerisms were classic: elegant posture, careful attention to her client's mood, foot nudging, whispering in the ear every seven and a half minutes.

Since we weren't allowed to speak at the Palace, stereotypes took precedence over communication, and I assumed that the Russians were cold. The freedom to speak with Katria in Heaven, however, did much to alter my opinion regarding these matters.

She and I had many conversations while waiting, and I lunged at the opportunity to foster a friendship with her, perhaps to make amends for my feud with Svetlana. By then I had reasoned that Svetlana and my rivalry had been the result of a great misunderstanding on my part.

"If a customer asks me to sing that t.A.T.u. song one more time," Katria once confided in me, referring to a popular Russian lesbian duo, "I'm gonna blow up!"

"I know exactly what you mean," I said, "except for me they are always requesting Britney Spears." By now it should be understood that when a client requests that a hostess sing a certain karaoke song for him, she cannot very well refuse, even if it is an artist she abhors.

While Katria and I usually spoke Japanese while we waited together, Anica preferred to address me in English.

"Your English is great," I complimented her one night. "Are many people in Romania so fluent?"

"Thanks," she replied. "Not many people at home speak English, but I don't know," the attractive brunette with large lips continued, "I have always loved to study it in school since I was a child. I really enjoy learning foreign languages."

"Me, too!" I happily related. As we continued to wait, Anica taught me some useful expressions in Romanian, phrases that I promptly forgot.

After we'd been friends a while longer, I insisted that Anica come visit me in New York as soon as we got the chance to go together.

"I'd love to," she said with enthusiasm, "but as a Romanian citizen I need official invitation papers."

"I can invite you!" I offered right away. "I just have to file some papers at the embassy, right?"

"I think that's all," she said. But as she contemplated the offer again, the look of excitement drained from her young face.

"I don't know if it's possible," she said sadly. "I will have to save a lot more money first. My house in Romania was damaged by a flood last month," she confessed, "so my parents need me to send them money for the repairs. My older sister also works as a hostess in Japan but she is not helping out the family in Romania because she has a family in Japan to worry about. Only I am single, so I have no choice but to give them my earnings."

"Oh," was all I could think to reply, not exactly able to relate.

"But maybe if I meet more rich customers," she said with a sad hopefulness, "I will make lots of money sooner."

Another coworker of mine was Yumi, a cute Korean national who was studying Japanese at a language school during the day. Just twenty years old, she loved to talk about popular culture in both Korea and America.

"Whitney Houston is not so popular anymore in Korea," she mentioned to me one night as we listened to Angela serenade her customer with one of the artist's latest ballads.

"Why's that?" I asked with interest.

"She did an interview once with a very important talk show host. When he asked her to sing just a little bit of one of her songs for the audience, she literally only sang two notes! She sang *"And I,"* you know, from "I Will Always Love You," then stopped. That clip of the interview was playing all over Korean TV for weeks. We thought it was so impolite."

"Which other American celebrities have acted rude in Korea?" I asked with interest.

"Meg Ryan!" she said without hesitation. "She did a television interview and sat with her legs wide open, and scratched her stomach like an old man!"

At that I began to laugh, her culture's great attention to detail being a source of great amusement for me.

"Which foreign celebrities do Koreans actually like?" asked Sara, a Mongolian native seated at Yumi's other side.

"There are many," she said, "We love Michael Jackson and Tom Cruise."

"It's the opposite in America." I smirked. "What female celebrities do you like."

"Britney Spears!" she exclaimed.

"Britney Spears?" Sara and I practically choked. "Why?"

"Well," Yumi said, "truthfully we were not expecting to like her when we heard she was coming to Korea. We thought she was going to be a typically rude American, but she wasn't like that at all. She wore traditional Korean clothes, complimented our culture, and waved back to everyone she saw on the street. Since then she has been very popular with Koreans."

Despite the varying topics of conversation among us, there was one thing that basically all the girls in Heaven had in common: a vile resentment of Mama Destiny. It was something we could all relate to when everyone sat at the waiting table at the otherwise empty bar at the beginning of the evening.

"Do you know who I am?" I thrust my chest out, my shoulders back, and my nose in the air in my best Destiny impression. "I ammmm . . . I ammm . . . I ammmmmmm . . . *Mama Destiny!*" At that, my caricature was met with uproarious laughter and a series of even more amusing Destiny imitations carried out by other women at the table.

When we tired of impressions, we also shared many stories concerning Destiny's undying love for herself and her unstable demeanor. One could call us the Destiny Hatred Society.

Early one night we were loudly mocking our ex-mama-san, as per usual, when Mama Mari emerged from her office and walked over to the waiting table.

"Who are you talking about?" she asked us sternly.

No one dared to speak. Mama's presence brought with it a panicked silence. I wondered whether Mari was a friend of Destiny's and had become angry at our bad-mouthing her. Or worse, she had decided to follow in Destiny's suit and forbid us from speaking to one another at the waiting table.

"I know who you were talking about," Mari said, cracking a warm smile that relieved our tensions immensely. "I used to work for her too a long time ago," Mari continued. "Mama Devil, right?" she said jokingly. "Oops, I mean Mama Destiny!"

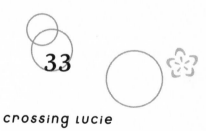

33

crossing lucie

ᴛнᴇ ɴɪɢнᴛ ᴀʟʟɪsoɴ and I met, I was in rare form. That is to say I was completely sober, and planned to stay that way for at least the remainder of the weekend. I had a huge gash across my left hand and was still feeling extremely distraught over the breakup with Nigel, to say the least.

Jadie worked during the day for a Tokyo modeling agency where Allison was an important client. The young woman's résumé was decorated with television appearances on children's programs and commercials along with magazine spreads, billboards, and voice-overs. Allison decided to stop by that evening in order to drop off her new portfolio for Jadie to take to the agency, and presumably to say hello as well.

"So you work as a hostess, too?" Allison asked me as she made herself comfortable in our small yet snug apartment.

"On and off." I peeked out from my corner of the room, still hiding my hand in the large pockets of my Tori Amos sweatshirt, an article of clothing I'd been treasuring for years since seeing the artist in concert.

"I used to work as a hostess," Allison related, "but I got fired pretty quickly."

"They fired *you?*" I asked. Jadie and I exchanged expressions of disbelief. The garden-variety of gorgeous, Allison was a tall young Australian woman with naturally blond hair and bright blue eyes.

"I think that I didn't have the right attitude or I didn't go on enough dōhan," Allison remarked.

"I practically got fired from the Palace last year," I sympathized, "for refusing to do *bira* one night."

"Were you working in Roppongi or Ginza?" Jadie asked Allison.

"In Roppongi," Allison replied, "at Greengrass."

At the mere mention of Greengrass, I gasped.

I looked over in Jadie's direction, but her back was turned so I couldn't tell if she shared my surprise. My gaze then returned to my laptop, where I was searching the Internet for methods of treating severe cuts to the hand without necessarily seeking medical care. (I didn't have health insurance at the time because I had fallen hopelessly behind on my payments.)

I decided to let the issue of Greengrass float; if by some odd occurrence Allison hadn't heard about Lucie, I wasn't about to be the one to tell her. Jadie fell silent as well. Even since the incident, Greengrass maintained its prominent position in the Roppongi district, just above the strip club Seventh Heaven and across the street from the twenty-four-hour pet shop. Only its name has changed. Everything else was the same, I'd heard.

Nobody ever talked about the Lucie Blackman murder anymore, but everyone knew who she was. It made us uncomfortable to talk about it, still everyone knew what happened to her. Since her disappearance in the summer of 2000, Lucie Blackman has been tragically symbolic of the dangers that face foreign hostesses in Japan.

But Allison did know. "At the time my mother kept sending me pictures of Lucie Blackman from the newspapers in Australia." Allison took a stab at the sudden silence, opening up an entirely new dialogue. "She was begging me to quit, so I suppose it was best I got fired anyway."

Most citizens of Tokyo know Lucie as the one-dimensional head-shot that circulated around the city above the caption SOMEBODY MUST HAVE SEEN HER for the six months she was classified as missing. Later on, the same photo was picked up by the foreign media as well. For those of us who never knew her personally, the mention of Lucie will always evoke a mental image of that photo, of the blond young woman with the bright smile and sad little blue eyes.

"I have mixed feelings about the Lucie Blackman murder," I admitted, the subject having been breached. "I think it's totally fucked-up that some people here thought she deserved it, and that business at Greengrass is doing as well as ever despite all the bad publicity. Still," I continued, "I'm really offended by the way that the foreign media paints Tokyo hostess bars."

Despite the valiant efforts of the sensationalist media to suggest that she went missing just yesterday, Lucie's disappearance predates me. I had just finished my freshman year of college during the summer she was murdered by a customer she met in Greengrass, which was then called Casablanca.

Lucie is significant because her death was a diplomatic affair which shed light on the darker side of *mizu shobai* culture. Tokyo police were originally slow to investigate her disappearance, since they do not usually dip their hands into the yakuza-controlled *mizu shobai,* and apparently did not press the case until Lucie's parents showed up in Tokyo with the support of Tony Blair.

After the case was stirred up and began to receive regular media coverage, some Japanese citizens used media outlets to initialize a backlash of sorts, during which time many editorials were written in the country's newspapers condemning Blackman for working ille-gally. These Japanese believed that Lucie got what she deserved for working as a hostess.

At the same time, though, the case also received a significant amount of attention by the foreign media who, to be fair, tend to be obsessed with tracking down missing white girls the world around. On the occasional American, British, or Australian nightly news spe-cial, shots of the dark and winding Tokyo streets are set to a sound-track that blends Oriental-sounding tunes with dark minor chords, resulting in what may otherwise be the score of a racist horror movie.

These news programs suggest that Tokyo is a hunting ground for dark and mysterious men to lust after innocent, ignorant, and bright-eyed young white girls. All the while, the murder rate is Tokyo is as-tronomically less than that of most American cities. In fact, it's precisely because Tokyo is such a safe city that certain rungs of the *mizu shobai*—ones that do not sell actual sex and employ "re-spectable" girls—can thrive. This in mind, many hostess bars will ac-tually refuse foreign clientele because the management feels they may be too aggressive toward the girls.

"You know they subpoenaed her journal at the trial recently?" Jadie said.

"Really?" I asked. Jadie often read the news in Japanese, which regularly contained some stories that never made it through the translation into English for whatever reason, so Jadie was an infinite source of information in that respect.

"Why?" Allison asked, perplexed.

"They read her diary in court," Jadie continued, "because she ad-mitted to using marijuana, being lonely, and was in debt."

"What the fuck does that have to do with anything?" I asked, sud-denly feeling angry and confused.

"The defense was trying to paint a picture of her as mentally un-stable," Jadie responded, her calmness with regard to the issue illu-minating her Japanese side.

"Honestly?" Allison asked in disbelief.

"What the fuck does that have to do with *anything?*" I exclaimed louder this time, perhaps shocking my companions with my charac-teristically American expression of my feelings. I suppose that I took such a personal interest in that specific aspect of the case due to my less than stable behavior over the past few days.

"I mean," I continued, "so what if she smoked pot and was sad? Is that really relevant in the context of murder?"

"It's unbelievable," Allison concurred.

"I don't care if she smoked all the pot in Tokyo and slept with the whole city"—I found myself in a fury—"does that mean that she somehow deserved to be drugged, raped, murdered, and hacked into pieces with a chainsaw? Does that mean she was asking for it?"

"Of course not," my friends agreed. After all, I had been preach-ing to the converted.

Somewhere between the Japanese media's portrayal of Lucie as an unstable whore who deserved what she got for working illegally as a foreigner, and the Western portrayal of Tokyo as a city where sexual predators hid behind dark corners to snatch up the next naïve and bright-eyed white girl who passed by, lies the picture of a girl who could have easily been me.

Unlike what the Western media will have you believe, no Tokyo hostess is ignorant about what happened to Lucie. Instead, her death holds a distinct meaning for each of us.

For me, Lucie's face in the newspapers carried the same symbolic qualities of a crucifix that has been planted on the side of a highway, marking a fatal traffic accident that had once occurred there. I saw myself following the same route on the map as Lucie did, with the same curves in the road and the same warning signs, except that only one of us veered out of control and crashed.

Lucie's face was a cross that I would have to drive by multiple times during my stay in Japan. Sometimes I was driving slowly enough to stop for a moment and pray for her. Other times, however, I would be speeding so rapidly around each tight corner that I failed to even notice a crucifix there at all.

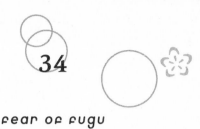

34

FEAR OF FUGU

"FUGU" WAS MY single-word response to a text message I had just received from my customer whom I called the Professor, inquiring which type of restaurant he should place a reservation at for the night's dōhan.

"Do you have a death wish?" he soon replied.

"Perhaps," I wrote back.

IT IS LIKELY that fugu, or blowfish in English, would not be such a popular and expensive Japanese delicacy if the fish did not contain a deadly poison called tetrodotoxin, a neurotoxin that is 1,200 times more lethal than cyanide. Seeing as the average fish contains enough poison in its internal organs—largely the liver—to kill about thirty humans, fugu chefs are required by law to possess a special license to prepare the fish.

A handful of people die every year in Japan from fugu poisoning. This mainly happens when people wish to eat the poison-containing liver because the tetrodotoxin, in extremely small doses, can produce a favorable tingling sensation on the tongue and lips. Through the course of twenty-four hours after consuming the fish, a victim of fugu poisoning will gradually lose control of all of his muscles, become completely paralyzed while fully conscious, and eventually die of asphyxiation.

Perhaps akin to culinary skydiving, it is the sheer danger involved in sampling fugu that makes the fish so desirable.

"You're lucky," the Professor told me after we met at Shimbashi Station and began walking toward Ginza, "fugu is in season right now. The fish bulk up in the fall and winter to keep themselves warm, so this is the season when fugu is tastiest. We have a reservation at one of the more famous restaurants on the Ginza."

"Excellent!" I replied, feeling grateful to him for taking my request seriously. After all, I would never have been able to afford fugu on my own.

The waitress sat us down at a Japanese-style table in a small room that smelled of tatami—what I had come to identify as the unmistakable smell of old Japan. The tables were separated by straw curtains to give the illusion of separate rooms. The first thing I noticed through the straw was the outline of a woman dressed in full kimono, sitting on the same side of the table as I, pouring sake for the man across from her.

"Is that a geisha?" I asked the Professor, intrigued.

"Perhaps," he responded, "there are some geisha establishments in the neighborhood, but I wouldn't really know. I don't have much interest in geisha."

While Western culture remains fascinated with the traditional Japanese geisha, the Professor's comment was indicative of a culture that, instead, is titillated by the modern.

"She is 'working' though, right?"

"This is Ginza," he replied, "all of the women you see in full kimono are working."

As I watched the outline of this unspeakably elegant cultural relic of a woman through the straw curtain, I couldn't help feeling as though I existed in her shadow, or she did in mine. We were the somewhat distorted reflections of each other.

Between the two of us, there were both striking similarities and stark differences. We were both out on working dates: we strove to become the image of femininity that society had created for us and for that our company was a high-priced commodity. We were human delicacies, pleasures reserved only for the elite. And at both tables, there was an approximate thirty-year age discrepancy between the client and his "date."

The skin of the fish came first, garnished with a seaweed salad.

"You will like the taste of the fugu skin," he informed me, "it is very gelatinous. It is among my theories that gelatinous foods are quite beneficial to our health."

"It's crunchy!" I exclaimed as I took a bite of the peeled skin. "What a fun texture!" My enthusiasm was exaggerated, as it often has to be when one is on a paid date.

"So how was your business trip?" I asked, changing the subject.

"Stressful," he said as he let out a huge sigh. "I had to make a report on a lawsuit that we have pending against a Chinese company."

"What did they do?" I asked, sincerely interested.

"Well, a few years ago in our labs, we developed a unique strain of a formula for a certain medicine. We were just perfecting it when we got word that a Chinese company was flooding the market with a cheaper version of the same product. So we took a sample into our lab and analyzed it, and we saw that it was exactly the same strain that we had developed. Scientifically speaking, this is enough evidence to prove in court that the company somehow stole our formula, still, nobody has any idea how the secret got out."

"Did you get too drunk one night and divulge the recipe to a Chinese hostess?" I jested.

"No," he said, "I never prefer Chinese women. But perhaps it was one of my lab assistants who did," he said more seriously. "When you make a new discovery some people just can't stop bragging about it. And hostess bars are one of the only places in Japan where bragging rights are allowed, so the girls end up knowing more than they should at the end of some nights."

"How interesting!" I said with a rare sincerity. It thrilled me to think about how some women in my profession had such a dangerous power over their clients.

"Is the same true for geisha bars?"

"Oh, I don't know," he said, somewhat irritated, "I don't know anything about geisha bars. Why is it you Westerners are always asking about geisha?"

"Sorry," I said humbly. At that the fugu sashimi arrived. Sliced so thin it was almost transparent, the small pieces of raw fish were placed in a perfect circle around a garnish.

"It looks so pretty"—I changed the subject back to the topic of fish—"I almost can't eat it. I feel like I am destroying a work of art."

"Perhaps all art is meant to be destroyed," the Professor responded, showing off his intellect. "I believe that nothing so beautiful will ever be permanent anyway."

"I'll take your word for it," I replied, beginning to eat.

When the Professor excused himself to use the bathroom, I took the opportunity to observe the outline of the geisha again through the straw curtain. At that moment I noticed that the woman's shoes were placed just beside mine, in the foyer of the room where we ate. It made me realize that neither my stiletto heels nor her geta slippers were particularly conducive to walking. And when we did move, her shoes forced her to hobble like a penguin while mine had me posed like a pigeon. Alas, when you are a human piece of artwork, a pawn for the male imagination, stillness is far more imperative than movement anyway.

When the Professor returned to the table, the main dish arrived. No matter how many times I see it, the sight of disembodied fish heads, still twitching with life, will always make me squeal. I would not touch the cut-up fish to place them into the bowl of boiling water, even though that was the woman's job.

The Professor pardoned me, however, as he placed the slices of moving fish into the boiling water to be cooked. More so, I was expected to completely freak out at such a foreign sight; it was almost part of my job description. The geisha seated across from us, on the other hand, could never have reacted in such a way.

Most of the real discrepancies between a hostess and a geisha occur in the male imagination. The geisha's appeal and attractiveness to a man lie in her essential Japaneseness, reflected in her knowledge of traditional Japanese music, dance, and etiquette. By contrast, the best-paid hostesses are typically non-Japanese citizens whose appeal lies in the exoticism of their snow-white complexions and bleach-blond hair.

Although she and I symbolized entirely contradictory projections of the feminine, when the dream fizzled at the end of each night, we had a lot more in common than most clients would let themselves believe, the least of which being that we both enjoyed the thrillingly dangerous taste of fugu.

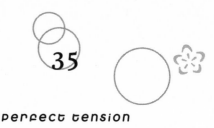

35

perfect tension

Imagine me; I shall not exist if you do not imagine me . . .
—VLADIMIR NABOKOV, *Lolita*

not all of my training in Heaven was as overt and matter-of-fact as the nightly orders I received each night from Mama Destiny at the Palace. Where Destiny and Rod at the Palace had me perpetually frustrated by their nonnegotiable orders not to move, Angela and Mama Mari taught me of a hidden power in stillness.

Mama Mari was often busy with administrative matters, so I received most of my training and advising from the chi-mama, Angela. A classic Asian beauty with high cheekbones, large brown eyes, and long eyelashes, Angela was nothing less than an artist. And all of the most useful tricks that eventually brought me success within the industry, I learned from her.

First of all, Angela taught me that although I was not allowed to move or speak to customers while I was outside on my assigned street corner, there were other ways to make my presence known. For one, there was eye contact. Japanese culture is one in which eye contact is usually avoided, so a glance straight into someone's eye is much more powerful given its rarity.

"Watch what I do when that man passes," she told me one night when we were out doing *bira* together. Then Angela, while holding her body elegantly upright and completely still, caught the man's eye at the furthest extent of her peripheral vision, and held his glance only with her eyes until he passed us and reached the other extreme of her sideways glance, his head fully turned by then while Angela kept her face pointed straight ahead.

I watched in awe as the man was seemingly dumbstruck and unable to look away. Then, at the last possible angle when eye contact remained possible between the two of them, Angela gave the stranger a subtle wink, at which point his face immediately turned beet-red.

"That was amazing," I cheered her on.

"Not really," the chi-mama lamented. "He didn't turn around and come to the club, did he? Let's try doing it together next time."

"Okay," I agreed, and we awaited our next victim.

And so Angela taught me how to speak with my eyes, and about the inherent power that lies in subtle gestures that I used to believe trivial. Angela often spoke to me with her eyes as well, which was necessary in Heaven, seeing as it was a smaller bar where most of the communication between hostesses went on behind the customers' backs.

If, for example, I had neglected to notice that my customer was pulling a cigarette from his front pocket, Angela could somehow catch my glance from across the room and make a sharp motion with her eyes to the lighter on the table. For me, the chi-mama's methods were far more favorable than Mama Destiny's nightly scolding.

With the chi-mama's own customers, however, she more than

spoke with her eyes: she could practically blind most men with a sharp glance forward. Still, most of the time, her gaze was subtle, and quietly hypnotic.

When she was entertaining, chi-mama always knew when to be quiet and when to speak. She seemed to possess an innate knowledge regarding what type of song her customer wanted to hear her sing, or which genre of dance to perform. And, of course, she always knew when to strike a smile, and which type of smile to fake. She taught her younger subordinates such tricks by both word and example.

Angela acted as both a clairvoyant and a hypnotist. First, she possessed an uncanny ability to read the feelings of her customers. Then, she could transform her image with each changing man, to become whatever he dreamed her to be, however he imagined "the perfect woman."

She could play the part of a shy and quiet companion just as well as she could become the outgoing karaoke singer or the aggressive dominatrix type.

Such a skill is the most important aspect of the hostessing industry. It is far more relevant than simple physical beauty or subservience, which can also be found in less extravagantly priced bars. This was what kept the customers coming, and paying out of their ears. This was what made Angela a "professional."

Angela also taught me, mainly through example, that hostessing is a lot like a balancing act. It is a game of getting as close as possible to someone without actually touching him. I watched and learned as she inched closer to her customers, then backed away when she noticed he was becoming too excited. Hostessing, like war, is a game of advance and retreat, and it requires strategy.

"It is a bit like pouring the perfect glass of beer," she would tell me. On the job, I became an expert at pouring the carbonated beverage into each customer's glass at the precise angle and for the proper duration so that the foam rises above the edge of each small glass without bubbling over. In Japan, much attention is always paid to the aesthetics of food and drink, so a perfectly poured glass of beer may be admired for its attractiveness, even if it's a temporary spectacle.

Angela likewise taught me that maintaining control through a pretense of submissiveness is an art form and requires practice, talent, and polishing. She also heightened my awareness to the power of subtle suggestion, erotic symbolism, and the power of "maybe."

"What do I do when a customer asks 'my price'?" I asked her one night in the dressing room as we were changing to go home.

"You mean, how much money to sleep with you?" She needed clarification, since English wasn't her native language.

"Yes," I said, "one of the more intoxicated customers asked me this last night. I couldn't believe it," I continued. "He was so rude!"

"What did you say?" she asked.

"I told him not to bother asking because there's no way he could afford it," I replied.

"That's clever"—she grinned—"but if a customer ever asks you something like that again, you should say 'It's free.' "

"It's free?" My confusion was apparent.

"Yes," she said, "say that 'It's free, but you have to court me first. And then if I fall in love with you, of course it will be free.' "

"That's brilliant," I replied, especially considering that "courting" within this context meant to become a regular customer, and required an investment that could range in the millions of yen.

"Angela?" Perhaps I was overstepping my boundaries with this question. "Have you ever fallen in love with a customer?"

"What do you think?" she answered as she looked away. Evasively answering questions with questions was among her specialties.

"You treat me like a customer!" I chided.

"Perhaps," she said with a smirk.

"Hey, come on!" It was the end of the night and we had both been drinking, so I was acting more inquisitive toward her than was my right.

"You know, Ellie"—she partially changed the subject—"it is important never to reveal too much about yourself to your customers."

"Okay, Mama." I resigned my inquisition. "Why?"

"If there is no mystery," Angela continued, "then there is no reason for them to come back." Another reason I preferred my job at Heaven to that at the Palace was because I would almost always get an answer when I asked why one rule or another was the case. This method was much unlike that of Mama Destiny, who would recite: "If you don't like what I say, you can go home." By contrast, working with Angela gave hostessing a third dimension for me. It became more than simply sitting still and following orders.

And Angela made a brilliant point when she advised me to always keep an air of mystery about myself. In fact, hostessing is a constant, never-ending process of unraveling, where the chase is pursued for its own sake. The customer is the perpetual hunter, and the hostess his perpetual prey. And when the process is executed perfectly, they chase each other around in circles eternally.

And it is this semblance of a hunt that is, in fact, what restores the customer's lost masculinity, what makes him feel like "a man."

The meaning was in the process of unraveling the woman herself, not in the end product, which was presumably sex. Real sex was not in anyone's interest, since its piercing reality would inevitably spoil the fantasy. Once the female is unraveled or found out or caught, the game is over.

After all, one cannot enter into a mirror without breaking it.

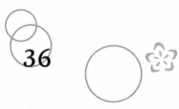

36

the little imeldas

It is terribly important to do certain things, such as wear overembroidered dresses. After all, the mass follows class. Class never follows mass.

—IMELDA MARCOS

I had only been working in Heaven a couple weeks, when Chimama Jackie stopped showing up at work. My new acquaintance Cheri seemed to be well informed on Heaven's gossip, so I decided to ask her if she knew anything about the disappearance.

"I heard that Jackie went back to Manila to have a baby," Cheri said, "but I'm not sure."

"Really." I was shocked, if only because I hated to hear about women close to my age who were having babies already. It made me feel old.

"Do you have any children?" Cheri asked me seriously.

"No way!" I responded, as if to a joke. I could hardly imagine having any children yet, especially within the context of my current lifestyle.

"Only her"—I whipped out my cell phone to show Cheri a picture of Pika—"but she is back home in America with my parents now. She likes it better there because there is more room to play."

Cheri glanced at the picture of Pika in her kimono for a few moments before smiling, passing the phone back to me, and enthusiastically saying, "*Totemo kawaii!*" Very cute.

"Do you want to see pictures of my children?" Cheri asked, looking like a skinny child herself, smoking her mother's Virginia Slims.

"Of course!" I replied enthusiastically.

"Right now they are also with their grandparents in the Philippines," she said, taking out her cell phone to show me the photographs. Once Cheri clicked a few buttons, her phone illuminated a picture of two beautiful children, smiling and hugging each other. "My son is six and my daughter is four," she told me.

"They're adorable," I assured her, although I'm sure she already knew as much. "Do you miss them while you're here?"

"Yes," she said sadly, "so very much. But I am working here in Japan so I can pay for them to have good food and clothing and education."

"Wow," I said, unable to believe that such a small woman could carry so much responsibility on her shoulders.

"Everything I do," Cheri concluded, "is for them."

For a split second I felt envious of the sense of purpose in life she seemed to have. Then the first customers of the night entered the club, forcing us to abandon all conversation and rise to our feet briskly, bow to the men, and chant "*Irasshaimase*" in unison.

A defining feature of the Filipinas I hostessed with, aside from their exotic beauty and their uncanny ability to sing, was the stack of photographs each had of the children they were working to support back in the Philippines.

They were devout Catholics, which for women of the Third World means that they begin to have many babies at a very young age. I found it terrifically ironic that these women found themselves working in the sex industry, albeit the top rungs, in order to support the by-products of their strict religious beliefs. But so much was not my place to judge.

Some nights later, I was called over to the table of Mama Mari's customer, on one of the rare occasions that Mama was actually working on the floor herself. He had never spoken with an American girl who could speak Japanese before, so my presence was requested. As the three of us shared a bottle of wine, the conversation turned to politics.

"I heard that there was a recent election in the Philippines"—I turned to Mari—"What is the government like over there now?" My question made the customer laugh, because, in my drunkenness, I had mixed up the word government, *seifu,* with the word for wallet, *saifu.*

"Well, it's almost the same thing anyway." I smiled and laughed, too, realizing my mistake. Then we both looked over at Mari, awaiting her educated reply.

"I'd like to pass on that question," she said, faking a smile.

"Oh, come on," her customer pried.

"Well"—since he was a paying client Mari would have to respond somehow—"it was much better under Marcos."

"Really?" I asked, somewhat shocked. "Why?"

"It was safer then," she replied. "At least there was a curfew every night so everybody had to go home. Now that there is no curfew in Manila, the city is much more dangerous."

"I didn't know that," I confessed, "but what about his wife, you know, the one with all the shoes."

"Yes," the customer said, "didn't Imelda Marcos have thousands of pairs of shoes?"

"That's not so many shoes really," Mari responded seriously. "Jackie has almost as many, and half of them are stored in the back room here. You should check it out."

"But weren't you upset that she used the government's money to buy shoes?" I asked, confused.

"If Imelda is the first lady," Mari said confidently, "then she should look stylish and nice. After all, she represents us to the rest of the world, and in the Philippines everyone loves high fashion. It is not like in America"—she turned to me—"where everyone is so casual."

"So shall I call you Imelda, Junior?" the customer chided.

"No, please don't," Mari responded, wearing her serious face.

I have never in my life understood the appeal of having so many shoes. Still, the case may have been different if I came from a different country, if, for example, I needed to look extra-posh in order to combat any assumption that I was poor just because my country was.

"Why don't you like to wear accessories?" Mari asked me later that same night, in a flat tone of voice.

"I don't know"—I hung my head in shame—"they just don't interest me."

This was a vast understatement. In reality, I hated them. Specifically, I detested the identical Louis Vuitton handbags that more than half of Tokyo sported in an expensive display of utter conformity. Outside of the club, I was extremely outspoken about such matters.

Within the international hostess bar, however, brand-name accessories carried a distinct significance. That is to say, accessories were signs of how much our customers were willing to spend on us. Truth be told, Angela possessed the largest Louis Vuitton handbag I had ever seen. "It's because I have so much stuff," she would say. "I like my bag to be big." Angela's monster of a handbag, for example, was a $1,000 gift from a customer.

All of my customers knew that I hated brands, seeing as I was sure to tell them so, and I consequently didn't receive such presents. And Mama Mari was inquiring into why. I did what I could to evade her questions until she took the ring off of her finger and gave it to me.

"Try this on," she said. "It is not so expensive, so if you like it then you can have it."

I put the ring, with a stone too large to resemble a wedding or engagement ring, onto my left ring finger and turned up my hand to her in order for Mama to inspect the ring.

"It looks good," she said, with a faintly warmer expression, "you should wear it often." It was, after all, in Mama's interest that I look good.

"Okay, Mama, thank you very much," I agreed, "but I have one more question."

"What's that?"

"Is this our engagement ring?" I joked, getting her to finally crack a smile.

Jewel and I shared a cab home again that night. There was no "night transportation" in Heaven because there weren't enough of us to fill a van, so our taxi bills were subsidized.

"Hey, Jadie," I said, "you awake?"

"Yeah," she mumbled.

"I think Mari is so obsessed with accessories, because she is one herself."

"What are you talking about?" she said without looking up in my direction.

"I mean that, she is just like an accessory for all the men who take her out, and that is why she is so into having expensive accessories for herself, too."

"You're not making sense," Jadie replied. "Are you drunk, Ellie?"

"Yes, very much so," I admitted.

37

of ants and elephants

Jewel and I sat practicing our karaoke, all dressed up in an empty bar. Heaven had a peculiar feel to it empty. All the bottles of imported whiskey and scotch, filled to the brim, the spotless water jugs, the ice buckets, were disturbingly clean and still untouched, like in an unrealistic promotional photograph. It was just us and Kento, the sharply dressed bartender. Anica and Cheri had gone outside to do *bira*, and the mamas never arrived until 9:30 or 10 P.M.

Suddenly, the first gentleman of the evening walked in. The two of us quickly turned off the karaoke machine and sat upright, looking straight ahead, as if we'd been waiting for him, as if we knew he'd come and were so happy he'd arrived.

"Irasshaimase!" Jewel and I chirped in unison. To my surprise he passed right by Jewel and me after looking us over and spoke to Kento at the bar. The man inquired who was in charge, and Kento explained that the mama-san had yet to arrive. Kento began to make a seemingly urgent call on his cell phone.

Jewel, in the meantime, opened the text screen on her cell phone and began typing something. She elbowed me and showed me the screen on her phone. She had written the word *yakuza* in capital letters. At that my eyes widened, I sat up even more straightly, and continued staring ahead of myself at nothing. She soon nudged me again, having cleared the previous screen and written: *He's going to complain.*

When the man finally left the club, I turned to Jewel in confusion. "Is he going to complain that we were using the karaoke machine for our own enjoyment?" I asked.

"No, it's just that whenever that one guy comes here, he's here to complain about something," she explained. "Last time it was because one of the girls doing *bira* outside accidentally handed a flyer to one of *them*."

"Uh-oh," I said, knowing that handing *bira* to yakuza members was strictly off-limits, but unsure of the reason. "So why do they get so mad?" I questioned my friend.

"Heaven pays the *ya-san* protection money not only to keep the club open, but they pay the boss a lot more money in return for his promise that the yakuza members will never patronize our bar"—Jewel really did know everything—"so when we tempt the gang members by offering them flyers they get frustrated."

"When that same guy came in a couple of months ago," she continued, "I overheard him complain to Mama that one of the girls outside was wearing jeans under her dress because of the cold."

"But why is that their business"—I was confused again—"since they don't patronize our bar anyway?"

"The *ya-san* basically control the street corners. They are like the landlords we rent from in order to do *bira*." I knew as much already, but I didn't know how seriously they took their "property."

"So if a girl is not dressed properly on 'their territory,'" Jewel continued, "they come in and complain. Sometimes they even ask for penalty money."

"So, um, Jadie?"

"It's Jewel in here," she corrected.

"Yeah, that's what I meant," I said apologetically. "So how do you recognize a yakuza anyway?"

"Don't say that word!" Jewel gasped.

"Sorry, I meant *ya-san*."

"You really don't know?" she asked, visibly dismayed at my general lack of knowledge. "Haven't you been living in Japan for two years? And haven't you done this type of work before?"

"Yeah," I said, "but at the Palace I was instructed not to give *bira* to anyone on the street unless they approached me first, so I never needed to tell the difference."

"Wow," she said, "it's hard to explain. Usually we can tell by just looking at them. It's a vibe they send out . . ."

"Like what?" I was more confused than ever.

"Well, first of all," she said, "they're completely different from *salarimen*. It's just *ya-san* and *salarimen* on the streets of Ginza, and you can't confuse them."

"I do!"

"But how can you?" she asked. "Maybe you don't look hard enough at the way they walk. The *ya-san* strut around like elephants, but the *salarimen* are like ants trying to get out of their path. The *ya-san* also move their arms and keep their chins up as they walk about Ginza; you get a feeling like they're inspecting the place. The *salarimen* keep their heads down and scurry about as if they are perpetually late."

"Got it," I said with a new confidence, "thanks, Jewel!"

"And another thing is," my friend continued, "the *salarimen* always have briefcases, but a *ya-san* might not be holding one as he passes."

I was about to thank her again profusely for the advice when the first customer of the night walked in and we arose to greet him and take his coat. Chatting time was over and I had to pretend like my sole purpose in my life rested in pleasing this man whom I didn't even know.

Only a night or two after my very informative conversation with Jewel, I met a *ya-san* on the street. It was as if the yakuza decided to take interest in me at the precise moment when I realized how to recognize them.

He did walk like he owned the street, just as Jewel said they do, and he wasn't holding a briefcase. I averted my eyes immediately, though I silently congratulated myself on my first successful yakuza sighting. I had to look up again though when I heard the sound of screeching tires on the street in front of me.

The yakuza I had just spotted had crossed the street, forcing the car to a halt, and was walking right toward me. He had a punch perm and leather boots and everything! I turned to look behind me, sure that there would be someone else who he would meet, but there was no one around. No one around but me.

I stuck my Heaven fliers in the pocket of my jacket and averted my eyes to the street, hoping he might just disappear, but he kept walking toward me until I was forced to glance up at him.

"Wheaa aa yuu furoomu?" he asked in barely understandable English.

"New York," I replied nervously.

"Aa," he said, "biggu shiiity." Then he abruptly kept walking.

When I returned indoors after my twenty-minute *bira* shift was completed, I couldn't wait for Jewel to show her customer to the door so that I could tell her what happened. When Jewel's customer finally left the bar, I ambushed her immediately with news of my curious encounter.

"That's not unusual at all," she said, somewhat to my dismay.

"*They* like to keep track of how many girls are at each club, and which countries they come from."

"Oh," I said, half relieved.

"You didn't do anything to make him angry, right?" she asked.

"I don't think so," I replied. "Actually he didn't give me the opportunity to talk so much—"

"Good," she cut me off. "You have to be careful of those people when you drink," she went on, "I know how you get."

"You know, I was reading a book about the *ya-san* in the bookstore today," I told Jadie as we shared a cab home from work a week later, "and they don't seem all that scary."

"Yes, they are," Jadie responded, seeming tired and slightly drunk.

"But seriously," I continued, despite her disapproval, "this book I was reading said that the *ya-san* organized a food drive for the earthquake victims in Kobe in 1995 and—"

"You're not gonna learn anything about them in books," she cut me off, her tone snappy and condescending.

"Okay, okay," I conceded, leaving it at that for the night.

38

all work and no play makes yoshiharu a dull boy

The men I saw on the train didn't leer at me or look at me; still, I felt nervous and uncomfortable, knowing they were looking at pictures of tied-up, naked women as they rode the same train.

—KYOKO MORI, *Polite Lies*

"It's fiction, it's just fiction!" my new client Yoshiharu pleaded apologetically when I took a pornographic comic book out of his briefcase while we were on a dōhan one night.

"I don't understand why you like this." I had to keep an affectionate tone of voice, like a mother scolding her son. This was a paid date after all.

"It's only pretend. Just drawings! Not real!" He restated his argument, cracking an embarrassed smile.

"And why do their sizes keep changing?" I continued, pointing to one frame in which a man and woman of the same height began to kiss and take off each other's clothing. When the man touched the woman's breast, however, he shrank to the size of her finger and clung onto one of her breasts, hugging it with his entire body.

"Because it's a cartoon," he replied, trying to take the book from my hands, since some other people at the restaurant were starting to stare at us. It was not at all strange that I was out on a date with a man more than twice my age, but once a foreign female is seen reading a *hentai* comic book, the sight becomes a spectacle.

My grip on the book was likely stronger than his, still I had to let go as he hid the book back in his briefcase, which he originally opened in order to retrieve his wallet. I had to let him win. It was a paid date after all, and others were watching.

"He's just too lonely," Angela told me later in the evening when I complained to her about Yoshiharu's penchant for cartoon porn, "you should try to feel sorry for him." Angela was always advising me that I should try to find something genuinely attractive in every one of my customers, so that when I complimented them it would seem most sincere. As a result, my job often consisted of finding the good in even the most unattractive, smelly, rude, old, fat, or dangerous of customers.

"He's just too lonely," Angela's words echoed in my head as I passed through Heaven's revolving door. Maybe Angela had been right. Men like Yoshiharu had so much money, still there was something terrifically sad about them as well.

On the way home I stopped at 7-Eleven, and observed all of the men reading comics there late at night. Since my presence was not being purchased anymore and I could behave as I pleased, I joined the group of well-dressed men and began to look through the magazines myself.

Magazine stands usually encompassed one entire wall of the typical Japanese convenience store. It is the most crowed section, as many customers crowd around reading manga, Japanese comics, with no intention of buying anything. This activity even has a name: *tachiyomi*, a word that is formed by simply linking the Japanese verbs to stand and to read. To say this word has precarious connotations, however, since most of these cheap comics are pornographic.

One of the older men in front of me was skipping around to pages with drawings of breasts. I wasn't standing there for a minute when a specific cartoon caught my eye. There I stood, staring aghast at a centerfold depicting a large-breasted woman who was tied up and crying as she was penetrated by a nonhuman but genitally gifted man-shaped demon.

When I looked up, all of the men who had been crowded around me just moments earlier had mysteriously fled from sight. There was not one left. The unusual presence of a female in this section of the store, not to mention a foreign female, had likely made them uncomfortable.

"Try to feel sorry for them." Angela's words echoed again.

Maybe, I thought to myself as I attempted to follow her advice, *the rape fantasies I so despise are precisely what make these men so lonely*. Could it be this fictitious image of women, this imaginary view of sex, that had these men feeling so lonely in real-life relationships? Inundated with fantasy, the men could not understand flesh-and-blood women at all. In fact, these unfortunate men had very little to live for besides work, sake, and pornography.

Despite rampant rape fantasies in the media, Tokyo remained an impressively safe and crime-free city. In my experience, young women can walk alone at night without fear or incident in Tokyo, to an extent that is unimaginable in other American and European cities.

Instead, the vast majority of sex crimes take place within the confines of the male Japanese mind. This begs the question, what is to be done with a criminal whose crime is imaginary? What sort of punishment is suitable? Maybe we could put the perpetrators, largely Japanese businessmen, the same demographic of white-collar workers who frequent hostess bars, into an imaginary prison?

But that's presuming they weren't there already.

While I lived in Tokyo, Japan's suicide rate was astronomical; it was the highest in the developed world, and per capita it was more than twice that of the United States. Journalists and even professionals often qualified this figure by contrasting Japan's samurai tradition of honorable suicides against the Christian view of suicide as sinful. Rather than belonging to any divine being, the soul of a samurai was said to live in his sword.

In more ancient times, members of Japan's warrior classes performed ritualistic suicides called *seppuku*. *Seppuku*, or hara-kiri, was a well-calculated and extremely painful way to die caused by driving the length of one's own sword through the stomach and intestines. It was done either to escape death at the hands of the enemy or to escape an unbearable disgrace in battle.

Despite this tradition, Jadie was fond of saying that "there are no real samurai left in all of Japan." And she had a point. There was a dramatic paradox within this so-called samurai culture. Much unlike the calculated deaths of their ancestors, the modern Japanese more often chose to die on impulse. Tokyo subway platforms were lethal in that respect.

Further, it was less than honorable that the family members of the deceased were made to pay for the inconveniences and loss of profit experienced by the Metro authority during such "accidents," a rule that was invoked to deter so many suicidal passengers from jumping in front of trains during rush hour. Such track jumpers were not samurai.

The other most popular way to die in Japan, carbon monoxide poisoning, also fell short of an honorable and painful departure by the samurai code. It was somewhat of a phenomenon for troubled and lonely Japanese to make suicide pacts with strangers on the Internet, who would help them die by placing a hose through a car window. Hara-kiri, in that it required slitting the stomach open with a short sword and pulling one's own intestines out, was considered one of the most painful ways to kill oneself. Suicide by carbon monoxide poisoning, on the other hand, is touted for its nonviolent and painless nature.

For the contemporary Japanese man, "honor" proved a paradox at best, a lethal illusion at worst. Yet the myth and the metaphor were powerful, even more so than reality itself, than life and death.

this in mind, it was rather miraculous that I only encountered one suicidal customer in Heaven. My thoughts turned to him as I left the convenience store on my way home. Kizuki came to the bar, usually alone, about three times a week. I was his regular hostess, private English teacher, and therapist.

Kizuki and his wife had divorced two years prior. One night he came in immediately after receiving word that his ex-wife had died of breast cancer. Because divorce was heavily looked down upon in Japan, he was forbidden by his wife's family to attend her funeral. Even if he had been an awful husband through all the years he was married, I gradually came to feel compassion for him.

According to Japanese social codes, he had lived his life exactly the way he was supposed to. He excelled in school, graduated from a competitive university, and entered a top corporation. There he put in long, hard hours six days a week and dutifully advanced up the corporate ladder. At the same time, however, Japanese society in general has little to say for treating one's wife with respect and dignity. So he did what everybody else did, he stayed out late at night drinking with his coworkers, had affairs, and never learned to even boil water for himself in the kitchen.

Fittingly, when he retired from his job with a handsome pension, his wife could not stand having him around the house all day long. Since their children were already grown, she simply packed her things and left. The phenomenon of divorce among older couples, usually a direct result of the husband's retirement, has become such a common trend in Japan that it has a name: *jukunen rikon*.

Kizuki's divorce was finalized some months later and now she was dead. He had never truly known her. There was a real sense of remorse in his voice when he spoke about her to me; it was sadly moving.

"Maybe I should kill myself," he lamented on one of the many nights we sat and talked.

"Don't do that," I replied, my eyes wide with concern, "I would miss you too much!" I was almost telling the truth.

"Okay, I won't," he replied, "because your eyes are too beautiful."

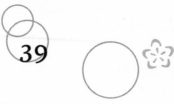

Dracula's Daughter

"Great Scott! Is this a game?"
"It is."

——BRAM STOKER, *Dracula*

It was family night in Heaven. That is to say, three younger men came to the bar together with their fathers.

Aside from the obvious awkwardness of this scenario, a great deal of shuffling went on as Mari and Kento tried to decide where each of the ladies would decorate the table. The entire group of men was acting extremely picky, and it was times like these that I really wished I couldn't understand Japanese.

"No, she's too tall," one of the men would say as Kento attempted to place me beside him.

"No, her breasts are too small," said another who refused to sit next to Jadie.

"No, she is not cute at all." Another demanded a shift.

"No, I hate Americans," said yet another man who refused to sit by me.

After about five intolerable minutes of this, each customer was sitting beside a lady whom he found at least adequate. At that, we began to pour their whiskey and the drinking party began.

I found myself sitting between a twenty-four-year-old man with a baby face and his father, who didn't have a baby face. We would have much rather engaged in conversation with the younger men, but there is an unwritten rule that the oldest men at the table should always get the most attention from the ladies. The reason for this was simple: he was most often the one who was paying, so it was he who would eventually decide whether or not to extend their stay.

But while the older man was busy introducing himself to Katria at his right, I could turn to my left and cordially greet his son.

"Do you go with your fathers to places like this often?" I couldn't help but ask one of the men in his twenties.

"Yes"—he surprised me—"but usually in Kabukichō."

I see, I thought to myself, *in Kabukichō, where you can touch the girls.* How charming. Ginza is a far cry from Kabukichō, we liked to think.

"What brings you to Ginza then?"

"My father said I should practice my English," he said, "so we all came to an international bar instead."

"Okay, I will speak English to you from now on," I said with a smile, switching languages immediately. Many a former English teacher who, in one way or another, finds herself in the hostessing world has remarked on how similar the two jobs are. Both jobs basically require one to act as both a cultural exhibition and an entertainer.

Then Katria asked one customer if she could have a drink, but he refused, telling her, "You are too fat.

"I'm not trying to insult you," he continued, "I am just worried about your health."

Sure he was. All the while, his beer belly looked like it might weigh about as much as Katria's entire body.

"Don't mind him"—the son looked over at me after I failed to hide my disgusted facial expression—"My mother is always telling him to lose weight so he's insecure about it."

"I really, really need a drink," I confessed to the younger man. He smiled at me then but made no attempt to order anything.

There is an entire class of customers in Heaven who come in only to insult the women who work there. They take a sick pleasure in pointing out our flaws. They also seem to know that they are slowly torturing us by refusing to buy us drinks, which we so dearly need to tolerate their company. On family night, the fathers seemed to be showing off in front of their sons, which made these men all the nastier.

"Where are you from?" I overheard one of the men ask Anica as I was dutifully wiping the condensation off of another customer's glass.

"Romania," she replied politely.

"That is where Dracula is from!" the man exclaimed, visibly proud of his insight.

"That's right," Anica conceded. "In the Romanian language, 'dracul' actually means 'devil.' "

"So Mama Destiny's new nickname should be Mama Dracula," Katria said under her breath, thrusting all of the women at the table into uncontrollable laughter.

Perhaps because he was irritated at being left out of our joke, from that point on the man speaking to Anica became noticeably meaner.

"You look like Dracula!" he told her. "Look," he exclaimed to everyone at the table, "her teeth even stick out like fangs! Don't you have braces in Romania?"

Anica's teeth did not, by any stretch of the imagination, stick out. This conversation was even more ironic seeing as the Japanese probably have, by far, the worst dental hygiene of any developed country. I racked my brain for a way to defend my friend. Just like we are permitted to slap the men if they ever try to grope us, we can repel their insults as well, but only if we have something wittier to say.

Still Anica, as a seasoned hostess, played along with the act.

"I am not Dracula," she first said in a somber manner. Then, after a short pause, she widened her dark eyes and exclaimed, "I'm Dracula's daughter! That is why I only come out at night." The men all laughed at this, so she continued. "And when I look in the mirror," she teased, taking out her pocket mirror and holding it at an angle, "I have no reflection!"

Switching to broken English, the man shouted, "I afraido, I afraido, itsaa durakura dautaa!" Everyone at the table broke into uproarious, haunting laughter.

"But instead of blood," Anica continued, "I have to drink red wine."

At that, Anica had done it. I let out a huge sigh of relief. Finally, an exorbitantly priced bottle of red wine was ordered for all the ladies at the table to partake. I winked at her in admiration when no one else was looking. We were all in serious need of a drink in order to tolerate the situation any further.

I learned much from Anica that night. To see an old, scrawny middle-aged man with bad breath insult a beautiful woman like that, especially a beautiful woman who is my friend, was certainly a hard pill to swallow with a smile. Still, there is a certain freedom in abandoning all pride, in remaining unaffected by insult, and in knowing that the entire environment was merely a fantasy anyway. And once a hostess can feel that sense of liberation from the real world, the game is on.

Still, I was very disappointed to witness the way these men were teaching their offspring to treat women. And when I saw their group off an hour and a half later, even though we had effectively sucked their wallets dry, it was with less faith in humanity in general.

They reminded me of a recent conversation I'd had with Yoshiharu, the lonely man with the cartoon porn.

"Your Japanese really sucks lately," Yoshiharu told me after I finished telling him a story about nothing in particular. Having been my regular for a while, I suppose he either wanted to stem my self-respect, seeing how often I was complimented on my Japanese by customers and ladies alike, or he had simply gotten to know me well enough to hit me where it hurts, to throw insults at my weaker points.

He knew I was insecure about my fluency in his language and that I was preparing to take the highest level of the Japanese language proficiency test that December, which I felt almost certain I was going to fail. If I had, for example, in some drunken mishap accidentally told him that I was a former anorexic, he would have probably been constantly telling me I was fat.

I know this sounds intolerable from the perspective of the modern woman, but it was just part of our job; it was how we received our nightly salary. Taking shit with grace, that was our job.

Tokyo hostesses really are as nocturnal as vampires, so when we finished work at 2 A.M. on family night, Anica, Jadie, and I decided to go out dancing in Roppongi. We were already dolled up from work, so we had no problem finding guys to buy us drinks.

We took turns asking a complete stranger—a male, of course—for the next round, then ditching whoever bought us the drinks as quickly as it took him to pay for them. The club was big enough to manage such a feat multiple times. In retrospect, I would not have been able to act this way if we hadn't developed a certain animosity toward men in general.

It made me think of Dracula again. After all, a vampire is essentially a victim turned aggressor. They are those who have been bitten, and as a result are cursed to crave the blood of others. In that respect, we were all Dracula's daughters.

40

the art of deception

I had done the unthinkable. Worse than the unthinkable: the unforgivable, the unmentionable, the inexcusable.

"Ima nan ji desu ka?"

I had asked a customer the time. Mama Mari, who somehow managed to be everywhere and hear everything at once like a true mama, immediately shot her glance in my direction from the spot by the vestibule where she often stood to greet all of the customers. The glare that met me during that instant was so cold that it could—no pun intended—stop a clock.

I managed to make eye contact with Mari while my customer checked his Rolex. In a split second, I gave Mari an extremely subtle nod of my head, to assure her that I wasn't too drunk and I hadn't gone mad. In fact, I had a plan. Raising her eyebrows as if to tell me to get on with my so-called plan, Mari then turned away again.

My asking the time was such an incursion on the rules because, as Tokyo bar hostesses, our job was to do everything in our power to make our customers forget that time ever existed. The ticking clock contradicts the flight from reality that all hostesses should symbolize. Heaven had no clock on the wall and no windows from which one may observe the sunrise.

Their losing track of the time was most profitable, since the men paid amply for every minute that was spent with us in Heaven.

"Eleven fifty-eight," my customer replied, somewhat confused.

"Oh"—I instantly flashed him a wide smile—"in two minutes it will be my birthday!"

"Congratulations!" Mr. Mitsubishi smiled back. "And may I ask how old the birthday girl will be?"

"I'll be twenty-three," I chirped in a childlike manner. "I am so quickly becoming an old lady!" When I said that, we both laughed.

"We should celebrate," Mitsubishi-san assured me as he patted my shoulder in a friendly manner. "But how?" He turned to face me.

"Champagne?" I asked him.

"Why not," he declared, summoning Kento over to the table.

Mitsubishi sang "Happy Birthday" to me on the karaoke machine as we toasted our respective glasses of Dom Pérignon.

"In two years"—I cocked my head slightly and looked him in the eye flirtatiously—"I will be a Christmas cake. Whatever will I do then?" I sighed. The tone of voice I used with him was of a higher pitch and was far more "cutesy" than my natural manner of speaking.

Popular slang in Tokyo dictates that if a woman reaches her twenty-fifth birthday before she is married, she is called a Christmas cake. The title refers to the fact that everywhere in Tokyo around the holiday season so-called Christmas cakes become very popular in stores and are sold for very high prices. Once December twenty-fifth comes around, however, the market value drops dramatically.

This disturbing outlook is so prevalent that, when the Japanese icon Hello Kitty reached her twenty-fifth year on the shelves, the company invented a husband for the fictional cat, whom they called Dear Daniel.

"You don't have to worry about becoming a Christmas cake," Mitsubishi assured me, "because you are so attractive."

"Will you marry me?" I joked.

"Maybe on your next birthday," he said, politely refusing.

"Oh," I sighed again. "Now I feel depressed because you won't marry me. I always eat when I'm depressed. Can we order something to eat so I'll feel better?"

"Anything you like," he assured me, summoning the waiter back to our table another time to place an order for an exorbitantly priced fruit platter.

An hour or two later, after seeing Mitsubishi off at Heaven's door, Mari let me look over her shoulder to glance at my customer's bill, which amounted to something around the ballpark of 95,000 yen, or enough to pay my rent for two months.

"You did well," Mama assured me.

"Thank you, Mama," I said as I beamed.

"But if you keep having birthdays like this," she jested, "you will become old very quickly. You might even turn thirty!"

At that, Mama and I began to laugh together. Truth be told, I think I had about six or seven birthdays in 2004 alone. Sometimes, I liked to think that I kept having birthdays in order to spite the society that would declare me a spinster at twenty-five.

Birthdays were not the only thing I lied to my customers about. Once, for example, I got sick of seeing Dōhanman all of the time so I sent him an e-mail telling him that I had to go home to America immediately because my grandmother, who was very much alive, had just died.

Through the course of our relationship, I attempted to cut all ties with Hideo two or three times because I feared that it was becoming too serious, but I always came crawling back eventually. This was likely because of his business, but I may have just missed him.

So, when I called him back to my club two weeks after the supposed funeral, I had to make sure my story was airtight. I notified every single hostess and staff member that, as far as Hideo was concerned, I went back to America last week and was not in Tokyo at all.

My plan was to avoid the topic as much as possible with Hideo, but when he bought a bottle of Jose Cuervo, poured us two shot glasses, and made a toast "To your grandmother," the lies just started flowing like the tequila.

"This isn't a sad toast," I declared with a sniffle, "my grandmother led a very good life. She lived to be eighty-five. If my life ends up being as productive as hers was, I will be very satisfied."

"I see." Hideo nodded sympathetically.

"She raised four children, and after they grew up she went back to college and got two master's degrees. Then she worked as a social worker until she was eighty-one. She loved to help people, my grandmother."

Everything I told Hideo about my grandmother that night was true, saving her being dead, so I suppose that there is a sprinkling of truth in every lie.

ᴀꜰᴛᴇʀ ᴡᴏʀᴋ ᴛʜᴀᴛ night, as we sat at the bar waiting for Mama to come reimburse us for our taxi receipts, Cheri and Angela inquired as to whether my plan had gone off without a glitch.

I proudly informed them that it had. "People will always believe only what they want to believe anyway," I admitted, "and Hideo really wants to believe whatever I tell him."

We sat there a while comparing stories.

"Six months ago," Angela said with a sly grin, "my customer said that I looked too thin and offered me this big wad of cash to go home to the Philippines for a week to rest."

"Did you take it?" I asked, interested.

"I took the money," she said, "but I stayed right here and just started eating more so I would look fatter next time he came back. So that whole week I was supposed to be back in the Philippines I had to tell everyone here to watch the streets for my customer, so that I could hide out if he found me. And whenever Kento answered the phone, he was instructed to tell all callers that I was not here."

"That's hilarious," I complimented her. "Well done, girl!"

"What did you do with the money?" Cheri asked.

"Shopping!" Angela exclaimed, and the two gave each other a high five.

"Did you feel guilty about lying to him about your grandmother?" Cheri inquired.

"I try not to think about it too much," I admitted, "and besides, they say 'all's fair in love and war'!" As I quoted Tolstoy, I noted to myself that the true difficulty lay in differentiating between the two.

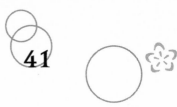

OF FAIRY TALES AND VISA MARRIAGES

cheri knew more about the underground goings-on in Heaven than any of us. I assumed it was because she shared a native language with Mama Mari and Chi-mama Angela. At the end of each night, I could always count on the red wine Cheri loved so much to loosen her tongue, and consequently I learned a great deal of Heaven gossip.

From her, I learned that most of the long-term workers in Heaven possessed "visa marriages." In other words, they had fake Japanese husbands whose sponsorship helped them to stay in the country without risk of deportation. The necessity of a "visa marriage" for a long-term foreign hostess puts an interesting twist on the old concept of the danna within the geisha world.

Although a geisha cannot get married without having to turn in her face paint and silk kimono, the closest step to a permanent relationship she may take is acquiring a danna. A danna is basically a cross between a husband, a pimp, and a patron of the arts. The geisha's danna is the rare man who is so exorbitantly wealthy that he can financially support his chosen geisha's lavish lifestyle. He does so in return for preferential treatment, if not sexual favors.

For most hostesses as well, the only incidence in which sex with clients might take place involves the exchange of total financial support, provided for the hostess by a client. This preferred customer's role in the relationship is strikingly similar to that of a geisha's danna. While in the geisha world, taking a danna has always had some features in common with getting married, in the hostess world of convenience marriages, our version of acquiring a danna is coming to mean just that.

With this in mind, it is fitting that in contemporary Japanese, the word *dana-san* also means "husband." When I am speaking of somebody else's husband in Japanese I will always use the word *danna*. It is much better than the alternative, the even more old-fashioned word *shujin,* which is formed by placing the kanji for "master" next to the one for "person," creating the compound meaning "husband." (Similarly, one Japanese word for *wife* is formed by a compound of the characters "house" and "inside.")

Visa marriages are how most foreign hostesses manage to remain working in Japan, especially for the long term. Among my other hostess acquaintances we refer to these arrangements as "sham marriages," seeing as the men who agree to such an arrangement are usually very old, perhaps widowed, and most likely act as a patron to the very young hostesses that they marry.

Sham marriages are on the rise between hostesses and their clients, especially now, as there has been a police crackdown on immigration law violations by hostess bars in the Ginza and Roppongi areas.

The tendency has added an extra element of fantasy to the already dreamlike atmosphere. In theory, the visa marriage phenomenon creates a fairy tale through the course of which poorer young women are whisked away from the ghettos of Manila or Vladivostok by corporate Prince Charmings who treat them to expensive luxuries. In practice, however, the picture of horny old men buying the affections of pretty young girls with few other choices to speak of reveals the inherent dark side of our cross-cultural Cinderella myth.

Of the Eastern European women in Heaven, Cheri informed me that Katria possessed a marriage visa, although it was not specified which one of Katria's many clients was her danna. Even more interestingly, Cheri also told me that Anica still did not possess a marriage visa, despite having worked in Ginza for three years, and in spite of Mama's constant urging that she consider such an arrangement. As a result, Anica was still working in Japan illegally, which meant that Heaven was paying a great deal of protection money to the yakuza on her account.

"What about Kaicho?" I asked Cheri about Anica's most loyal customer. Everyone in Heaven called him by the nickname Kaicho because he was the president of a company. *Kaicho* literally translates into "boss," while the word can also loosely mean "master." "I hear he is divorced," I continued.

"Yeah," Cheri confirmed, "he is the one Mari has been pressing her to marry for the visa."

"Any idea why Anica's holding out?" I asked. I could think of about one thousand reasons why she shouldn't marry him myself, the least of which was that Kaicho was fat, old, and smelled bad, but I wanted to hear Cheri's take on the matter.

"Maybe she's religious," Cheri suggested. It was true Anica would go on these Romanian Orthodox religious binges, and stop drinking or smoking for weeks at a time. But she would always start up again. It was really quite impossible to do the job without the help of some sort of anesthetic, no matter where you came from.

"Maybe it's Kaicho's face," I countered. Although I was half-joking, Kaicho did have the sort of decrepit countenance that persuaded one to believe that fairy tales were originally horror stories for a reason.

I had been in Japan two years when my visa I had acquired at my previous teaching jobs expired.

"I hear you are spending much time with Marui-san—the dōhanman—outside of the club," Angela told me one night, although I still have no idea how she found that out.

"Yes." I hung my head in shame, preparing for a scolding that didn't come.

"We appreciate your effort," she said, "but just remember that we are Ginza hostesses, and we never get physically involved with a customer, that is, unless he is a danna."

"I know, Chi-mama, I know. Don't worry, I'm not touching him, okay?" I quickly responded. "Marui is just an old friend, I guess."

"Have you considered marriage?" she asked.

"What?" I was taken aback, "Um . . . no. I don't like him that way."

"Well, maybe you should," Chi-mama continued, "most of the hostesses here have Japanese husbands. You don't have to live together but it makes it a lot easier when it comes time to renew your visa. Do you understand?"

"Yes, Mama."

"He is very rich and such a gentleman," Angela continued, "so you should consider it."

"Yes, Mama," I lied.

I chose not to tell Angela that just a week earlier I had received a tempting offer from Marui-san. Hideo Marui always became more generous as he continued to drink beer, and at one point in the conversation he offered to pay the rent and utilities for my apartment. In the past, I had accepted many times the amount of my rent from Hideo each month in the form of gifts and meals, but the actual payment of my monthly rent by him was where a line would have to be drawn between us. If he paid for my accommodation, this would be the mutually understood first step in his becoming my danna-san, and that was an offer I would have to refuse. Rather, it was an offer that I *was able* to refuse, given the fortunate circumstances of my birth in America.

Still, instead of accepting or refusing Hideo's offer, like a true Japanese I simply changed the subject.

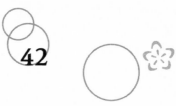

42

Heaven's Little Whore

Jadie worked at Heaven only one or two nights a week for a period that extended more than a year. I, on the other hand, was not suited for a routine so stable. As a result, I usually worked every night for a couple of months or so at a time. I dove into the job at full speed until I burned out entirely, until I was so saturated with alcohol and attention that I didn't recognize myself anymore. At that point I would usually take a break, during which time I would let the alcohol drain out of my system and engage in more respectable forms of employment, such as substitute teaching for elementary schools.

It was during one of my off periods that Jadie informed me of an interesting new development on the Ginza scene.

"There is a new girl working at Heaven," Jadie told me during a phone conversation one evening, "and she is a total whore!"

"A whore?" I asked in disbelief. "No way!"

"Yes way," she reassured me, "her name is Michi, and I have no idea why Mari hired her. She is old, and ugly, and a total whore!"

"Does she have her own customers?" I asked.

"Yeah," Jadie reflected, "she has tons of customers. Maybe that's why Mari hired her. The other girls and I were talking, and we think that she sleeps with all of them. Ew!" Jadie's voice echoed with utter disgust. "She is so nasty!"

"What makes you think she has sex with them?" I asked.

"Well, the other night I was sitting beside her and this nasty customer, and he was totally massaging her boobs. Ew! I don't understand why Mari is allowing such things. She brings down the level of the whole club and it makes us all look like whores, too. She's so disgusting!" Jadie explained.

"Ew," I concurred.

"We think," my friend speculated, "that at her last job she was a prostitute."

"Really?" I asked in disbelief.

"Yes!" Jadie insisted. "And her behavior reflects negatively upon us all!"

The following week, my curiosity having been peaked by many similar discussions regarding this mysteriously infamous Michi, I decided to rejoin the ensemble in Heaven for another run, if only because I wanted to investigate whether Michi really was the whore everyone said she was.

The Monday evening I resumed my job in Heaven was one of Jadie's nights off, so I arrived alone. Upon entering I immediately scanned the room for the notorious Michi, but there were a few new girls there so I wasn't sure which one was the whore. Plus, there were some customers who had arrived early, so I had to hurry up and change into my dress and makeup.

anica nodded in Michi's direction with her eyes, and whispered, "*Saseko,*" in my ear with the most malevolent tone of voice I had ever heard her use. *Saseko* is the Japanese slang for "whore," although the literal origin of the word refers to a public toilet.

I looked to Saki, across the table from Anica, for reassurance. "It's true," she said. "The only reason she has so many customers is because she lets them touch her breasts. We've all seen it. And the worst part is," she continued, "she has been getting the ten-thousand-yen bonus at the end of every week that is always reserved for the hostess with the highest sales of the week."

"I know!" Anica said, her anger renewed. "And it's totally unfair because that bonus is reserved for the hostess with the highest sales, not the whore with the most sales!"

At that, Maki and Anica began to cackle mischievously. I let out a giggle myself, so as to fit in.

Soon afterward, Mama Mari sent the three of us home in order to catch the last train, while Michi stayed on, seeing as she had a client with her. To my disappointment, circumstances did not allow me to actually meet Michi that night. Still, there would always be the next night.

I woke up the next morning, and before remembering where I was, I advised myself that the subject of my recent dream was worth remembering. Alas, when I came to I could only recall that I was supposed to remember my dream, while its subject matter slipped my mind. It took five minutes of head-in-hands brain-racking on my pillow until one word, a name from my past, floated into my consciousness: Jenny. My dream had been about Jenny, a classmate from my past I had done such a good job of forgetting. *Jenny*. Despite our unyielding reputation as rivals in high school, it occurred to me that we'd never actually spoken to each another until the night of my dream.

As the high school soap unfolded, Jenny lost her virginity to an older college kid she'd been dating named Mike. A week later said

Mike and I met at a party, became respectively wasted, and ended the night by hitting it off in the hostess's bathroom. I didn't know much of anything in those days, least of all that Mike was dating anyone in particular prior to our meeting, let alone a preppy brunette in my math class named Jenny Blake.

By the following week everyone in my school had heard, with varying levels of detail and intensity, how Mike and I had fucked extensively in the bathtub at Christie Jordan's party, which, in a twist of irony, did not actually happen, as I was still a virgin. I begged my so-called friend Christie to set the record straight and tell everyone around school that Mike and I had only kissed in her bathroom.

"But, Lea," she protested, "everyone thinks it's really cool! All these hot college guys keep asking me when my next party is!" Although my group of friends was delighted with their sudden popularity around school at my expense, I felt unbearably guilty. To make matters worse, said Jenny sat two rows ahead of me in our advanced math class.

Every day I wanted to say something to her, pass her a note even, to tell her what really happened, and that I had no idea she was dating Mike when I hooked up with him. But I never found the courage to approach her and soon she dropped out of advanced math. The entire class surely figured I was the reason for Jenny's short-lived math career, yet no one could blame me as intensely as I blamed myself. I never saw Mike again.

Even more ironic, the make-out session with Mike was actually the only action I had experienced since my sixth-grade boyfriend, Brad Brewer, told every boy in school that I was a "prude" when I refused to let him kiss me on the lips (I was eleven at the time), and since then no boy had taken the trouble to ask me out.

It was in such a manner that my high school reputation soared from "prude" to "slut" in the course of one night, a night that didn't

even happen. Given that it was more than five years prior, I had generally blocked the sticky situation that tainted my entire high school
reputation out of my conscious mind. Which was why it was so surprising to come across Jenny and Mike in my sleep.

In my dream, I was sitting on a hill of grass, and Mike and Jenny
were standing at the bottom engaged in a conversation I couldn't decipher. While I pretended to be studying and not noticing them, I
couldn't help but note some hostility in their tone toward each other
and tried to hide myself as Mike drove away in his car and Jenny
walked in my direction. My hiding somehow graduated to rolling up
into a fetal position on the grass, unwillingly exposing my anguish to
Jenny.

"Why are you so confused?" She spoke to me first, sitting down a
safe distance behind me and to the right.

"I'm not confused," I replied gloomily. "I'm depressed." Seizing
the opportunity to finally clarify the situation, I turned around to
speak to her. "Jenny, I . . . , Jenny, it didn't really happen between
me and Mike the way people said it did, please believe me. *Jenny,
I . . . I'm so, so* sorry!"

"I never thought badly of your intentions," she said calmly, almost gently.

"But you switched out of advanced math because of me!" I reminded her.

"Seeing you made me think of him," she said, "but I never
thought badly of you. It wasn't your fault."

I don't remember if I responded to her understanding before
waking up. Recalling the dream, I realized that this was the only conversation the two of us had ever had, fictional or otherwise. It was
such a warm feeling to hear that she forgave me, even if it was all just
in my imagination.

My waking thoughts also led me to feel an odd sort of sympathy with Michi. I've always had sympathy for those deemed sluts since the "Jenny fiasco." Even the girls who actually do sleep around, since they usually end up doing so because of some deep-seated loneliness or depression. So the title is basically like a kick when you're already down. I wanted to meet Michi more than ever, and to hear her story. I would do so that night.

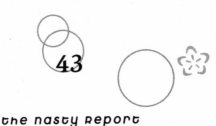

43

the nasty report

"you're meeting her?" Jadie stared back at me with an expression of utter repulsion, once she realized that she hadn't heard me wrong.

"Yeah," I said, "before work tonight. We're going to drink some beers together at the Pronto across the street."

"But *why?*" my friend asked, still in disbelief.

"Michi is my new project," I rationalized. "I invited her out because I've never known any prostitutes before. I really want to know her life story and what she's about. I met her last night in Heaven and we were talking about New York. When she said that she lived uptown before, at first I was sure she was lying, but then I drilled her about directions and she knew her shit. Michi really did live in New York last year."

"Okay," Jadie said carefully, as if her approval were imperative, "but you'll have to report back to me everything she says, because now I am curious to know, too."

"No problem," I replied, "we can call it 'The Nasty Report.'"

"Yeah," Jadie said with a grin, "because she is fucking nasty. Next time we work with her we should sing that song 'Nasty Girl' by Destiny's Child. . . ."

"Anica sings that song pretty well," I added. "We can ask her to do it."

"Just don't get herpes or anything," Jadie continued.

"Chill out"—I patted my friend on the shoulder—"I'm just going to drink with her, not have sex with her!"

"Still, one act can turn into the other rather quickly," Jadie jested.

"Fair enough," I conceded. "Besides, Michi's gotta have some crazy issues." I continued to justify myself. "And you know me, I love people with issues, they're much more interesting than most."

Michi arrived at the Pronto restaurant-bar across the street from Heaven about a half hour late. It is quite un-Japanese to show up even a few minutes late, so I had conceded that she was not coming by the time she walked in the door and found me. We had both been a bit tipsy by the time we had made the plans to meet, after finishing work the night before.

"I'm so sorry," she said. "I have been very busy today," she continued, though with what she did not specify.

"No worries," I replied calmly, already on my second beer.

"It's so nice to see you outside of the bar." Michi treated me cordially. "Usually I am so busy working that I don't get the chance to talk to any of the other girls."

"How did you meet all of your customers?" I asked her, wasting no time.

"Well," she said, "I moved back here from New York six months ago, and I worked at the Palace for a while."

"I worked at the Palace, too!" I exclaimed. "So did basically everyone else in Heaven."

"Really?" she asked. "Yeah, I worked there for about four months, then one night Mama Destiny just fired me without any explanation."

"Yeah, that happened to most of us," I related.

"I had no idea that was the case," Michi said, the surprise evident on her face. "I am so occupied with my clients in Heaven that I have no real opportunities to gossip."

"You do have so many customers," I remarked and then segued to, "tell me, Michi, what is your secret?"

"I'm not sure." She smiled and laughed an evasive laugh that let me know that I would not be getting much information out of her that evening.

"How old are you?" I asked anyway.

"Twenty-six," she said. I knew she was lying. I'd already heard from Mari that Michi was thirty-two, which is very old for a hostess. Still, we were all professional liars, so there wasn't anything unique about her particular fib, no real cause for offense. "And you?" she asked.

"Twenty-four," I replied, "so you're my oneesan." *Oneesan* is literally Japanese for older sister, but in its practical use it is a respectful way to address a woman who is slightly older than oneself.

"Since I'm your oneesan"—Michi took a deep breath—"can I ask you a personal question?" she inquired.

"Of course," I replied, a bit taken aback.

"What's that on your wrist?" she asked, nodding at my parallel scars.

"Umm." I paused and took a large sip of my beer. "Are you sure you really want to know?" I asked, hoping she would forget about it.

"I think I already do"—she put a hand on my shoulder—"I hope you don't mind my asking, but it's just that my best friend does that, too, and I don't know how to get her to stop."

"Therapy is a good thing," I replied, being purposely vague. I would have to remember to put more makeup on my scars the next time I went out.

"Yes," Michi reflected, "but there is such a stigma about going to therapy within Japanese culture."

"More of a stigma than cutting your wrists?" I asked in disbelief.

"It's a tough question to answer," she replied, in all seriousness.

"That's really a shame," I said, reflecting on my awful experience with the first and only Japanese psychiatrist I would ever visit.

"So where is your hometown?" I grabbed the first opportunity I could to change the subject.

"Matsumoto," she replied, "in Nagano Prefecture."

"Nagano, like the Olympics, right?" I asked.

"Yes!" Michi replied with a smile and an exaggerated nod of her head.

"The town of Matsumoto also rings a bell for me," I confessed, "but I forget why."

After a long pause I suddenly remembered why I recognized the name Matsumoto, but decided not to press the matter further as a matter of tact.

A year before the Aum supreme truth cult launched a sarin gas attack on the Tokyo subway system in 1995, the same cult executed a separate but equally lethal sarin attack in Matsumoto. A small town in the countryside, Matsumoto is basically known throughout Japan as the location that suffered Aum's first sarin attack.

"How many people are in your family?" I asked instead.

"I hate to spoil your fantasy," I told Jade upon arriving home later that night, "but Michi didn't work as a prostitute before she joined the staff at Heaven. She worked at the Palace first like everybody else."

"Does she have sex with her customers after-hours then?" my friend inquired.

"I really don't think so," I responded half-honestly.

"Are you sure?" Jadie asked in disbelief.

"Of course I don't know for sure," I admitted, "but I don't think so."

By that point I'd realized that if Michi had, in fact, slept with one of her customers, there was no way that I was ever going to find out. When such unusual events do come to pass, this is the type of secret that most every hostess will take with her to the grave.

I'm not sure if it was a consequence of the proliferation of my nasty report, or a result of Michi's realization that the other hostesses became offended when she let the customers touch her, but she subsequently cleaned up her act, and in the weeks to follow, the bashing of Michi by the other hostesses toned down quite a bit, and she was almost accepted into our tribe.

I was sitting next to Michi at the waiting table, around that time, when I received a text message on my phone from Marui-san:

"There's a typhoon out at sea, I want to drive to the beach at Kamakura to watch the waves tomorrow morning."

"Let's go!" I typed a reply immediately.

As an afterthought, I turned to Michi by my side and asked her if she might like to join us.

"I'm sorry," she said, "but I will be very busy tomorrow morning," although again, she didn't tell me with what. Still, I could see from her reaction that she really would have liked to come along if she had had the opportunity. Perhaps we were both storm chasers at heart.

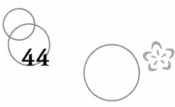

44

the tempest that wasn't

the air was especially crisp one night in autumn. After exiting the taxi, I walked briskly home, despite my utter inebriation. The clicking of my heels was rhythmic, and an original verse came to mind that fit the meter:

> *I'm usually a bitch*
> *But you're rich*
> *Lord, I can't believe*
> *I've succumbed to this*

I chanted so many words out loud, over and over again, as I walked alone along the deserted street to my apartment. Jadie hadn't worked with me in Heaven that evening. Actually, most of my coworkers had not shown up, either, seeing as a typhoon was forecast to strike the metropolitan area that evening. Tokyo was experiencing its worst typhoon season in recent history.

"Are you fucking crazy?" Jadie had asked me when I told her that I would brave the storm and head to Ginza.

"Of course, I'm crazy." I answered her criticism. "I thought you'd know that much about me by now."

"Seriously, Lea," she went on, "you should just stay home. People are dying in all these storms we're getting lately because they are stupid enough to go to work. The Japanese workaholics are dropping like flies this typhoon season!"

"I'll be careful," I rationalized in an attempt to get her off my back.

"Why do you have to go in tonight anyway?" she asked, disappointed that she couldn't dissuade me.

My reason for defying the weather was rather simple: Mama had asked me to.

As it happened, when my longtime client the Professor had called Mari earlier to inquire whether Heaven would still be open despite the storm, he mentioned that he would like to see me that evening if possible. When Mari admitted to him that she wasn't sure yet what would become of the evening, the Professor convinced her that the typhoon's behavior suggested that it would likely veer out to sea, narrowly missing the Japanese archipelago. Taking the Professor's word to heart, Mari decided that Heaven would brave the storm after all. At that point Mama called my cell phone to request my presence that night, seeing as the Professor was my customer after all.

When I arrived in Heaven late, at 9:30 P.M., I saw that Mari was vacuuming the floor and washing the tables herself. Usually this was Kento's duty, but he had taken the night off for the storm as well.

Alone in the bar with Mari, I realized that Mama still made me quite nervous. My behavior was certain to be under a microscope that evening, since I was the only hostess working so far. Being alone with Mari made me feel as if I had to do and say everything right that night, or else. I never wanted Mama Mari to feel disappointed in me, not ever. In fact, I'd braved the threat of angry weather because I didn't want her disappointed in me.

"Do you need any help?" I asked her when I entered and saw she was cleaning.

"No, no," Mari replied, "just hurry up and get changed. The Professor will be here soon."

When my customer arrived, he spent an hour lecturing me about various scientific aspects of the cyclical pattern seen in typhoon winds, and I pretended to be interested. He then took out his cell phone to check the weather on its wide screen.

"Look," he told me as he showed me a live satellite picture of a funnel storm barely brushing the edge of Honshu as it veered out to sea, "I told you the storm wouldn't hit."

"Mama Mari," the Professor called across the bar, "check out this satellite image! I told you the storm wouldn't hit!" At that, the Professor spent the rest of the evening with a more pretentious air than ever, as he was extremely proud of his accurate prediction. (Although the compliments had to come from me.) The storm itself may have likely been more tolerable.

although the skies were dry, there suddenly came a flood of unexpected customers that night. As one may expect, Mama and I were in a state of emergency seeing as there were only two of us working. Mari had to call Anica, Katria, and Saki to request that they rush into Ginza immediately to work. The three showed up at the door one by one, changed into their evening gowns, and were ready to begin pouring drinks all within the course of a half hour. It was as if they were entirely at Mari's disposal.

After more hostesses arrived, the panicked expression on Mama's face gradually subsided and gave way to a look of contentment, probably a reflection of the profits that were coming into Heaven that night.

Then, to make the mood even more heavenly, a man for whom money was no object walked into the bar just then. Upon entering he pointed to Katria and me, and said, "First request," to both of us even though we did not know the man at all. "I really am in Heaven." He made the unoriginal pun with his arms extended around both Katria and me. *So am I,* I thought to myself as he ordered an entire bottle of tequila for some 30,000 yen. His name was Mochizuki-san.

I did not feel this way because I'd be able to drink high-quality Jose Cuervo for the remainder of the evening, or because Katria and I would receive a good percentage of his expenses for being named "first request," but because Mama would be happy with me.

It is good to make money and all, but for me cash has always been a necessity rather than a passion. I neither hate it nor love it. The passion was in making Mari happy, and the way to do that was by making money. Whereas Chi-mama Angela was my teacher, Mama Mari was my muse.

Later in the night, when I convinced this man to stay for another *encho* (an extended stay), Mama-san pinched my cheeks, stared me in the eyes for a split second, and puckered her lips in a mock-kiss to express affection for me—for my role in keeping the club open for this lucrative night of business, and for doing my job right.

The night of the supposed storm had unexpectedly become a splendid evening, the stuff on which dreams were made. I felt like I was finally doing something right for a change, seeing as in the space of a year and a half after graduating from college I had been fired from two English teaching jobs and had quit my job at the Palace in an abrupt and shameful manner. I had nearly been deported more than once for my stint selling fake handbags, and all this was supplemented by the traumatically failed relationship with Nigel. I basically felt like a complete failure in my attempt to enter the real world after college, so as a result, I ate up Mama Mari's approval like chocolate.

As I've mentioned, the affinities that I tend to develop for older maternal figures are maddeningly severe. I would do anything to please Mari, anything to earn her approval, her affections, her compassion. From that night on, I realized that the road to Mama's approval was paved with good sales.

"Did I do good, Mama?" I actually asked her this, night after night, my English having been dumbed down a bit, as I was one of the only native speakers around.

"Yes, of course you did good, Ellie, you always do good," she would say, and I would just melt.

Anyway, back to the night of the storm. Mochizuki-san insisted on paying my cab fare home, so we ended up sharing a taxi that dropped me off at my apartment before taking him home. I gave the taxi driver an address about four blocks away from the apartment I shared with Jadie, since Mama had warned us to never let the customers know exactly where we lived.

Somewhere between Heaven and home, Mochizuki leaned over me in the backseat of the cab and started to kiss me. I usually slap and scold any customer that even comes close to me, but I was already in such an ecstatic mood that I felt like kissing him back. Drunk on tequila and Mama's approval, I willingly made out with a man older than my father's age in the back of a taxi for a good five or ten minutes.

Naturally, I left the cab and began to walk home with mixed feelings.

I'm usually a bitch
But you're rich
Lord, I can't believe
I've succumbed to this

lost in ukiyo

ꜰᴏʀ ᴘʀᴀᴄᴛɪᴄᴀʟ ʀᴇᴀꜱᴏɴꜱ that summer, I eventually moved into the Shinjuku apartment that Jadie had formerly shared with her ex-boyfriend.

"Did you know that you talk in your sleep?" Jadie asked me one morning, peering up from the stack of papers she was translating.

"I've heard that I do"—I had just woken up—"was I speaking in Japanese or English this time?"

"A little of both," she said, "but most of it was unintelligible."

"Oh, sorry," I mumbled, still in a semi-sleeping state, "next time I do that you have permission to hit me. Do have any idea what I was talking about?" I inquired.

"You were saying *'moshi-moshi,' 'irrashaimase,'* and 'Marui-san.'"

"Marui?" I replied disgustedly. "Ew!"

"That's what I thought, too," Jadie replied flatly.

As disturbing as it was that I was dreaming about my customers, it made perfect sense that I would see Marui-san in my sleep, seeing as Hideo Marui and I had been spending a ridiculous amount of time together since I recommenced my hostessing career.

It was a side effect of my master plan to please Mama Mari that I ended up spending much of my free time with my customers, in hopes that they would in turn feel obliged to patronize me in Heaven. This strategy worked very well, especially on nights when I waited for my customers to become extremely intoxicated before inviting them to join me for an exorbitantly priced date at my place of work. At the same time, however, I had begun to completely lose track of whether I owned my own time or not.

On the weekends, Hideo and I took trips together on the bullet train to historically rich Japanese cities such as Nikko and Kamakura for sightseeing. We also attended the world's fair expo being held in Nagoya, Aichi, that year, with the intention of sampling one glass of beer from each of the restaurants that accompanied the cultural exhibitions held by most of the world's nations. At the Asian pavilion we managed to drink domestic beers of China, Cambodia, Vietnam, Laos, the Philippines, Korea, Indonesia, and Mongolia. It was in the European pavilion, somewhere between Belgium and Germany, where we lost track of what we were drinking altogether.

As expected, Jadie was not terrifically impressed with the amount of time Dōhanman and I were spending together, even though it was completely platonic, and this became a subject of animosity between Jadie and I.

"Sometimes," Jadie would say, "you have to know when to refuse a free drink, Lea."

In retrospect, she was right.

It is Japanese custom to refill another person's glass after it is less than half empty. In such a fashion it is easy to lose track of how much one is drinking, which may partly explain how often Japanese businessmen become overly intoxicated at hostess parties or other such events. When one does not wish to drink anymore, he must leave a full glass of beer in front of himself on the table so that he is not offered any more, so a significant amount of Japanese beer gets wasted in this manner every night.

I, on the other hand, could never leave that figurative full glass in front of me.

Jadie was concerned that I was taking my hostess career too seriously. "You have to remember that this isn't a real job," she said to me on various occasions. "It's for people who don't have that many other options. But you, Lea, you have so many options. Remember that!"

I knew that Jadie was right, and every morning I woke up with a hangover I thought about quitting and finding a job that was not so treacherous for my body. I wanted to stop hostessing and I wanted to stop drinking, but I couldn't.

I didn't care about the money. Actually, I was addicted to the attention. Going out on fake dates five out of seven nights each week was not so much about the free extravagant meals, but instead, it filled the space inside of me where a real relationship was missing. The Nigel debacle had completely turned me off to the idea of a "real boyfriend," and perhaps I became entranced by all of the dōhan culture because I was afraid of another meaningful relationship.

It has been my experience that the more money that a customer spends on a lady, the less "real" emotions need be involved. So in dōhan culture, no one usually gets hurt. In this regard, the floating world is a perfect oasis for those of us who fear love. In this light my motivations were not so different from those of my customers, and I became as addicted to their attention as they were to mine.

My customers and I were "breaking up" and reconciling all of the time with little emotional repercussions. If I got sick of one customer, I simply stopped answering his calls (after all there were plenty more *salarimen* where he came from), and a customer might act the same way toward my invitations if he saw fit.

Perhaps it was then when I stopped feeling, and when I gained the ability to treat my customers in a manipulative and deceptive way that no human being should ever be treated. And when emotions stop, profits soar.

I was on fire. Mama Mari told me that I was the best hostess Heaven had ever had, and Angela constantly seated me next to the most important guests at each party. "Because you are the best," she'd tell me. The best. I swam in their approval.

On nights when I drank myself to the edge of oblivion, I was not afraid of anything, and I mistook that feeling for freedom. I was playing the part of a girl who was not me. Living and working in Japan for extended periods of time, especially in the entertainment industry, makes it easy for you to get very confused about who you are. The most successful Tokyo hostesses spend so much time acting that we fall into the part altogether, and that is why many of us stay in Japan for much longer than we intended to.

"I can't tell my dreams from reality anymore," I confessed to Jadie that morning. "Every night when we come home from Heaven and pass out, my dream begins where Heaven left off. The night just continues and the party never ends."

"Yeah, sometimes I dream that I'm still at work after a day when I work too hard," Jadie related. "I really hate those dreams."

"Then sometimes," I continued, "I wake up in the middle of the night and I think that I'm still at work in Heaven. In the dark, my clothes sitting on the dresser look like Mari, the mess of makeup on the top of the bureau is the face of a customer. Cheri is the refrigerator, and Anica is the bedpost.

"And in the morning," I continued, "I'm not sure how to distinguish my dreams from my memories."

"That's the floating world for you," Jadie replied in a cynical tone.

Once again, Jadie had made an excellent point. You know you're living in *ukiyo* when you can't tell the difference between dreams and memories anymore. You know you're lost in *ukiyo*, however, when the difference between the two becomes obsolete.

I was floating through the streets of Tokyo just as aimlessly as the smoke from the pack of cigarettes I smoked every night. Still, on the inside, that same smoke was turning my lungs black.

On one memorable night, I sat at a bar-café a block south of Heaven, waiting for Hideo to arrive. Earlier in the day, Hideo had explicitly stated that he did not want to accompany me to Heaven that evening, but only desired to have a few drinks together before-hand. Therefore my strategy, as per usual, was to wait for Hideo's face to become red with lust and alcohol, then shamelessly beg him to reconsider his decision and follow me to Heaven where he would have to pay a dōhan fee as well if we entered together.

The sheer number of times that this precise strategy had worked for me during my career as a Ginza hostess is a very sad reflection on the intellect of the male race.

I was thinking as much to myself as I took out my journal to ease my boredom, and began to write.

I am like an addiction, I'm realizing. Hideo's addiction, Mochizuki's addiction, the Professor's addiction, and so many other what's-his-name's addictions. They think they can come see me at the club just once. But no, no, my dear no. If you come to the club especially to see me, I will beg you to come back, and when you do I will drink up all the money in your bank account. Then I will ask you for dōhan, and you will accept, because you can't resist me. Yet I will not stop there, instead I will keep asking for dōhan, and you will continue to accept, because I

*will hint that the ever elusive after-party is just around the corner. But
it's all a lie; there are no corners in this circle. I have no choice but to lie,
because I have my own addictions to answer to as well: most notably,
beer and Mama.*

I looked out the window and noticed a young woman crossing
the street in front of the café dressed in full kimono, a geisha perhaps, talking on her cell phone. Geisha on a cell phone, that's Japanese modernity for you. I looked back down at my notebook, reread
what I had just written, and continued to reflect.

*And addiction is the most horrible nightmare ever inflicted upon the hu-
man race. Yet it's more real than any dream, because no one ever really
wakes up—it's there with you every day. You can have a wonderful
breakthrough one day, saying with all the sincerity you've ever known
that you hate it and you never want to see it again. But the next day it
will be back, asking you to join it again on its little crusade to hell, and
you will want to and have to with everything you are and more.*

At that, Marui-san arrived.

46

a somber mood came over all of Japan in early August of 2005 as the sixtieth anniversary of the atomic bombings of Hiroshima and Nagasaki steadily approached. The feeling was intensified for my friend Jadie, as she was working during the day as an interpreter for a documentary being made by an independent American filmmaker on the subject of atomic bomb survivors.

I had already been doing some written translation work around Tokyo, and was interested in making the bridge over to the much more challenging field of simultaneous interpretation. Therefore, Jadie invited me to shadow her at her interpretation job, as a sort of interpreter-in-training. It was there that we had the unique experience of meeting a survivor of the nuclear bombing of Hiroshima.

When we arrived together at the train station nearest to the location of the day's filming, the director's assistant was late to meet us.

"Is she not Japanese?" I asked Jadie jokingly.

"She is Japanese," Jadie replied with a frown, "that's why I'm beginning to get worried."

The two of us peered over the edge of the station platform onto the street below.

"Hey, there's a little old lady down there," I informed my friend. "Maybe she's the one we're interviewing," I mused, nodding my head at a less than five-foot-tall older woman with a hunched back and a cane.

"What are we going to say to her," Jadie jested, *"sumimasen, hibakusha desu ka?"* Excuse me, are you a *hibakusha? Hibakusha* is the Japanese term that specifically refers to the survivors of the atomic bomb.

"No, I guess we can't say that," I conceded.

"I think today's interviewee is a man anyway," she continued.

In due time, we were met by the director's assistant and an avalanche of profuse apologies for her being seven minutes late. At that, she walked us to the tea shop where the filming would take place.

"It is Japanese custom to take your shoes off," a small man with a gentle face told us as we entered in Japanese.

At that, Jadie and I gave each other the first of many knowing glances. It would have been nice if he assumed that we knew as much already, seeing as we were the interpreters after all, but we let it go because he was old.

"So who's the *hibakusha?"* I whispered to Jadie as we changed into our slippers.

"I think it's him," she said, nodding at the man who had just told us to take our shoes off.

"Really?" I asked. "But he doesn't look old enough." Between his small stature and his red suspenders, the man looked almost child-like to me.

"There are some very old Japanese people who look much younger," she said, having full authority on the issue, being half Japanese herself.

As a matter of course, we had to be treated to tea and cakes before any actual production could take place. It was there that Jadie introduced me to the director. We explained that while Jade was the main interpreter, I had come along as her assistant, and would clarify her translations only when needed.

At that he instructed Jadie to sit opposite where the *hibakusha* was seated, just outside of the camera's bright lights, and me, slightly further out of sight among a group of assistants at a different table.

Since filming hadn't started yet, the two other women at the table immediately introduced themselves to me as members of a peace organization in Tokyo, volunteer assistants at the taping. I explained that I was a volunteer, as well, because I was studying to be an interpreter, and that I was very interested in what would transpire at the taping.

"You know that woman?" one of them asked, nodding at Jadie.

"Yes," I said, "very well. She is helping me train to be an interpreter."

"She is so great," the other woman said to me, "she is so professional and stylish, and she speaks perfectly in English and Japanese. Is she *hafu?*"

"Yes," I confirmed, "half Japanese and half American."

"*Erai ne,*" the two declared almost in unison, expressing Jade's distinguished position at the taping, although she was out of the spotlight. Only the director and the *hibakusha* would be on film. The three of us recognized, however, that it was Jade who was really making it all happen. The two men would not have been able to communicate upward of two words together if not for her assistance.

"That's my best friend!" I wanted to proudly declare. But with pride being an unacceptable emotion in the cultural context, I simply nodded my head knowingly.

After a couple of false starts, it was decided that the cast would take a break while the crew made some necessary adjustments to the lighting. At that, Jadie and the director moved over to my table.

"What I'm trying to do in these interviews," the director told us in a slightly pretentious manner, "is humanize the A-bomb survivors. I want to bring out aspects of their personalities—aside from their experience after the bomb—that everyone can relate to."

Jadie and I nodded quietly, as if at work in Heaven.

"The last man I interviewed," the director said with a grin, "when I asked him about his hobbies, replied that his favorite activity was drinking beer and watching girls, and that was just a perfect example, I think."

When the director left our table to attend to other business, Jadie and I looked at each other again, and smirked. "Drinking beer and watching girls," I mumbled sarcastically.

"I can certainly relate to that," Jadie chimed in, "how about you?"

"Watching girls is my favorite activity," I said in a sarcastic tone. "Something everyone can surely relate to indeed."

Soon after, the filming of the interview began. Through its course, I realized that I had much more studying to do in order to achieve the degree of bilingualism that Jade was fortunate enough to have been raised with. The man used many complicated words and phrases that had me constantly glued to my electronic dictionary.

I could follow his story in more detail when he began to speak directly about his experiences on the day the bomb hit, if only because it was similar to the countless other stories I had read or heard about: a blinding flash of light, a deafening bang, then, the closest thing to hell on earth that humanity may have ever experienced.

This man was in Hiroshima when the bomb went off, I thought to myself as I watched him speak, and it felt surreal for some reason. He was nine years old at the time, and was trapped beneath his house with his younger brother, aged six, for hours after the explosion.

Of all things, I saw myself developing a new admiration and re-spect for Jadie as she translated the director's questions and com-municated the man's responses as literally as possible without being able to give any direct input of her own, saving the careful choice of words.

It was a stern topic for all involved, but visibly more difficult for Jadie than anyone else involved in the filmmaking process, save the A-bomb victim himself. She had to process his wrenching story in Japanese, then attempt to give it justice in English. In order to do so, she had to fathom his tragedy in Japanese, in English, and also in-side of a certain gap between the two languages where there were only ideas and no words.

There was no escaping the harsh reality.

Then, the inevitable happened. "When he and his brother were finally rescued from underneath his collapsed house by his parents," Jadie began to translate, then paused. The entire room was silent as she searched for the right words, which seemed to not be coming. When I got an opportunity to see Jadie's face, however, I saw that the reason she had stopped speaking was because my friend was fighting back tears.

A few moments later, Jadie took a deep breath. "They realized that his six-year-old-brother was already dead," she quickly uttered before tears began streaming down her face uncontrollably. At this, the director's assistant gave Jadie a tissue and a hug, and the filming continued without further incident.

When the interview was finally complete, I put my arm around Jadie and we walked back to the train station in silence, both of us visibly moved by the *hibakusha*'s story.

As we approached the station, one of us finally spoke. "This is the second time this has happened to me!" Jadie exclaimed. To my sur-prise, she was livid with herself. "This is the second time I've cried while translating an interview. This is so unprofessional! I totally suck!"

"That is so untrue!" I exclaimed in surprise. "You did not suck at all! In fact, you were awesome! We were all so impressed by your language skills, and everyone in the room was moved by your empathy. It was not an easy story to translate."

"I should have kept my composure," she said, nodding her head with her eyes to the street.

"Not at all!" I retorted.

"Really?" she asked.

"Everyone thought you were great," I reassured her, "and I was so proud to be your friend today."

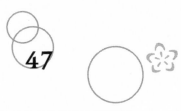

the art of destruction

Women's bodies . . . what peculiar creatures they were;
and the continual flux between the outside and the inside,
taking things in, giving them out, chewing, words, potato
chips, burps, grease, hair, babies, milk, excrement, cookies,
vomit, coffee, tomato juice, blood, tea, sweat, liquor, tears,
and garbage . . .

—MARGARET ATWOOD, *The Edible Woman*

three days later, I lost my voice from singing and throwing up.

Belting out karaoke tunes on a nightly basis takes a natural toll on the vocal cords. And when drinking is your job, everyone has her own strategies for keeping it down, the most popular among which are taking speed and throwing up. Personally, I was partial to vomiting.

Having much experience in the precision of self-induced vomiting, I could throw up and start drinking again at a rate faster than anyone else at the Palace. And I was almost proud of this. After all, everyone knew that the more I could throw up, the more I was worth. Literally.

That night, I came to work after a dōhan with the Professor. Dōhans were dangerous for me lately, inasmuch as the expensive meals and drinks involved almost always resulted in my arriving at Heaven already drunk, despite the night of drinking I had yet to undertake. Such was the case that Friday night, when the Professor and I drank copious amounts of fine sake at one of Ginza's more traditional Japanese restaurants.

After we arrived at Heaven, I threw up as much sake as I could while pretending to touch up my makeup for him in the rest room. Then I went to change into my evening dress, where I had a brief opportunity to speak to Mama in the dressing room.

"Sorry about my voice," I rasped. "I wasn't going to come in tonight but the Professor wanted a dōhan so I had no choice."

"Don't worry," Mama said with a grin, visibly pleased with the business I had brought into the club that evening, "your voice sounds sexy like that."

It was sexy to be in pain, I was coming to realize, as I joined the Professor at his table. For an hour and a half we drank tequila and I listened to him sing karaoke, unable to join in—as I usually liked to do—for my lack of voice.

The strain has to go somewhere, I thought to myself after the Professor left and I was standing over the toilet again for the second time that night. *The men who come in just to insult us, the men who come in to steal our energy, the men who project their dreams onto us, the strain has to go somewhere.* I liked to think that all the stress I was feeling was disappearing down the porcelain toilet as I pressed the electronic flush button. In the real world, however, there is no such perfect metaphor.

Next, Angela sat me next to a *kaicho* again.

"This man is very important," she told me, "so *gambatte ne.*"

After I did my job dutifully again and convinced the important man to extend his group's stay two times, Angela took me aside and looked into my quite drunken face with one hand on each of my shoulders.

"I sat you there because you are the best," she admitted. "Even without your voice you are the best. I knew you could do it, Ellie." At that, I bowed my head to hide the melty smile her approval had brought to my face. Then I headed toward the bathroom to throw up again.

When I saw blood hit the porcelain, however, as aesthetically pleasing as the red on white appeared to my blurry vision, I knew that I'd reached my limit. I had to stop vomiting for the night. *I want to throw up my life,* I thought to myself, standing over the same toilet for the third time that evening. *This lifestyle I have now is just not working.* My throat stung like I'd swallowed a handful of thorns.

Superstar though I was, there's nothing so humbling as having your head in a toilet.

I wish that I had some heartrending reason for doing what I did after that, some poignant story to tell. But I don't. I wish I could say that my next customer tried to touch me, or tried to grope a friend. That might have justified what I did, and it was what I would claim happened afterward, still, the truth was nothing of the sort.

Basically, I had just reached the edge of emotional oblivion, which left me feeling indifferent to everyone and everything

From all I remember, the man was sitting with a male companion, whom apparently he hadn't seen in years. I tried to strike up a conversation with him, but all he wanted to do was speak with his friend. I was not used to such a lack of attention. Perhaps it was the sheer drunkenness, or my unconscious reluctance to be the best. It was nice to be loved, just as well to be hated, but God forbid I ever be ignored.

"Urusai," I said, my belligerence exceedingly inappropriate for the situation. Jewel looked over at me, the fear evident in her eyes, but before she could intervene on my behalf the man signaled Kento. He pointed to me and then made a gesture that suggested I be taken away from the table, as if he were swatting away a bug.

So I hit him. Actually, I punched him, straight in the face with a fist. It was the first time I'd ever punched anyone, and it hurt my hand. Kento saw. Jewel saw. Still, everyone else at the club was looking away at Anica, who was singing "Girl" for the second time that night.

After that, all hell broke loose. The man was obviously very upset, and threatened to call the police on the club. Within a few minutes, Mari instructed Jewel to take me home since we lived together, and all of the hostesses in Heaven who did not possess a proper visa were asked to go home as well.

"What the hell were you thinking!" Jewel screamed at me, with reason, as we walked down the Ginza to rush into the cab. "If the police come, then Heaven is going to have to pay a huge fine!"

"I didn't like him," I said calmly.

"What?" Jadie asked me in disbelief.

"I don't know." I somehow managed to put a sentence together out of my daze. "I don't know anything anymore."

I didn't dare open my mouth again for about ten minutes, then my cell phone rang.

"Everything is okay," Mari informed me. "The man is not going to call the police."

"Really?" I asked. "I'm so sorry about this, Mama." Mari's voice had brought me back to a semblance of sanity, if only for the moment.

"Everything is going to be fine," she continued. "In places where people drink, things like this happen all the time. I will see you again tomorrow night, right?"

"Yes, Mama," I said gratefully.

I may well be the only Ginza hostess to have ever punched a customer and kept her job.

"What did she say?" Jadie asked me, her tone flat.

"Everything's fine," I replied. "Mama says everything's fine."

" 'Everything's fine'!"—to my surprise, Jadie's anger began to overflow—"Do you really believe that? That everything's fine? Lea, you almost gave all of us a heart attack! Don't you feel sorry about that at all? If he called the police everyone might have gotten arrested. Do you even realize what you've done?"

"Mari told me that he's not going to call the police," I restated. "Sorry," I said as an afterthought.

"Sorry isn't good enough anymore," Jadie said angrily. "I'm so sick of your drinking too much and getting out of control. I could be working for two more hours, but instead I have to take you home. When are you going to fucking grow up?"

"Leave me alone." I turned toward the window of our cab, accidentally lighting a cigarette backward. Upon realizing as much, I casually threw it out onto the street and lit up another one, as if the mistake had been intentional.

"You don't even consider the consequences of your actions." Jade's fury was relentless. "And you care about nobody but yourself. You think that you are the queen of your own little universe, and I am fucking sick of it . . . you should have gotten fired for this."

"You're just jealous"—my drunken belligerence had reignited— "because Mari said that I'm the best hostess Heaven's ever had."

"Big fucking deal!" Jadie exclaimed, "I love how you think that's anything of an accomplishment! As if hostessing were a real job."

"It's stressful, you know," I retorted, "being seated next to the most important clients all night long. But I suppose you don't know what that feels like."

"Are you gonna hit me, too, now?" she slurred sarcastically, being a bit drunk herself.

"No, but I'm moving out." I tried to shout back despite my lack of voice.

"Good! When do you leave?" my ex-friend exclaimed.

"As soon as possible!" I assured her.

After that, there was a sad and angry silence that endured for the rest of the night.

weekend at Bread man's

When I called Hideo the next morning, inquiring about a place to stay, once again it was not a matter of why, if, or how, but of when. That is to say, how soon I could move into the extra room he had in the apartment above his family's store in Nihombashi. At present, he was sharing the apartment with his younger sister. My room would be adjacent to hers.

Hideo was the one customer I could always count on to save my ass in times of trouble, if only because he wasn't married and therefore had the extra time on his hands. I was slightly confused as to why he was unmarried. After all, he wasn't that hideous to look at, but his appearance paled in comparison to the simple fact that he was filthy rich.

On top of that he was a pretty nice guy, as far as Japanese men go, so it shouldn't have been the case that he couldn't find a wife. He was most likely single by choice, a bit of an oddity in Japanese society, where maintaining the bloodline is so important. Perhaps Hideo just didn't want to grow up.

The song "Tsunami," which we often sang at karaoke together, contains a lyric that reads *"otona ni narenai,"* meaning "I can't become an adult." There was always a certain passion in Hideo's eyes when he sang that lyric, so maybe he was still unmarried because he couldn't manage to grow up and settle down despite his age. Then again, his eyes may just as well have been reflecting only the passion in mine as I felt the words of the song myself.

For the entire weekend I stayed at Hideo's apartment, I was basically inconsolable. After all, I had just lost my best friend. Hideo tried to remedy my depression in the only way he knew how: by buying me things, buying me many, many things. After we went jewelry shopping and dress shopping and shoe shopping, I did my best to pretend to be cheered up, still the weight of the shopping bags just made my soul feel heavier.

Hideo and I ate out for every meal, and every time I ordered a significant amount of beer. Sometimes it made me feel better, sometimes it made me feel worse.

I was also in the company of Akiko, his younger sister. As Hideo explained to me, her husband had recently died of cancer the previous year at a very young age, leaving Akiko widowed at barely thirty. All of her Japanese girlfriends, Hideo had told me, were married and too busy with their families to visit Akiko very often.

Spending time with Akiko was the only thing that could cheer me up in the slightest degree, if only because I knew that by keeping her company I was doing something good instead of something bad for a change. When I visited her room, she showed me her deceased husband's golfing trophies and a photo album of the two of them together.

On Saturday night, the three of us went out to a Thai restaurant in Odaiba, then sang karaoke. I let Hideo and Akiko sing most of the songs, which was uncharacteristic of me. I only plugged in a song to sing myself if I sensed that Hideo was worried about my mood. Since he was the one paying for the evening out, it was imperative that I pretend to be having a good time, despite circumstances.

While inside the karaoke box, I received a text message from Jadie on my cellular phone. I opened it carefully, holding my breath. I read the first line: "Dammit I hope you're happy . . ." she had written. That was enough, I snapped my phone shut as if by reflex, I couldn't read anymore. I would have gone into convulsions with grief. As we walked home that night, I took Dōhanman's arm in mine. When I was with Hideo I was not myself, and pretending to be someone else entirely was the only coping mechanism I had left.

When we returned to his apartment, I said that I felt dizzy and was encouraged to lie down. If Jadie and I were no longer friends, I pondered, then Dōhanman would insist that I stay at his house indefinitely, and this could not happen. Our entire fake relationship was based upon fantasy and mystery, and if we spent too much more time together it would all be spoiled. Not to mention, he might start expecting things. Staring at the possibility that I was gradually becoming that girl who I pretended to be in my customer's presence, a new wave of desperation hit me.

Truly at my wits' end, I locked the door of the room where I was supposed to be resting and called my mom. When my mother answered the phone, she knew it had to be important, because I never called. In fact, I don't think I had called my mom even once during my entire stay in Japan before that night; it was always she who called me.

"I think I might be ready to come home," I told her.

"That's good!" she exclaimed. My mother had been a proponent of my coming home since I first got fired from my teaching job.

At that, my mother remarked that she would inquire whether it was already too late to apply for tuition remission at the graduate department of the private university where she worked as faculty. I had already taken the GREs years ago, before leaving the country.

"Are you sure you're okay, Lea?" she asked as our conversation wound up. "You don't sound so good."

"I'm fine," I said, brushing her off.

After hanging up the phone, I lay on the unfamiliar bed and stared at the ceiling. One week earlier I would never have even pondered going home, I was at the top of the Ginza hostess ladder after all. *I am just so volatile,* I thought to myself. *I am habitually volatile, even, like an earthquake waiting to surface: over and over again. This happens over and over and over again.*

"Tomorrow," I told Hideo before going to bed, "I want to go to that place you've told me about where you go into a room and go through the simulated experience of a great earthquake." In retrospect, I was coping with my instability by applying such symbolism to my own moods. The entire situation made me wonder if people sometimes use metaphor because the truth is too painful to grasp on its own, without some distortion.

So on Sunday, Hideo took me to the natural disaster safety learning center in Honjo. Seeing as I had a curiously morbid fascination with earthquakes in general, I had been begging Hideo for months to take me to the museum where they could simulate an 8.0 earthquake for guests to experience.

When we first arrived, we saw a 3-D movie that simulated the destruction that might befall the city of Tokyo if it were to experience an earthquake of the same magnitude as the one that destroyed the entire city in 1923. Then we had to put on wet suits to enter the typhoon simulation room. Last came what most of the guests were there to experience, the earthquake simulation chamber, where we had to stand in a foam-covered semblance of a kitchen. When the chamber began shaking, we had to see how quickly we could turn off the gas stove, put a pillow over our heads, and duck under the fake table. The entire experience felt disturbingly like Disneyland, except with natural disaster simulations instead of rides.

On Sunday night the two of us went out to dinner again with Akiko, and before we went to sleep that night we were all watching TV together in the living room. For a while Hideo stopped the remote on a news special commemorating the anniversary of the bombings of Hiroshima and Nagasaki, but almost as soon as the program appeared, Hideo changed the channel to a program about cute little puppies. Personally, I would have rather watched the documentary about the war, but Dōhanman was holding the remote control.

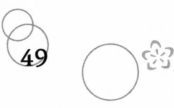

49

tears in Heaven

that monday morning I woke up with a blinding hangover, compounded by the knowledge that I would have to face Jadie in Heaven that night. Still inconsolable, I had to keep going. *I have to be like Courtney Love,* I thought to myself, *that night last year when she performed in New York just out of jail.* In order to disguise how miserable I had been feeling all weekend I would have to give the performance of my life that night, and I knew it.

Jadie and I completely ignored each other for the first two hours of the night, which was nothing less than excruciating. Later on I was outside doing *bira*, pondering how I was going to tell the mamas that I would have to quit, when Mama Mari came outside with some *bira* in her hand and stood beside me. Mari never did *bira*, so it seemed as if she had come outside specifically to speak to me, under the pretense of doing *bira*.

This is it, I thought to myself, *she's come to fire me. Jadie talked to her and convinced her to fire me.*

Instead, however, Mari's intentions were nothing of the sort.

"Inside the club," she informed me, "Jewel is very upset. Did the two of you have a fight or something?" Mama inquired.

"She is upset?" I was honestly surprised. I honestly thought that I was doing her a favor by leaving the apartment. She had seemed so fed up with my presence after all.

"I can't talk about it now," I warned Mama. "I'm going to cry."

"What happened between you two?" Mama asked. "I thought the both of you were such good friends."

"The things that were said," I explained, "the damage is unfixable. We can't be friends anymore." At that I lost my composure and tears began streaming down my face.

Mama took me by the elbow and we moved from the street, into the foyer of Heaven's building, as if my well-being was more important than drawing customers into the bar, if just for the moment. There, Mari took a tissue out of her handbag and dutifully dried my tears in the subserviently maternal manner that she, and all mamas, were accustomed to.

"I'm sorry," I told her, knowing that crying on the job would have been grounds for dismissal at the Palace. Still Mari paid no attention to my apology.

"She is only angry at you because she cares about you," Mari lectured.

"But she treats me like a child!" I lamented.

"You are a child," Mari reminded me.

"No, I'm not," I whined, "I'm already twenty-four." At that, Mari's cell phone rang, which she had to attend to immediately.

"I can go back outside now," I said, my tears having stopped.

"Okay," Mama replied, "just thirty more minutes, okay?"

"Okay," I assured Mama, as she reentered the building to attend to whatever business she had been called about.

And for ten minutes I stood there, still as usual, trying not to cry.

Then I took out my phone and reread the message I received from Jadie the morning after I left. I read it through again, since it had been too painful to read it thoroughly before.

"Well, I hope you're happy," she had written. "Maybe you are so used to hurting people that you don't care, but when I realized that you had left the apartment, my heart felt like it had been ripped out. The worst part is that drinking too much and hurting people is an habitual behavior for you. So go ahead and keep associating with people who don't give a shit about you, and alienating your real friends who care about you. I don't give a fuck anymore. I hope you're happy."

Until that moment I hadn't responded. I opened my phone with a shaking palm, and began entering text. *There really is a freedom in abandoning all of one's pride when necessary,* I reminded myself.

> Jade, Jewel, I am so, so, so sorry that I hurt you. Everything was my fault. If you could find some way to forgive me, can we ever be friends again? I miss you. You're my best friend. I love you. Lea.

After pressing the SEND button I shut my phone immediately. I didn't know how I was ever going to enter Heaven again if I didn't receive a reply from Jadie within the remaining twenty minutes I was designated to be standing outside. I had to leave the street and go back into the foyer again, where at that moment I shed more tears than I had during the course of our entire fight.

After about five minutes of crying, my phone buzzed. I checked the number to see that the message was from Jadie inside the bar.

"When can you move back in," she wrote.

"I can stop drinking," I replied. "Your friendship is worth so much more to me than alcohol."

"You don't have to stop completely," she wrote, "just learn your limits."

At that, my cell phone rang. "You must come back inside immediately," Mari's voice announced, "there is a customer here who likes to talk to American girls." As she said that, Mari hung up before I could reply at all. I can see why she did so, because my next question would have certainly been whether I was about to work opposite Jewel.

As I reentered the bar, stopping first in the bathroom to wipe the mascara off of my face, I was not surprised to find out that this would be the case. If the customer had wanted only one American girl, Jewel would have sufficed. But no, he wanted both of us at his table. In this respect I can see how it was in Mari's interest that Jewel and I be on civil terms with each other again.

Jewel and I were not really allowed to talk to each other while entertaining a customer, but there were other ways of communicating.

"Can we sing a song for you?" I asked the customer.

"A song just for me?" he replied, blushing.

"Yes," Jewel joined in, "a special song just for you."

"Wanna sing Madonna?" I glanced in Jewel's direction.

"Okay," she said, putting in the song "True Blue."

Entertaining drunken Japanese men gives one an unwritten license to exaggerate all sentimentality and push the limits of utter cheesiness. As we sang Madonna's kitschy lyrics about love and friendship, I couldn't help smirk at the idea that this man actually thought we were singing about him.

Then after we finished singing, the inevitable happened: the customer asked us if we wanted to order drinks for ourselves. After Jewel ordered a glass of red wine, it was my turn.

"Yes!" I said impulsively. Refusing drinks simply didn't happen at hostess bars, since our salary depended on how much we could drink.

"And what would the lady like?" He turned to me.

"Orange juice!" was my reply, which cost him just as much money as it would have if I'd ordered a cocktail. Still, I was exhibiting such a beaming smile as I uttered the words that he could hardly question my choice.

Jadie was smiling as well by then, and both of our smiles, although they were actually intended for each other, were enough to knock out any man who got caught between us.

One of the last songs that night was sung by Katria's customer, with whom Jadie and I were also sharing a table. Mama had placed two extra ladies at the table in hopes that he would buy all of us drinks, a strategy that was working well as usual.

"Would you like to sing something?" I asked, taking the remote control in my hand as Katria fixed the man's drink.

"You know Eric Crapton?" he asked.

"Do you want to sing 'Tears in Heaven'?" I guessed correctly, somehow keeping a straight face. "Tears in Heaven" was one of the more popular karaoke songs in Japan at the time, and Japanese businessmen are strikingly predictable. I entered the song into the machine.

"The song called 'Tears in Heaven,' and we in Heaven," the man said through chuckles. "But I not sad. I very, very happy!" he said as he put one arm around me and the other around Katria. Jadie and I let out a few giggles, as if we didn't hear some version of that same pun every night, and soon the man began to sing.

In spite of his intoxication, this particular man's singing voice was not really that bad. The customer wrapped up the song's final verse with more clarity than most, expressing the heartrending lament of a songwriter who questioned whether he belonged in Heaven.

"It's true, you know," Jadie said to me through the applause as she placed a tipsy head on my shoulder, "we don't belong here."

Her comment made me sigh, as I took a look around the bar to witness the usual scene.

"Who does?" I replied.

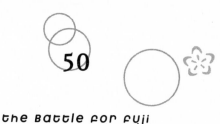

50

the Battle for Fuji

"So how long will you be in New York?" Jadie asked.

She and I were sitting beside each other on the two-hour-long bus ride from Shinjuku Station to the foot of Mount Fuji. Although it was August, our backpacks were nonetheless packed with sweaters, mittens, scarves, and fleece hats.

"The first semester is four months," I told her. "Then I plan to come back here for the holidays to work and make more money. There's no way I would be able to move out of my parents' house unless I can bring in a hostess's salary over the break. The cost of living is way too high."

"I don't want you to go," she said.

"I don't want to go, either," I reminded her, "but at the graduate program at the university where my mom works I can only get tuition remission as a part of her benefits package before I turn twenty-five. A free ride at a private university these days is no joke, so I've gotta take it before it's too late."

"You lucky bitch!" Jadie snapped affectionately.

"You think?" I asked. "I'm pretty indifferent to it all."

"What will you study?" she asked.

"Asian Studies," I sighed.

"You should be teaching Asian Studies," she complimented me.

"Yeah, right." I brushed her off. "I see it as a way to kill time until I figure out what I'm doing with my life."

"Join the club." My friend could relate. "But really, Lea, what am I going to do here without you?" she whined.

"Relax. You just like having me around because I'm crazier than you," I teased. "When you're standing next to me, you look completely sane!"

"Hey," she said, mockingly, "that's not *entirely* true—"

"Jade-chan!" a male voice interrupted as someone playfully kicked the back of my friend's seat. We turned around to greet our company on the trip: Jadie's recent boyfriend Taro and two of his Japanese male friends, all of whom occupied the seats behind us.

"How do we look?" Taro asked. The three young men were sitting upright with their new matching climbing hats. Each headpiece consisted of various black elastic head straps that attached to a flashlight which protruded from each man's forehead.

"You look like you're wearing your underwear on your head," Jadie teased him before turning back around.

"So you're definitely coming back in December?" she asked as she continued our conversation.

"Yeah," I said, "I've even gotten the Professor to buy my ticket."

"Wow," she reflected, "you're good."

Outside the window of the bus, the sun had nearly completed its descent. It was all according to schedule: we would disembark from the bus by ten in the evening, then complete the approximately seven-hour climb through the course of the night. If successful, we would be able to view the next morning's sunrise from the summit.

Climbing Mount Fuji, or Fuji-san as it is called in Japanese (the "san" means "mountain" in context) was something I had been meaning to do since arriving in Japan. The third climbing season was about to slip by when I finally braved my hangover and set off for the infamous hike among some friends.

There are ten stations of Mount Fuji, with the first being at the base of the mountain and the tenth at its highest point. The road only runs until the fifth station, after which point the terrain becomes too treacherous for driving. Like the majority of climbers, the fifth station was where we disembarked.

When we got off the bus, our group of five immediately began to put on our winter clothes in order to adapt to the altitude's low temperatures. After having a snack, we began our climb. The first couple of hours consisted of a walk along a gradual uphill slope in the darkness, through the course of which the guys warmed up their muscles while Jadie and I played flashlight tag.

When the course got rough, I didn't want to let on to Jadie that I was getting tired at all, so I made sure to keep my pace. I did not want to do anything to confirm Jadie's belief that my less than healthy lifestyle of drinking and smoking was catching up with me.

Once our trail ceased to be so gentle an incline and began to require the gripping of designated chains and ropes in order to climb nearly vertical sequences of volcanic rock, it became harder and harder to pretend everything was okay. Somehow, however, I continued the same pattern for long enough that my body kept pushing ahead without protest.

I remembered how years earlier it was one symptom of my eating disorder that I insisted on running six miles every day, even when it was ninety degrees outside. So truthfully, climbing the mountain at night didn't seem so challenging by comparison.

Around the time we all had reached the seventh station, I started to wonder whether Jadie was going to make it to the top. She had this look of anguish in her face that seemed to express the very depths of human pain and exhaustion.

"You should go ahead," she told the group. "I need to rest here before going any farther." I wanted to stay with her, but I also wanted to get to the top in time for the sunrise. So Taro stayed behind with her while his two friends and I walked on.

After leaving Jade and Taro in the volcanic ash at station seven, Taro's friends and I kept a steady pace at first, as we climbed together upon the rocks and volcanic ash. Ryo led our group, followed by Akira and then myself. When the path widened for a while, however, an interesting dynamic began to take place. Akira passed ahead of Ryo casually, which led to Ryo's accelerating his pace to regain the lead. I noticed the pattern repeat itself a few times although the two men did not utter one word to each other concerning their silent race.

It did not occur to me until after the fact that Akira and Ryo may have been trying to impress me. Instead, I recalled something that a customer in Heaven had told me when I told him of my plans to climb the mountain.

"Please be careful," he told me, "the climb to the top of Mount Fuji is so challenging that it was forbidden for women to climb it until the beginning of the Meiji era."

This customer had never actually climbed to the top of Mount Fuji himself, but to point that out was against the rules of conversation.

There was never a doubt in my mind whether I would reach the top of the mountain without giving up. Quitting is not something I do, especially in the face of a once-in-a-lifetime experience. At the same time, however, I never could have anticipated the burst of adrenaline that befell me.

The rush I felt gave way to a competitive spirit so instinctual it felt almost primal. I suddenly had something to prove. If this was indeed a race, I wanted to play, too.

So it was that I casually passed by my two acquaintances on the uphill trail, and maintained my lead until I looked over my shoulder from station nine and the two were no longer in sight.

Hostessing had really instilled in me a certain competitive and even warlike mentality concerning my relationships with basically all members of the male race. So when I could no longer see Akira and Ryo, I was still in competition with every penis-wielding human on the mountain.

And there was the clock as well: I had to reach the top of Mount Fuji before the sun rose again. The wind was blowing in my face, as if its intent was to push me off the mountain entirely. Still, the resistance and my refusal to be blown back only made me feel stronger. It was an unspeakably thrilling phenomenon, the likes of which I had never experienced before.

The feeling lasted until I was almost at the very top, when something very, very irritating happened: there was a traffic jam. Looking up in the gradually brightening sky, I could see a line of hikers, much like myself, standing neatly in line for what was the last half mile of the climb.

I was utterly disappointed. I fucking hate waiting in lines. In fact, I avoid Disneyland and other amusement parks for this very reason. The crawl to the top took up a sluggish hour and a half of what should have been my ten-minute victory run. I ended up watching the sun rise while sandwiched between strangers, all waiting to get to the peak.

When I did reach the top, I fell asleep on a rock until my entourage found me and woke me up. "Sorry we lost one another," I mumbled to an audience who was too tired to care. At that, the five of us ate ramen and napped in a crowded hut. Some hours later we circled the crater at the summit, then headed back down.

The route down the mountain was different than the one we had taken on the way up, and it was largely composed of zigzagging trails of volcanic ash and rock. Jadie had hurt her ankle during the upward climb, so I let her use my shoulder as a crutch.

It is far easier to be a good friend while walking down a mountain than it is to be supportive on the way up.

"Now I know why the Japanese say that no one ever climbs Mount Fuji twice," she whined. "Anyone who would put themselves through an experience so hellishly difficult for a second time would have to be a total masochist."

"It wasn't all that bad," I countered. "Some aspects of the hike were kind of fun."

"You're crazy!" my friend replied.

A week later, as I took off for "home" from Tokyo's Narita Airport, a part of me wondered if going home again might feel like the descent from Mount Fuji. That is to say, if it might somehow resemble lowering my head out of the clouds and planting my feet back on the ground. It might be good for me "to touch base," or at least that was what my mom had lectured me over the phone.

As my plane landed, however, there was no way I could have known how little foundation existed for me in New York anymore.

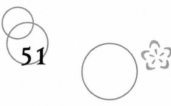

51

my so·called escape

ıt was hard to believe that just six weeks earlier I had been standing at the top of Mount Fuji. By the fall of 2005, I was feeling fully deflated.

"You're aware that we don't have the resources to be calling Japan to verify any of these references." The gray-haired woman peered at me over the rims of her glasses while she scanned my résumé. "Don't you have any former employers in the immediate area?" she asked.

"I left the country when I was eighteen," I explained, "and haven't lived here for any significant amount of time since." I'm sure I appeared awkward, seeing how preoccupied I was just trying keep myself from bowing during every instance that would have called for such a thing in Asia. It seemed that whenever I gave a greeting, received an introduction, or felt some form of gratitude, this caused my backbone to inadvertently liquefy. Before I knew it I'd be staring at the ground.

This woman was only one of many human resources workers

who viewed my lack of local references as a red flag. After the same situation more or less repeated itself in the company of various potential employers, I decided to set my sights lower.

"Isn't it time you got a *real* job?" the woman at the clothing store in the Walt Whitman Mall inquired after realizing that I was a graduate student.

You have no idea, I wanted to reply.

Seeing as I had expressed no interest in relearning to drive on the right side of the road, my mother drove me home from the mall that day. I felt like a teenager again.

How did this happen? I silently asked myself as I sat in the passenger's seat observing the familiar blocks and street corners of the village where I grew up. After all, I had left this town six years earlier with plans of global domination. Presently, however, I couldn't even find myself a part-time job so that I might afford my own apartment. The fact was dawning on me that I would have no other option but to live with my parents for the duration of my stay in America, and it depressed me immensely.

This is not what my homecoming was supposed to be like, I lamented to myself.

Then again, I reminded myself, *I never did like it here.*

I moved to Montreal after high school, largely because McGill was the farthest from home of all the universities I had been accepted to. Instead of coming home during my first summer vacation from college, I left the continent entirely to go study in Paris. It was this progression of events that brought me to Tokyo, where I began my adult life in one of the farthest places from home that I could find while managing to remain on the same planet.

This in mind, my return was a lot like the fated snap of an overextended rubber band that has finally run out of stamina: it stung. I wondered if I had finally burned out, as my mother had always warned me would happen if I kept rushing through life stages, overextending myself and diving headfirst into any goal-oriented endeavor I could either find or create for myself.

What if she has been right? I asked myself. Just the thought made me cringe.

As far as university was concerned, my graduate courses were easy enough. This allowed me to jump onto a fast track that would get me a master's degree by the following June. Still, I couldn't seem to fit in at my new school.

Other people said that they wanted to hear about life in Japan, yet they generally started to lose interest when they noticed that Japan was the only topic on which I could manage to hold a conversation. Everything else was scarily unfamiliar to me, and I was always making others snicker at my pop culture slipups. When attempting to hold conversations regarding television shows, for example, I had to be told what the acronyms CSI and OC actually stood for. As well, I was partially corrected when others learned of my honest belief that Paris Hilton was primarily famous for being a porn star.

At that, I made an attempt to become culturally educated by flipping through various late-night talk shows. In this I discovered the maddening degree to which contemporary media in America is almost entirely self-referential, making it largely impossible for any cultural outsider to understand. Comedy isn't funny when you don't understand any of the pop-culture references, so I tired of the new hobby quickly. Having been out of the country for so long, American culture felt like a constant joke whose punch line I would never get.

Still, some forms of cultural illiteracy can be more harmful than others.

In addition to heightening my desire for liquor, life in Japan for the past few years had made me incredibly naïve in some respects. In fact, I realize now that I was in such a hurry to leave North America after graduating college that I never learned how to act like an adult within my own culture. And since I'd never been legally allowed to drink in my own country before, I had no idea how dangerous it is to be a drunk girl out at bars in America. As it turned out, I had been taking Tokyo's low crime rates entirely for granted.

For the first month or so that I spent in New York, I went out drinking with acquaintances in the city at every opportunity I could. Yet these nights never ended well. On nights when I was lucky, I'd wake up in a public bathroom in a train station, missing my purse. On nights when I was not, I might regain consciousness in a situation so compromised that after running away, I would spend a week barricaded in my room writing raw poetry about cultural necrophilia.

As I was learning, the relative safety of Japanese society certainly did cater to the rampant alcoholism that flourished there. More than once, I have walked along on the narrow streets of Kabukichō—the area considered to be Tokyo's most dangerous neighborhood—in the early hours of the morning to find otherwise respectably dressed businessmen passed out in the doorways of closed venues, their briefcases at their sides, and their Louis Vuitton wallets half-hanging out of their pockets, untouched. In a similar light, I have yet to meet any Japanese men who possessed the same sense of entitlement that I have seen in some men in the United States when they encounter an unconscious woman.

Japan is a heavily rule-governed society, and perhaps such unfair fights are not regarded as honorable. It is one of the more curious quirks regarding the country that produces the most violent video games and the most perverse pornography in the world, yet is so safe that children as young as six or seven often ride the subways home from school by themselves.

Even if I was not respected as a woman or as a person while working in a hostess bar back in Tokyo, the club regulations that banned any of my clients from laying a hand on me inside its doors most often were. When one is living her life as a piece in this game, as a flower in this arrangement, or even as an animal in this zoo, the rigid rules that confine her can likewise keep her safe from outside harm. My brief return to America had made me acutely aware of this fact.

I had spent only a few months back in New York during my first semester of graduate school, yet enough had happened to convince me that I was not safe in that environment. As a result, I felt a keen nostalgia for my life at the zoo.

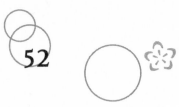

52

the floating sisterhood

to my great pleasure and relief, December came about eventually. Thankfully, I found Club Heaven to be basically the same as I'd left it. One evening that month, Michi, Cheri, and I were sitting at Heaven's bar at the end of a long night, discussing dreams.

"What is your dream for the future?" I had asked them.

"I want to own my own beauty shop one day," Cheri revealed.

"I want to have my own bar, just like this, where I will be the mama-san," Michi said, adding, "And what about you, Ellie, what's your dream?"

"I want to be an interpreter at the United Nations," I said to their raised eyebrows, slightly embarrassed that my dream didn't quite fit in with the others.

"You really do have the same eyes as Mari," I told Cheri, changing the subject. I wouldn't have said such a thing if I were sober. I would have been afraid that it might come across like a racist assumption that all people from their native country looked alike.

"Can you keep a secret?" Cheri asked. The alcohol had apparently loosened her tongue as well.

"Yes, I can," I lied.

"Mari is my half sister," she revealed.

"Wow," I said, astonished that no one had ever told me such information in the months I adorned Club Heaven. "But why is it a secret?" I asked.

"Really," Michi joined in, "why don't you tell anyone?"

"It's complicated," Cheri said, unwilling to elaborate.

Secrets are not nearly as fun when you don't know the reasons why they must be concealed. Still, I had to be satisfied with my progress on the puzzle.

Cheri and I didn't get a chance to speak honestly again until some weeks later. Specifically, there was one evening that January when Heaven had no customers to speak of. And since our jobs depended upon our being well-versed in matters of economy and politics, not one of us didn't know why.

Besides their inextricable dependence on each other, the Tokyo Stock Exchange and the *mizu shobai* have a lot in common sometimes. In both the water trade and the TSE, there are only processes of going up or going down; certainty is always in flux and nothing is ever a "sure thing."

Still, it was being called Black Wednesday. It all started on the evening of Monday, January 16, when prosecutors raided the offices of a fast-growing Internet services company called Livedoor Company, resulting in an indictment for fraud, a suicide, and an avalanche-like dumping of market shares.

Jadie and I first learned of the crisis as we characteristically flipped between CNN and MTV while enjoying our morning coffee in the afternoon. She and I were having the same conversation that went down so many times during my six-week stay with her over the holidays.

"I don't want to go back to New York," I whined. "It's just so much safer here in Japan!"

"I can understand why you'd feel that way," she replied, "but ge-ography is not so cut-and-dried. There are plenty of assholes here in Japan, too. Just because you haven't encountered much danger here yourself doesn't mean it doesn't exist."

"I just like it better here!" I hopelessly oversimplified matters. "Tokyo is cool and New York totally sucks. I don't know how I will ever get back on that plane."

"Of course I'd rather have you stay here with me," my friend comforted me, "but you should finish your degree. Then, after an-other semester you can come back to Tokyo again with a master's degree and maybe even get a *real* job. Plus, if you quit school now then you will totally regret it, and the assholes of the world will win."

At that we noticed the news.

"I'm so skipping work tonight," Jadie rejoiced. "It's like a snow day!"

As Wednesday progressed, the situation worsened as the TSE was forced to close all trading early, at 2:40 P.M., due to the market's spectacular plunge into the red.

After dark in Heaven, no one was particularly vexed that no customers were coming that night. It was just a matter of course that such events would come to pass sometimes, just as there was always a flood of clientele when the market took a turn for the better.

Anica and Katria convinced Mari to let them go early that night, seeing as nobody would likely show up anyway. Saki left shortly after, and Jadie—true to her "snow day" proclamation—never bothered coming into work at all. This left only Michi, Angela, Mari, Cheri, and me, all dressed up with no one to en-tertain.

Then, after the bartender himself went home, there transpired a very unlikely event: a group of Ginza hostesses began drinking together at their own bar, without a customer in sight. Mari sold us the drinks at cost, which amounted to about five times cheaper than what a man would have to pay for each drink. And for once, the flowers of the bar were given the freedom to arrange themselves.

Perhaps it's because we all experience—to varying degrees—a similarly oppressive shyness while sober, drunken women the world over really do love to talk about sex. It all started innocently enough . . .

"Your skin is so smooth!" I complimented Angela. "How do you keep your face so glowing?" I asked.

"Okay," Angela said sternly, "I'm going to tell you all a secret." Chi-mama had captured our attention to the degree that Michi even took out her notebook and a pencil to jot down Angela's upcoming advice.

"In order to achieve a perfect skin glow," Angela continued, "you have to orgasm every day!"

Our serious mood suddenly burst and erupted into laughter. Cheri and Angela gave each other a high five across the bar, the way women from the Philippines are apt to do after someone makes a witty comment.

"Every day!" Michi exclaimed. "But how do—?" She stopped herself mid-sentence, not sure how to phrase the question to her superior. Michi was Japanese after all.

"But how is that possible?" I finished Michi's inquiry, not being Japanese.

"Is your boyfriend that good in bed?" Cheri asked earnestly, with a hint of envy.

"No, no, no, no," Angela corrected. "No man is that good in bed. I prefer to do it by myself."

This made another occasion for Angela and Cheri to slap hands across the bar. Even when speaking explicitly about masturbation, Angela had a quiet magnetism about her. It made me admire my teacher more than ever.

This naturally led to an hour or so of conversation debating masturbation techniques and lamenting the inability of men—the world over I found out—to understand and appreciate the magic of clitoral stimulation.

We had a similarly grand time explaining to one another a variety of slang terms for precise sex acts, as they were pronounced in our respective languages. When our mangled English or Japanese did not suffice to communicate such matters, we relied on explicit hand gestures to get the meanings across. I had never seen Cheri's face turn so red as she sucked back one Virginia Slims after another.

"So you have a boyfriend?" I asked Angela.

"Yes," she said, taking out her cell phone. "This is my boyfriend"—Angela showed me a picture on her cell phone—"he is Japanese but he acts like a Latin lover!"

"My ex-boyfriend from college was Brazilian," I related.

"Ooh, Brazil!" Cheri and Angela said almost in unison.

"Latin lovers are totally my type in bed," I admitted.

"Latin lovers are everyone's type in bed!" Angela jested.

"Yeah, but he totally smothered me emotionally," I qualified. "I like to have my own space, to think my own thoughts, you know? But he wanted us to be together all of the time and it bored me."

"American girls, so independent," Cheri said in Angela's general direction and they looked at each other knowingly.

"It's not all that great there," I mumbled.

"It is our culture in the Philippines"—Cheri turned in my

direction—"that the man always makes the first move. Is it like that in America?"

"I think it used to be," I said. "Maybe it still is that way in the South or something. I'm not so sure, it's a big country.

"But when I am working here," I admitted, "I act more aggressive toward the customers than I would be in a normal dating situation, because I feel like if I am the one to touch his hand or stroke his hair first, then I feel like I am in control of the situation, which makes it more tolerable."

"Oh," Cheri said, "I'm studying lots of cultures this evening!"

"Do you like Japanese men?" Cheri asked me.

"No, not at all." I could finally reply honestly.

"Why?" she asked.

At that I held up my thumb at an angle.

"That's a stereotype!" Michi pleaded. "Most Japanese guys aren't really that small."

"I speak from more experience than I'd like to admit," I countered. "They really are less endowed than most."

Meanwhile, Mari missed out on most of this conversation, as she had been tidying up all corners of the bar. When she finished cleaning, she handed the keys over to Angela.

"Don't wreck the place," she told us half-jokingly. "I have to go home."

"Please stay, Mama!" I pleaded.

"I have to go home to my son," she said as she turned to me, sashaying out of sight before I could ask her about her family.

With Mama gone, I went behind the bar and playfully flirted with Cheri, as if she were a customer.

"Welcome to Heaven!" I said in my most exaggerated hostess voice. "I love your tie. Your singing voice is *soo* good! You should be a rock star! So your name is Hiro? Will you be *my* hero?" I jested, to everyone's amusement.

When I returned to my seat, Cheri let out a huge burp, presumably from all the beer she was drinking.

"Cheri!" I turned to her. "What a demure little butterfly you are!" I joked, secretly wishing that the Tokyo Stock Exchange might crash more often.

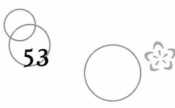

53

eighteen years

We know that a dream can be real, but who ever thought that reality could be a dream? We exist, of course, but how, in what way? As we believe, as flesh-and-blood human beings, or are we simply parts of one's feverish, complicated nightmare.

—"SHADOW PLAY," *The Twilight Zone*

"Mari's got a kid?" I asked Angela and Cheri, after Mama left on the night of the stock market crash.

"Yes," Cheri answered. "She has one son."

"How come I never knew any of this?" I asked.

"Mari never talks about her personal life," Angela said, entering the discussion. "Haven't you noticed?"

"I suppose," I said, realizing that I'd been so obsessed with fearing Mari or trying to please Mari over the months I had worked in Heaven that I had very little idea who she actually was.

"Cheri, how long has Mari been a hostess in Tokyo?"

"She has been the mama at Heaven since she opened the club, four years ago," Cheri said.

"I mean before she was a mama," I clarified, "wasn't she a regular hostess for a while first? She said she worked for Destiny, right?"

"Yes," Cheri said, looking uneasy, "but I don't know how long."

"Yes, you do," I replied with more aggressiveness than Cheri was likely used to. "For how long has Mama Mari been a Tokyo hostess?"

"Okay, don't tell her I told you," Cheri said with the typically loose tongue of a drunk.

"I promise," I slurred.

"Eighteen years," Cheri said.

"Eighteen years?" I pulled my head back and dropped my jaw.

"Eighteen years," Cheri confirmed.

Eighteen years. I fell silent, making a few mathmatical calculations in my head.

"Shit," I whispered to no one in particular.

Eighteen years as a hostess. Wow.

I mean, it wasn't eighteen years of selling her body, which was fortunate. Still, it was eighteen years of emotional prostitution, of pretending to be in love with paying customers: eighteen years of selling her soul. Night after night of it. Mari had been doing this kind of work since 1986. That was the year I entered kindergarten and cried for my mother all day long on my first day of school. That morning in New York was evening in Tokyo, and Mari was already pouring drinks. To be treated as a vessel of fantasy for that long, night after night of it, is more intense than I'll ever be able to imagine.

I could not pretend to understand what Mari's life had been like. The countless streams of childlike men, how they treated her over the years, and how they must have made her feel. The businessmen who wore the same suits, sang the same songs, and told the same jokes. What a nightmare it must have been, reliving a single night forever. Eighteen years.

Yet Mari did not turn cruel and cold like Destiny had. A part of her was still alive. More than alive, it sparkled even and touched other people. That amazed me. Despite how life had treated Mari, she still had a warm heart. That was a feat in itself. It was another quiet accomplishment that, unfortunately, no one gives out trophies for.

"I have to go back to school in America again next week," I told Mari. "But don't worry, Mama, I'll be back soon. Heaven is my favorite bar in Ginza."

"I'm disappointed to lose you," she replied with a sigh, "but it is best you go back to school."

"Thanks, Mama," I said, feeling sad that I was leaving but relieved that she understood.

"Me," she said, "I never got to finish my studies."

"That's a shame," I said. "You can still go back, can't you?"

Mari gave a sarcastic laugh. "I'm pretty busy right now," she said.

"You have family here?" I asked a question to which I already knew the answer. I felt as if I could finally take the liberty to ask Mari about her personal life, since I was leaving Heaven after all.

"Yes," she said, "I have my son." At the mention of her son, her face lit up with a glow I had hardly seen before.

"He keeps you busy?" I asked, in hope of keeping the glow on her face.

"Yeah," she reflected, "I'm busy with getting him to school every morning and finding good baby-sitters for the nighttime. Besides, I run a couple of other businesses during the day. My life is a bit too complicated for school."

"If I ever get a job in journalism when I return to New York," I asked on a whim, "would it be okay if I could interview you? I think that there are a lot of people in America who might want to know what the life of a Ginza mama is like."

"Oh, it is not so interesting." Mari shrugged off my request. "I live only for my son; he is what keeps me going. It is not such a glamorous life as you think."

"How old is he?" I asked, feeling moved.

"He's eleven," she said.

"Isn't your son the same age as Destiny's son?" I asked. "Destiny once told me that her son was eleven."

"Ha!" Mari exclaimed. "Did she really tell you that?"

"Yes," I responded, confused.

"Destiny is a dirty liar," Mari said with a smirk.

"How so?" I inquired.

"Destiny's son is seventeen or eighteen by now," Mari said. "She just wants you to think she is younger."

"How old is Destiny?" I couldn't help but ask.

"I'm not sure exactly," Mari said, "but she is a lot older than you think. Destiny has had lots of plastic surgery to hide how old she is becoming, I'm sure."

"I see," I replied.

"But never mind that." Mari changed the subject. "When you go home to New York, I don't want you to drink so much alcohol as you do now. It is very bad for your body. And beer is not good for studying, do you understand?"

"Yes, Mama," I said, rather moved by her advice, especially since a cure for my alcoholism was not directly in her interest.

"I wish you happiness in your life," Mari then told me, "sincerely."

I nodded. "I'm going to be fine, don't worry about me. I wish you happiness in life as well," I said, reciprocating the gesture.

"Yeah, right," she retorted sarcastically. At that Mari averted her eyes, snickered, and nodded her head back and forth as if she held some terrible secret I would never understand.

"I mean it, Mama," I said seriously.

"Okay." Mari turned to me then, looked me in the eye, and said, "Let's fight."

"Okay." I held up my fists jokingly, reminded of the many times Mari and I had feigned such bantering battles over customers, to make them feel special.

"Not that type of fight," she said, putting a gentle palm on my shoulder. "I mean, let's fight for life," she corrected. I narrowed my eyes and nodded.

"Did you not understand my English?"

"No, no, Mama." I shook my head vigorously. "I understand you perfectly now. Let's fight!" I repeated with zeal, thinking that for some reason, at that moment I had just heard some of the most touching words I'd ever been told by anyone.

Not long after my talk with Mama Mari, I left Heaven for New York with a renewed passion to fight for life.

54

a bar of her own

and right I did. Upon returning to New York, I found a job teaching at an Asian-run preschool in Queens, took up some freelance translation work out of Manhattan, finished my graduate work, and wrote a book proposal. I also met a nice boy in one of my graduate classes, and actually began to form a relationship with a man who did not drink.

All of this occurred in the space of four months. That was how much Mari had inspired me.

When my long-awaited Tokyo homecoming finally arrived, however, I was much dismayed to learn that Club Heaven had gone out of business. Everyone I talked to had a different explanation as to why the club closed its doors, but I tend to believe that Heaven's closure was due to a lack of commerce.

It's hard to explain why I returned to work for Mama Destiny at the Palace then. Goddess knows I wanted to quit hostessing. And now that I'd come back to Japan with a master's degree I wasn't just working below my skill level, I was working ridiculously below my skill level. Still, rather than mopping the floor of the mailroom, a job typically reserved for the new members of a Japanese company, hostessing allowed me to shine. I'm not sure whether I was more addicted to the attention or the alcohol. Regardless, I couldn't seem to stop.

The turnover rate among hostesses being so high, there was only one woman I recognized at the Palace from nearly three years earlier. And I didn't even notice her until she told me her name, because she looked about ten years older than the last time I saw her. Unlike my acquaintances at Heaven who worked their way up in the hostessing world because they were fascinating conversationalists who understood the art of flirtation, Destiny had since hired for herself a pretty pile of young blondes from Europe, Canada, and Australia who were basically as dumb as bricks.

The Russians, as much as they disliked me, had been a much brighter pack. Most of them could speak conversational Japanese quite well. These new girls, however, could barely speak a word. This was for the best, though. Women that beautiful with such little brainpower are much more attractive before they open their mouths anyway.

Unlike Heaven, business at the Palace (which I took to calling Club Hell after my first night back) was booming. The rules were as strict as ever, and the *ikebana* arrangement had picked up speed due to the influx of clientele. Rod was gone, but in his place were three much shorter men, whom I likened to "mini-rods." They seemed to enjoy telling each of us what to do even more than the original Rod. Truth be told, there is an entire subculture of such men who occupy jobs in such bars largely because they like to boss around pretty girls.

Luckily, my homecoming at the Palace was short-lived. On my second night there, Destiny called me aside into her office.

"You're too old"—Destiny seemed to have decided on a whim—"so don't come back."

"I'm twenty-five," I protested.

"You look older," she said flatly. "Don't come back."

Although twenty-five is moderately old for a hostess, I don't think that my age was the real reason that Mama Destiny fired me. Most likely, she had heard that I had been working for Mari, and it was no secret anywhere in Ginza that the two were rivals.

It was then that it struck me completely that Destiny had no soul. They say that only the dead are forever young, and this could most accurately explain Destiny's seemingly eternal youth.

"Who the fuck do you think you are?" I challenged Destiny, furious, in a sudden rush of self-respect.

"Ask me that one more time, I dare you." She was absolutely fuming.

"*Who. The. Fuck. Do. You. Think. You. Are?*" I responded immediately. Entirely unaccustomed to being answered back to in such a way, she made a horselike huffing noise and closed the white curtain around her small office.

"Is that all you're really going to do?" I said, poking my head back through the white curtain on impulse. At that, I realized that the fragile curtain really did represent the true width of her power. In this culture of obedience, no one had ever tried to break through her silk curtain before.

"I'll tell you who you are"—my temper, flared by tequila, was unstoppable—"you are *nobody!* Yours is not a real career! All you do is exploit people! You are *nobody!*"

"Get her out of here, she is crazy," Destiny ordered her little Rods. They were tiny men who wouldn't know the first thing about bouncing someone out of a club. All they could do was keep pointing their arms toward the door, with open palms, the same way they instruct each girl to sit by the side of each customer. I finally gave in.

I was embarrassed to tell Dōhanman that I was fired from the Palace so soon and in such a manner. So without a second thought, I did what is common practice in the termination of fake relationships: I stopped returning his calls.

"michi has a bar?" I questioned Jadie in disbelief on the following evening. *"Michi?"* There had been too many changes in Tokyo in too short a time. "I leave for four months and everything in Tokyo changes on me!" I exclaimed.

Of all things, the recollection made me start to feel old, like I should have done more with my life. If Michi had a bar of her own already, why wasn't I working at the UN by now? Luckily, however, my feelings of inadequacy soon took a backseat to my general elation for my friend Michi, who had realized her dream in life so quickly.

"Haven't the tables turned!" I jostled Jadie. "I knew there was a reason to be nice to Michi!"

"So what if one of her customers bought her a bar," my longtime friend retorted. "It's probably because she had sex with him. Ew!"

"What's her bar called?" I asked Jadie.

"No no no no!" Jadie said, half joking and half in a panic. "You cannot go working for Michi! No! I won't allow it! Why did you go home to get a master's degree if you're never gonna get a real job?"

"My parents made me get a master's degree, because tuition wouldn't have been free after I turned twenty-five," I said, "because my mom's on faculty, remember?"

"Do they know what you're doing now that you have this degree?" Jadie said sarcastically.

"Ha!" I laughed. "They're on a need-to-know basis, and they don't need to know."

"Her club is called Nami," Jadie relented, "and it's in Kinshichō. Kinshichō is much rougher than Ginza, so be careful."

"Nami," I said to myself, "cool." Nami meant "wave" in Japanese. How very *ukiyo*.

I went to Kinshichō the next night, and asked around the neighborhood for the location of Nami, where I planned to surprise my old friend Michi.

"But you cannot go there," one man told me after giving me directions, "it is a Japanese bar. The international club is around the corner."

"But I *am* Japanese," I told him to his great confusion, then walked in the direction of Michi's club.

"How quickly you've realized your dream!" I finally was able to tell Michi, after an hour or so of searching for her bar and then waiting for the all-important mama-san to come out and meet me.

"What should I call you now?" I asked as I agreed to her request to work. "Mama Michi or Michi-mama?"

"Michi-chan is fine," she said, "as usual."

"That's not respectful enough," I said. "You are important now!"

"How about Mama Michi-chan, then," she replied.

"Very good," I replied on my way down to the changing room.

Jadie had been right about Kinshichō being rougher than Ginza. The customers at Nami were not as rich, and were significantly less polite. There was even one regular at Michi's bar who took to running around naked after he had too much to drink, forcing the waiters to chase him around with his pants, insisting he put them back on immediately. No, this was not Ginza.

To my surprise, since Heaven's unfortunate closure, Anica and Katria had become the top hostesses in the neighborhood of Kinshichō. And to my relief, Anica never had to marry Kaicho, since

Kinshichō is one of the few neighborhoods left in Tokyo where the police haven't cracked down on the illegal immigrants.

As a result, basically no one working in a Kinshichō hostess bar had a valid visa. It is the neighborhood where all of the Roppongi and Ginza hostesses fled to when the immigration inspectors raided their bars in recent years.

Kinshichō is quite a few steps below Ginza in terms of class and price, so anyone in Kinshichō who has also worked in Ginza is greeted with a raise of the eyebrows and a deep bow. Thus, I took a liking to the area. On top of that, I was not only the only American working in a Japanese-only bar—an exception, seeing as I was a friend of the mama-san—I was also the only American in town.

This is perhaps why word of me spread rapidly. So quickly, in fact, that two weeks into work at Nami, I was propositioned with an offer that I never, even in my wildest most drunken dreams, thought I would receive.

A bar in the neighborhood was looking for a new mama-san.

On my way home the night after I'd received the offer, I replayed the conversation in my head ad nauseam. Me, a mama. A mama-san at twenty-five. Me, Mama Ellie. No, no, the name Ellie was too childish for a mama. I would have to invent something more elegant and grown-up sounding. I could be Mama Annabella, Mama Katarina, or Mama Krystal (like the champagne). This was the real sign that I'd made it to the top.

In fact, I was so flattered by the offer that I almost forgot what the job would entail. A mama had a completely different job description. Instead of one flower in an arrangement, I would be the arranger. What control.

Was it possible, I racked my brain, to be a "nice" mama? Unlike Destiny? Mama Mari was the closest example I'd witnessed to a kinder mama-san. Still, it was not always possible. If I didn't press the girls for dōhans and if I didn't insist that they get marriage visas, the club would quickly go out of business.

So I felt flattered, but not fulfilled. It was like finally achieving a longtime goal, then realizing the pot of gold at the end of the rainbow was empty. I thought as much to myself as I walked home from work at three in the morning.

In spite of the title, this job was not nurturing. Instead, it was the opposite. It was worse than the opposite, it was acting as a destroyer under the guise of a nurturer. *I can't treat my own kind like a flower arrangement,* I thought. This was not my dream.

"I want to work for the UN," I'd said.

To be a mama was someone else's dream. When, I wondered, was I going to tire of living everybody else's dreams and find my own? Yet in order to do that, I had to let go of the full glass of beer that was placed in front of me.

"I'm sorry," I said, "I can't accept your offer." I spoke into my cell phone, having dialed the owner's number on an impassioned impulse.

"I want to," I lied, "but I have to move to Paris." Paris was simply the first place that came to mind, since as I spoke I was walking past a Japanese coffee chain called Vie de France. After shutting my cell phone and putting it back into my pocket, I turned around, retraced my steps, and walked into Vie de France. I needed to sit down and think. Since I was "moving to Paris," I would not be able to show my face in Kinshichō any longer.

As I ordered a late-night coffee at the empty café, I pondered the literal translation of the Japanese saying, *Nana korobi ya oki,* Fall over seven times, wake up eight.

Wake up eight.

The coffee I purchased there tasted bitter and repulsive, like most coffee in Japan. Still as I sipped from the mug, I knew that I had begun the process of opening my eyes from what had been a very long waking dream.

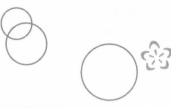

epilogue
filling in the blanks

this is the epilogue I never thought I would write. When I first took on this project, I could not have foreseen that this book might end with my decision to abstain from alcohol. To even attempt such a thing was out of the question, ridiculous even. The alcohol abuse that took root on the shiny tables of Tokyo hostess bars, then followed me out the doors and kept me company even after I swore that I had quit hostessing for good, had become a far too integral part of my lifestyle.

Writing this memoir, however, forced me to face the cyclical nature of my own destructive behavior on a deeper level than I was prepared to comprehend. Although I was writing these chapters in the first person, I often felt as if the girl I followed around Tokyo on drunken misadventures and fake dates was simply not me. She was reckless, self-destructive, indifferent, and if she didn't do something about her excessive drinking soon, she was doomed.

I never want to have to write a book like this again, which is largely why I began attending AA meetings shortly after I completed the first draft of this manuscript.

I should have expected to meet a handful of former hostesses in the program. In recovery, I am meeting women of all ages who worked in Tokyo hostess bars in the seventies, during the bubble economy of the eighties, through the economic recession in the nineties, and as recently as the past decade. With all of our stories, our small group could very well write an alternative narrative concerning the history and development of Tokyo's culture during the past forty years.

"If I could have invented the worst possible environment for someone with my predisposition to alcoholism and desire to escape reality," one women who had worked during the bubble told me after a meeting, "it would have been a hostess bar, hands down."

"I know how you feel," I related honestly.

I quit drinking after reading over my memoir and barely recognizing myself in its pages. The more I keep sober, however, the more I see that the strange girl in these chapters actually is me. What's more, she is hurt and very pissed off. I also know that I am never going to get to the bottom of her rage if I keep drinking myself in circles of overindulgence and guilt, of countless temper tantrums and subsequent apologies.

For the moment, I still miss alcohol along with all of the debauchery that it enabled. Perhaps I continue to yearn for its taste much like one might long for an abusive former lover. I know that I am in a safer place now, yet life without alcohol is lonely and frightening.

"I'm afraid that I will be bored to death in sobriety." I shared my concerns honestly over coffee with an older woman named Zoey, whom I had met in the meetings.

"What's even more boring," she replied with a smirk, "would be if you continued to abuse alcohol and kept making all of the same mistakes over and over again."

"Touché." I admitted to being caught red-handed in my own contradiction, "but still, what will I do with all of my spare time now?"

For me, committing to sobriety contains an element of uncertainty, and that is perhaps what scares me the most. It is like staring at a blank page on my word processor, without a clue as to what I should write next. And for the most part, I still don't know what I'm going to do with all the free time that abstinence allows and will continue to provide me. So for now, I have to be satisfied only with the knowledge of what will not be written there.

Without the influence of alcohol to alter my personality, I can confidently predict that the next chapter of my life will contain no shoplifting, no beer-based relationships, no meaningless sex, no cutting, no punching customers, no screaming matches with those I love the most, no vomiting blood, and no getting lured back into the world of hostessing. And that is enough to keep me motivated for the time being.

"I know how hard it is to enact such a drastic change in your lifestyle," Zoey said, taking my hand and looking me square in the eyes. "But trust me: things can become better than you've ever imagined."

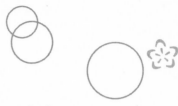

acknowledgments

This book would not exist if not for the help of Sharlene Martin, the best literary agent ever, without whom I might have taken on a career as a lifelong bar girl. Special thanks also to Anthony Flacco, for his early criticisms and encouragements, Diane Reverand, the acquiring goddess whom I hope to actually meet in person one day, and Hilary Rubin, my editor at St. Martin's Press, for understanding my story and helping me to tell it here.

Also at St. Martin's Press, thank you to Linda Friedner Cowen and Pete Garceau. Plus, my thanks to copy editor Sabrina Soares Roberts.

I cannot forget Liz Roberts, for making possible my first visit to Japan, or any of my later Japanese instructors: Merken sensei, Hasegawa sensei, and Uesaka sensei. Although this book was not what any of you had in mind when you shared your language with me. Thank you for everything.

Thanks to *The McGill Daily* for giving me a creative outlet when I needed it the most, especially Jaime Kirzner-Roberts—whom I secretly idolized—and J. Kelly Nestruck, whose word-count restrictions I habitually ignored.

For saving my life more times than I'd like to admit: Martha Macdonald; Meredith Warren; Chris Brown; Siu-min Jim; Hillary Vipond; Astrid Lium; Hikari Kambara; Dr. Sharon Goldblum Ranzman; the

Canadian Health Care System; and everyone at the McGill Eating Disorders Unit, especially Donna Kuzmarov.

I feel particularly grateful toward: Jonathan Colford, for believing in me through my most scandalous exploits, and for the long and inspiring arguments over pitchers of beer on St. Denis; Scottish Dave, for all the conversations about world literature; and the great Janice Erlbaum, I'll always be your biggest fan.

I would be lost without my longtime friend Tomoko Yasukawa, who stuck by me at the Happy Learning English School when no one else did. Thank you for sharing with me your youthful energy.

Crystal, many thanks for helping me take care of Pika, and for not throwing her out the window after she peed on your bed.

I feel infinite gratitude toward the Destiny Hatred Society (you know who you are). May you always fight for happiness in your lives.

That goes for you, too, Laura Fumiko Keehn. You are the best. I love you.

I must also thank my mom and dad, for allowing me to pursue my plans of global domination, for promising never to read this book, and for doing a much better job as parents than they give themselves credit for.

Special thanks to God for all the late-night insight, chapter ideas, creative energy, and for keeping me sober thus far.

And, of course, Trevor Coombes, my love, for crossing the globe to be with me, for saying that I looked cute despite the taped-up glasses, frizzy hair, and lack of showers I displayed while entrenched in this manuscript, and for washing the dishes disproportionately often. Thank you for making me feel at home wherever it is that you are.